Title:	The Double Life of Katharine Clark
Author:	Katharine Gregorio
Agent:	Elaine Spencer
	The Knight Agency
Publication date:	March 15, 2022
Category:	History
Format:	Trade Paperback
ISBN:	978-1-7282-4841-7
Price:	$16.99 U.S.
Pages:	368 pages

Please send all reviews or mentions of this book to the Sourcebooks marketing department:

marketing@sourcebooks.com

For sales inquiries, please contact:

sales@sourcebooks.com

For librarian and educator resources, visit:

sourcebooks.com/library

THE
DOUBLE LIFE
OF KATHARINE CLARK

The Untold Story of the American Journalist Who Brought the Truth about Communism to the West

KATHARINE GREGORIO

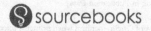

Published by Sourcebooks
P.O. Box 4410, Naperville, Illinois 60567–4410
(630) 961-3900
sourcebooks.com

[Library of Congress Cataloging-in-Publication Data]

Printed and bound in [Country of Origin—confirm when printer is selected].
XX 10 9 8 7 6 5 4 3 2 1

For Will and Sophie, may you always seek the truth and have the courage to defend it.

CONTENTS

List of Key Characters   xx
Author's Note   xx

Prologue   xx
Part I: Hope   xx
Part II: Truth   xx
Part III: Justice   xx
Epilogue   xx

Acknowledgments   xx
Reading Group Guide   xx
Conversation with the Author   xx
Notes   xx
Selected Bibliography   xx
Index   xx
About the Author   xx

LIST OF KEY CHARACTERS

PRIMARY

Katharine Clark: correspondent for International News Service (INS), NBC, and the *Washington Post* and then a researcher at *Reader's Digest*

Edgar Clark (Ed): correspondent for *Time-Life*, husband of Katharine Clark

Milovan Djilas: former vice president of Yugoslavia; author of *The New Class*, *Land Without Justice,* and *Conversations with Stalin*

Štefanija Djilas (Steffie): wife of Milovan Djilas

Aleksa Djilas: son of Milovan and Steffie Djilas

SECONDARY

Politicians

Aneurin Bevan (Nye): leader of the British Labour Party's left wing

Vladimir Dedijer: Tito's biographer, Central Committee member of League of Communists of Yugoslavia

Edvard Kardelj: vice president of Yugoslavia

Morgan Phillips: secretary of the British Labour Party

Josip Broz Tito: president of Yugoslavia

Publishers

William (Bill) Jovanovich: president of Harcourt, Brace, and World, which became Harcourt, Brace, Jovanovich. Published *Land Without Justice* and *Conversations with Stalin*, among many others.

Felix Morrow: New York publisher, University Books. Served as Milovan's agent for *Land Without Justice*.

Frederick Praeger: New York publisher, Frederick A. Praeger. Published *The New Class*.

Newsmen

Stella Alexander: writer and friend of Steffie Djilas

James Bell: bureau chief in Bonn, Germany, *Time-Life*

Stojan Bralovic: correspondent in Belgrade, United Press International

Al Friendly: managing editor, *Washington Post*, and Ed's classmate at Amherst

Milton Kaplan: features editor in New York, INS

Joseph Kingsbury-Smith: chief of correspondents, INS

Paul Underwood: *New York Times* correspondent in Eastern Europe and friend of the Clarks

AUTHOR'S NOTE

Like many of us, I grew up hearing family stories, but it wasn't until I was an adult that I discovered my great-aunt Katharine Clark had a secret. An award-winning foreign correspondent who overcame personal obstacles and social expectation to pioneer a career in a man's profession, Katharine provided essential eyewitness reports of postwar Europe and life behind the Iron Curtain to the American public at the height of the Cold War. As I investigated her life, after spotting a plaque for a special collection with Katharine's and my great-uncle Ed's name in the basement of Georgetown University's library in 2003, I discovered one of the most unusual adventure stories of the Cold War, one that has gone untold until now.

While posted in Belgrade in the mid-1950s, Katharine befriended a man who by many definitions appeared to be her enemy. But she saw something in Milovan Djilas, a high-ranking Communist leader who dared to question the ideology he helped establish, that made her want to work with him. It became the assignment of her life—taking her on a journey from amanuensis and editor to friend and advocate. Along the way she ferried his ideas to the West: pitching articles, pigeoning mail, and smuggling manuscripts out of Belgrade. The papers she helped shepherd included *Land Without Justice*, Milovan's autobiography of his youth, and *The New Class*, his first political book, which carried a powerful analysis of the Communist system. Published in August 1957, *The New Class* blasted the Cold War world order with a criticism of communism from an unimpeachable source, making it an instant bestseller in the West and automatically banned in Communist countries. It eventually sold over three million copies across translations into more than sixty languages.

The events in the pages that follow are remarkable as much for their unpredictability as for the fact that they really occurred. Anything between quotation marks comes from diaries, cables, correspondence, newspaper and magazine articles, or other documents as written.

This story takes place primarily in Yugoslavia, a country that no longer exists but that, from 1918 to 1992, comprised landmass now recognized as the countries of Bosnia and Herzegovina, Croatia, Kosovo, Macedonia, Montenegro, Serbia, and Slovenia. Due to the nature of the job of a correspondent and the fact that important events were taking place in the region outside of Yugoslavia, there is travel to neighboring countries—Austria, Bulgaria, Germany, Hungary, and Poland. It is in this movement where we see two very different worlds—East and West, Communist and democratic—exhibiting the divide Winston Churchill described in his speech at Westminster College in Fulton, Missouri, on March 5, 1946:

"From Stettin in the Baltic to Trieste in the Adriatic, an iron curtain has descended across the Continent. Behind that line lie all the capitals of the ancient states of Central and Eastern Europe. Warsaw, Berlin, Prague, Vienna, Budapest, Belgrade, Bucharest and Sofia, all these famous cities and the populations around them lie in what I must call the Soviet sphere, and all are subject in one form or another, not only to Soviet influence but to a very high and, in many cases, increasing measure of control from Moscow. "

Beyond the curtain, away from its shadow, this book is about the prism of truth: why some systems abide freedom of expression while others engage in its distortion and suppression. In the end it is a story of transformation—how one woman, uniquely placed to see what others did not and driven by the bonds of an unusual friendship, broke through to expose truth to the world, changing both her and history in the process.

—*Katharine Gregorio, San Francisco*

In matters of truth and justice there is no difference between large and small problems, for issues concerning the treatment of people are all the same.

ALBERT EINSTEIN

PROLOGUE
BELGRADE, YUGOSLAVIA

November 1956

As the footsteps on the cobblestones behind her grew louder, she willed herself not to turn around. Her only chance now was to blend in, to make everyone believe she was a local. She knew no one from Belgrade would dare look back to see if the secret police were in pursuit.

She wanted to run, but she forced herself to slow her gait, shivering a little despite her sensible wool coat. She tried to count to three between each footstep the way her mother had taught her so many years before in preparation for her wedding.

Luckily, the steady drizzle that had been falling since morning had stopped. She was grateful it was still a few degrees above freezing so the wet streets had yet to turn to ice. But she knew that wouldn't last. The weather forecast for this cold afternoon called for a blizzard. As if to confirm her thoughts, a strong gale of wind whipped up and stung her cheeks like a sharp, frosty wasp. No matter. Biting her lips together, with her head forward, she tilted her face down and leaned into it, the angle also allowing her to avoid eye contact that might attract suspicion.

A minute later, she walked by the window of a brightly lit dress shop, stopped, and lifted her gaze, pretending to examine the boldly colored frocks on display. She knew enough from her years living in a Communist country that inside there would be nothing for sale like what was advertised in the window. The same was true at every store like this. Only when there was a line wrapping outside of the shop and around the corner like a trail of breadcrumbs was there anything to buy inside.

But shopping wasn't her aim. She studied the reflection of the pedestrians behind her. A handful of men and women carrying umbrellas under their arms and shopping bags in their hands shuffled by.

The footsteps were closing in on her. Clenching her jaw and forming tight fists with her gloved hands, she readied herself. A moment later, a fat, middle-aged man with an ushanka—the traditional bushy fur hat with ear flaps for warmth imported from the Soviet Union—and a long, dark coat that strained against his girth, appeared in the glass. Quickly he was upon her. But he passed where she stood, hurrying on his way, the footsteps echoing loud in his wake.

She let out a shallow exhale.

Nothing out of the ordinary, she thought.

Still, she knew she wasn't safe.

Not yet.

She squeezed the handbag she was carrying over her right shoulder tightly against her ribs, patting it to make sure everything was still inside. Grabbing the collar of her coat and drawing it in closer, she began to walk again, allowing herself to move faster now along the remaining two blocks to her hotel.

As she hurried, she thought about what was next. She needed to get out of the country. She had to deliver on her promise.

Everything depended on it.

PART I

HOPE

ONE

BELGRADE

January 1955

At half past seven on the twenty-fourth of January 1955, Katharine Clark shivered as she left the dark, run-down lobby of the old, central district courthouse and stepped outside onto its front steps. On this frosty winter morning, gray clouds from an overnight storm still troubled the sky, casting a long shadow over the city. Pedestrians wearing black overcoats and fur hats hurried by on their way to work or to the many shops that lined Masaryk Street, leaving the freshly fallen snow tarnished in their wake. In the street, a pair of grimy sedans grumbled past, their engines sputtering in the raw, wet air. And then, from close behind, she heard the raspy sound of a man clearing his throat.

Ed.

She could almost see her husband trying to signal to her, masking it as a cough to hide it from everyone else. His long, slender hands that could build anything balled in a tight fist just below his mouth to show the curve of a smile, a clue to his wry sense of humor. It still amazed her how he could cultivate so many

high-placed sources behind the Iron Curtain, keeping them anon-
ymous even from her, but when it came to the everyday, he was
hopelessly transparent.

It had been that way since they had first met, as college juniors
in New England working the same story as campus stringers for
The New York Herald Tribune. She couldn't even remember what
the story was about now. She just remembered Ed looking at her
in a way no man had ever done. Before him, she'd been a tall,
gawky girl, a general's daughter, who rebelled against anyone and
anything when it took her fancy, which was often.

Try to behave, her mother implored when Katharine's parents
dropped her off at Smith College. She had tried, keeping herself
busy beyond her studies by writing for newspapers. Katharine
dreamed of moving to New York to be a journalist after graduation.

Yet, the disappointment on her parents' faces when she told
them she was pregnant eclipsed their reaction to everything else
she'd ever done. Her father had tried to dissuade her from mar-
rying Ed when Katharine had informed him Ed had done the
proper thing and proposed. Katharine knew the only thing her
parents thought she and Ed had in common was "youthful enthusiasm for newspaper work." But although her father was a decorated army general used to having his orders followed, he failed to
change Katharine's mind. Trying to make the best of the situation,
Katharine's parents threw them a small wedding at West Point.
Shortly after, Amherst and Smith expelled Ed and Katharine for
being married—a status neither institution permitted in its student
body. The newlyweds moved to New York City. But Katharine's
life there was not how she had envisioned it from her dorm room

in Northampton. Instead of covering stories for one of the city's daily papers, she was confined to bedrest in a rundown studio apartment on Morton Street in Greenwich Village, while Ed followed his dream working as a newspaperman covering breaking news for the *New York American*.

Katharine had almost been felled by it all—the pain of her parents' disapproval, the stark change in her circumstances, her reluctance for motherhood, and, more than anything, her deep envy of Ed's career. But their poorness had saved her, and she'd been able to overcome obstacles, taking advantage of opportunity and luck to finally become a reporter.

Although she had come a long way in the last twenty-two years, Katharine could feel the old, familiar mantle of jealousy wrapping itself around her again.

She had come outside to collect her thoughts. Everything inside the courthouse that morning had happened so fast.

The day before, the government of Yugoslavia had confirmed the trial would be open to the public and the press—both domestic and international. Anyone was welcome as long as they held tickets for admission. That was typical; tickets gave the selection process an air of fairness if not efficiency, two characteristics the Communists in charge of Yugoslavia valued the most.

The foreign correspondents, instructed to arrive at seven, joined a growing cluster of people in the lobby, including family of the defendants and members of the general public waiting outside the office of the court secretary. The short, plump court secretary emerged from his office to deliver a last-minute statement from the Yugoslav government. With an air of importance typically reserved for someone at least a foot taller and a rank higher, he'd declared, "The foreign newspapermen have not received tickets because we are not persuaded they will report truthfully about the trial."

Trials of men accused of anti-state activity were quite common in Communist Yugoslavia—President Josip Broz Tito used them to punish those whom he grew weary of or to send a message. They were so common that even the local media rarely covered them, let alone the foreign press. But never before had two men so close to Tito been on trial. The defendants stood accused of criminal violations of Article 118, attempting to "undermine the authority of the working people" via hostile propaganda against Yugoslavia and Communism. It was a grave accusation. Conviction carried a possible prison sentence and up to twenty years of hard labor.

The timing was curious. Tito was currently out of the country. Several weeks before he'd departed on a grand tour to India and Burma. But everyone knew he communicated with Edvard Kardelj, vice president of Yugoslavia, who was the acting head of state in Tito's absence, several times a day. It was Kardelj who would have given the order, with Tito's blessing, barring foreign correspondents from attending the trial.

Even before the court secretary slammed his office door behind him, Ed, Katharine, and the dozen other Western correspondents huddled together. Other than Katharine, they were all men.

There was Jack Raymond, the hard-charging reporter from the Bronx, who now wrote for the *New York Times*. His friendly eyes and warm smile masked the sharp skills that allowed him to get his sources to share more than they had bargained for, breaking stories that often graced the front page, above the fold. Like Ed, Raymond had served as a reporter for *Stars and Stripes* during the war, where he had seen more than his fair share of action as a journalist across five major campaigns, earning him a Purple Heart. It was an open belief that Raymond's front-page Christmas Day article entitled "Purged Yugoslav Asks Two Parties, More Democracy," carrying the first in-depth interview of one of the defendants, was the reason for today's trial.

John Earle was the tall, brawny correspondent for Reuters who had film star looks and an adventure backstory to rival anything Hollywood could dream up. At the start of the war, Earle had parachuted behind enemy lines in German-occupied Yugoslavia. It was to be a quick mission, but Earle never left, meeting his future wife weeks after he landed. As a result, Earle spoke excellent Serbian and served as the group's unofficial spokesman.

Other Americans and Europeans who worked for various global wires and publications rounded out the group. The only one missing was the Russian.

Everyone except Katharine began talking all at once. Arguing about freedom of the press and Communist contradictions was not helpful to her right now. She went outside to escape the chatter and think about her next move.

She needed this story.

Eighteen months ago, when she and Ed moved to Belgrade, after she'd received yet another rejection letter commending her for her wartime coverage but conveying the news that the position had already been filled, she'd settled to serve as a stringer for the

Chicago Tribune, paid only for what ran in print, always one article away from redundancy. None of the other foreign correspondents in Belgrade faced this problem. Instead, each man received a sizable salary enhanced further with rich expense accounts and an organized secretary who helped schedule trips and made translations. Katharine was intimately familiar with the trappings because she was married to one of them: Ed was *Time's* man in Belgrade.

Don't worry, Katharine, you'll get a story.

Ed's whisper from behind reminded her why she'd come outside. Drawing her shoulders back, she turned around and took in the familiar look of concern on Ed's rugged face. She could see the dozen other reporters just over his left shoulder, lined up like schoolboys eager to escape the confines of the classroom for the playground.

She let out a grunt of exasperation before she turned forward again. She immediately forgot about the other correspondents as her gaze shifted down the stairs to where a crowd of several hundred gathered, spilling from the steps out onto the sidewalk. *Where had they all come from?* Katharine marveled. Just a half-hour before, when she and Ed had entered the courthouse, the street had been empty.

The question consumed her senses as she stepped sideways, planting her size ten boots down firmly in an open corner of the landing. She was a tall woman, with chestnut-brown eyes and hair that shined despite her inattention to it. She had never been vain—her towering height prevented that—but she was always composed, pulled together, a by-product of growing up in a household that was both military and southern.

As Katharine shifted her large, burgundy leather bag brimming with papers and pens higher on her shoulder, the other correspondents squeezed in around her, Ed closest to her. The police appeared and asked them to move, but all the foreign reporters ignored them, refusing to budge. When the police moved on, Katharine concluded they had orders not to use force.

A *positive sign*, she thought, before it was interrupted by someone inside the sea of dark overcoats and fur hats who started chanting, "Traitor! Bandit!" More of the group joined, some booing, so that soon the sound pierced the frozen morning like howls from a pack of wolves.

Katharine sought the source of the commotion and saw several figures of varying shapes and sizes at the end of Masaryk Street approaching the courthouse on foot and splashing through the now melting snow. Katharine studied them with the investigative lens she'd honed during two decades as a journalist. The man at the front walked with a lightness in his step that belied the severity of what loomed before him.

Milovan Djilas.

The former vice president of Yugoslavia, regarded as Tito's heir apparent until a year prior, had told Raymond a month prior in their December 1954 interview that democratic trends had been stifled in Yugoslavia and the government needed to permit the establishment of a second party to foster freedom of expression. Milovan acknowledged through a translator, "I thought that the Communist party must permit freedom of discussion. Now I see that this is impossible." He explained, "I am giving this interview to encourage free discussion as an act of legality. I am taking a risk, but one cannot go on without some risk. In our present system, we cannot know what will happen. However, I think that nothing bad will happen, and it will mean a lot for our country to have a citizen say what he thinks."

At the time, Katharine had not known if Milovan had been brazen or naive. As she looked at the former revolutionary who carried about him an air of authority acquired by those who had achieved the highest positions of power, Katharine believed this handsome, tall, and lanky man with a mop of wiry black hair knew exactly what he was doing. Katharine assessed the woman walking next to him for a brief moment. She was clinging to his arm as if her life depended on it. Katharine guessed this was his wife, Steffie.

Turning her attention back to Milovan, she summarized her thoughts: *a man whose time has come*. It was the predominant belief among all the Western journalists that Milovan was a Communist party man whose luck had simply and finally run out.

Satisfied, Katharine's eyes turned in search of the second defendant. She skipped over two men carrying black briefcases who she assumed to be the defendants' lawyers and found the reason she was here today. At the back of the group, walking with a limp, was Vlado.

Vladimir Dedijer was a six-foot, three-inch hulk of a man with a barrel chest, big nose, and thick lips. He was a former journalist and high-ranking party member who had authored Tito's 443-page official biography in 1952. He'd been the only other Communist Central Committee member to support Milovan at a party plenum the year before where Milovan had been stripped of his government posts. And over the past year, Dedijer persisted in his refusal to join the official boycott imposed on Milovan by his former comrades. Although Dedijer did not agree with what Milovan had to say, he believed Milovan should have the freedom to voice his opinions.

But seven weeks prior, in early December, after almost a year of quiet following the party plenum, a three-man control board had called Dedijer to a hearing to account for his defense of Milovan in January 1954. Dedijer told anyone who would listen how he had walked out after several minutes. He attempted to call a press briefing at his house to share what had transpired, but when reporters turned up for the briefing, they found a dark house barricaded by police who informed the correspondents the event had been canceled.

Undeterred, Dedijer persisted. He knew the power of the press. Because the Yugoslav government controlled what the domestic press wrote, Dedijer turned to Western publications to make his case. He gave an interview to *The Times*. Milovan followed his course and provided his own remarks to Raymond at the *New York Times*. And then as the pressure on Dedijer and Milovan mounted, Dedijer granted an interview to Ed for *Time* as well, sharing details about how the government was applying pressure on him for his continued support of Milovan.

Dedijer and Ed had been friends since they'd both landed at the same hospital in Naples, Italy, during the war, bonding over their fondness for New England—Vlado's brother had studied at Princeton—while recovering from life-threatening wounds. Ed had been badly wounded on the beach at Anzio, and Dedijer had suffered mighty blows to his skull and leg as a Partisan fighter in

Yugoslavia against the Germans. When the men first met, there was no guarantee Dedijer would make it. But Dedijer defied the odds, living longer than any of his doctors predicted. The only evidence of his wounds now was the fact that a large part of his skull was silver and he walked with a limp.

Now, as Katharine studied Dedijer's red face, angry but controlled, Katharine's heart went out to him despite the fact she still didn't understand how he had gotten himself into this mess. When Ed had asked Vlado about it the week before over dinner at the Clarks' house, Vlado had simply responded that the entire affair was a big conspiracy. He had refused to back down from his support for Milovan. But when he tried to cable Tito, the message had been returned with a note on the reverse side: "The very fact that you should try to cable Tito shows that you need discipline and should be punished." It was signed by someone from the Central Committee.

Suddenly, Katharine felt herself being pushed toward the center of the stairs. The entire crowd seemed to be moving in unison like a wave cresting and falling toward the shore. In all the bustle, Ed jostled her handbag and several items spilled out. Stooping to collect them, she heard the assault before she saw it. *Kersplat.*

It sounded like someone was spitting.

Katharine stood up quickly to see Milovan now standing at the base of the stairs blocked by a wall of people. Vlado was a few feet behind him. The scene reminded Katharine of the picture she had seen after the war of a man being led in front of a firing squad—the soldiers standing shoulder to shoulder, staring forward with hard, unsympathetic expressions singularly focused on their target, who stood equally stoic, resigned to the fate before him.

Out of the corner of her eye, Katharine spied a short man with a big nose tilt back his head and purse his lips. The spittle that launched from his small, red mouth landed squarely on Milovan's cheek. *Kersplat*. She grimaced, taken aback by the man's action. Revulsion flooded her senses.

Katharine looked around, wondering where the police had disappeared to. But finding them absent, she knew the answer. This had been planned. In that moment she remembered the speech Kardelj had given in Sarajevo to combat the foreign press coverage in several Western publications ahead of the trial. He had declared, "Every honest man should spit in the face of these politicians." The crowd was merely following those instructions, she realized.

During the fifteen minutes that went by without a police presence, anger flamed inside her as the crowd continued to heckle the men, although it was clear Milovan was their main target. She had come today to support Vlado and to write a story about the trial and its high-ranking defendants for the *Chicago Tribune*. But now Katharine wanted to do something about this injustice. Her mind wandered across the possibilities as she watched uniformed policemen appear and quiet the onlookers, parting the group to clear a path for the defendants up the stairs and into the courthouse.

As the crowd pressed back to make way for the men, Katharine saw Milovan lean down to kiss an old woman who now stood beside him. Dressed in black from the shoes on her feet to the shawl draped over her head in the traditional style of a Balkan peasant woman, she was hunched over a cane, her long, lean arms clutching it to hold her steady. Katharine recognized her from the courthouse lobby. It was Milovan's mother. Earle had learned from a neighboring group in the lobby that the court secretary had refused Milovan's mother a ticket to the trial, arguing that the proceedings would be too much strain on the elderly woman. The court secretary also refused admission to Milovan's sister and younger brother, but Earle informed the rest of the correspondents that the court secretary made no mention or specific excuse why Milovan's siblings were not given tickets to the trial. It had been the last thing Katharine learned before she'd gone outside.

The crowd hushed enough that Katharine heard Milovan's mother say "*Sretno sine*," wishing her son good luck before she watched him scale the stairs as he held his wife's hand.

At the top, just feet away from Katharine, Milovan stopped before turning back to the crowd to yell "Kush" before he and his wife entered the courthouse. Katharine smiled, recognizing the word her neighbors used to quiet their barking dogs. It was the perfect thing to say to the pack on the steps.

Vlado, too, kissed Milovan's mother and then followed Milovan and Steffie up the stairs and inside with his wife, Vera.

Katharine saw an opportunity and hurried to find the men and their wives inside. At the main stairway she called up the steps, "Mr. Dedijer, did you know the Western media would be barred from today's trial?"

Vlado stopped climbing the stairs and turned to look down at her. His gaze locked with hers before he replied, "No." Then he added that he had no further comment, and he turned away and continued to climb the stairs.

Katharine repeated her query to Milovan.

Not bothering to stop, Milovan replied he was aware the media would be barred from the trial and added he also had no further comment.

Katharine felt a burst of disappointment. This couldn't be it.

She wove through the other people on the stairs, skipping steps where she could, trying to close the gap between her and the defendants. At the second-floor landing she pushed open the heavy wooden door into the narrow, dimly lit hallway. Milovan was ahead of her, nearing a door midway down the hall where two uniformed police officers stood at attention in front of a double-doored entrance. She broke into a jog, reaching Milovan as the doors were opening to admit him and his wife. Katharine paused for a moment before she reached out to tap his shoulder.

When Milovan turned around, she found herself looking into a pair of deep-set, dark eyes glimmering with activity. She could feel him cataloguing her, taking her in. She returned his stare. As she did, she noticed something else behind the sparkle—a look she recognized in herself. She saw cold determination that was wholly unbreakable. A guard said something to him, and Katharine blurted out, "Mr. Djilas, if there is ever anything we can do to help, you know where to find us."

Milovan remained still, maintaining eye contact for another moment, his dark eyes unblinking, and then he abruptly turned and walked into the courtroom. As the doors closed behind him, Katharine realized he hadn't said a word. She wasn't even sure he had understood her.

She stayed rooted where she was, watching. Dedijer was now

at the door, but realizing Vera was no longer with him, he turned back, saying, "Vera, Vera, come on, Vera."

Hearing the faint whimpers of someone crying behind her, Katharine looked to find Vlado's wife caught in the middle of a nearby group. Katharine reached for her friend's hand and pulled Vera forward through the crowd before pushing her toward the door. As Vera slipped her hand in Katharine's, she managed to wish Katharine, "Good morning," in between her sniffles.

Instinctively Katharine asked Vera if she had any comment.

Vera stopped crying long enough to respond, "No, please no," before her eyes flooded again. Her body heaved into deep, guttural sobs that shook her from head to toe as she took her husband's arm and the courtroom swallowed them up.

With the courtroom doors closed, Katharine sized up the two uniformed men guarding the entrance, considering whether she could try to force her way inside. Raymond came up beside her, and the two of them made a go of it together, trying to propel themselves inside, but they were pushed back, hard. Katharine made eye contact with one of the guards, holding his gaze even as he curled his upper lip to snarl at her, his yellow teeth and beady eyes reminding her of a childhood run-in with a rabid dog. As if he could read her mind, he sputtered out four words at Katharine: "No ticket, no entry."

Undeterred, Katharine lingered outside the courtroom entrance, taking in the rank smell of sweat, cigarettes, and wet wool from the coats of the growing crowd around her. Everyone was jostling, hoping like her to sneak a peek into the courtroom. With their hats removed now that they were inside, Katharine saw most of the crowd were just teenagers, perhaps students from the university sent by the Communist Party. She scanned the crowd for Ed, assuming he'd be nearby, wanting to share her observation with him. But before she could locate him, from somewhere behind her, a hand grabbed her shoulder and pulled her back forcefully. Katharine stumbled a little before quickly steadying her footing.

She turned around to confront her aggressor, whose hand still gripped her shoulder, and came face-to-face with a twenty-something man with a sneer. "No tickets, no entry," he spat at her, repeating himself several times before letting go of her and shoving her sideways as he pushed himself forward to stand in between the two uniformed guards blocking the door. Finding his post, the youth glared back at Katharine.

Katharine stood there dumbly, the whole thing throwing her slightly off-balance. By then, most of the other foreign correspondents had flanked her. She turned around to accept their concern, still shaken by the incident but trying not to show it, when she felt a new force pushing against her back. When it stopped, she and the other reporters were halfway down the hallway. A small group of teenagers stood near them, jeering in Serbian: "We hate you as the supporters of the traitors of our country." Katharine tried not to roll her eyes, and after a few more minutes, the hecklers receded.

The foreign correspondents stood around deliberating what to do next when a local lawyer, whom many of them knew, came up with a suggestion: why not call on the court president? Katharine expected little to come from the effort, but since neither she nor anyone else had a better idea, their entire group set off to find the court president.

They made a funny sight as they turned down an adjacent hallway, fourteen correspondents walking in a pack like lions searching for their prey. Earle was at the front and Katharine at the back, with the twelve others taking up the entire width of the hall in between.

The group reached their destination and filed into the open office door one by one, so that by the time Katharine got there, the small office was packed tight. A white-haired, pompadoured man in his midfifties sat at a desk stacked high with papers before a dark wooden bookshelf displaying books by Karl Marx and Vladimir Lenin. As Katharine entered, Milivoje Seratlic jumped up from where he'd been sitting. At five feet, eight inches tall, Seratlic was still several inches shorter than every reporter, a fact everyone in the room—including himself—noted. Seratlic knew all of them well. Some of the reporters routinely asked him for quotes, and Katharine guessed that to some he also disclosed secrets.

But this morning, maybe because it was all of them together, maybe because he was following orders, or maybe because he felt threatened, he lashed out when Earle addressed him. Making up for his height with animation, Seratlic clenched a fistful of papers in his right hand so tight his knuckles turned white. He waved them around vigorously as he spoke. "I have nothing for the foreign press, and I have no time to talk with you," he sputtered. He added that no details would be provided to them that day or any other day—they could not see the indictment or talk to either defense attorney, and they would receive no announcements about progress. Katharine finally lost count of how many times he said "*nista, nista*," nothing, nothing.

"Is this trial secret?" someone asked.

"No, it is public," Seratlic replied.

Then he shooed them all out of his office, his face so red Katharine wondered if he'd even taken a breath, and slammed his office door ceremoniously behind the last reporter out.

In the hall, they regrouped. They knew technically Seratlic was right. The Yugoslav penal code, something all Western reporters learned cold, prescribed that all criminal trials be open to the public except those members of the public that the court president chooses to exclude in the public interest.

After a half-hearted effort to get into the courtroom one last time as Katharine's attempt to tell the guards the court president had said the trial was open failed, the group disbanded. Some went to their offices to await a report from Tanjug, the official Yugoslav Communist news agency. Others hung about the halls or went outside to wait for news. Someone made a report to the American embassy, but there was little hope the bilateral agreement between Yugoslavia and the United States guaranteed the reporters the ability to cover trials. It only guaranteed mutual amounts of publicity in both countries.

Ed and Katharine found a hard wooden bench at the end of the hallway to wait. She shrugged out of her camel wool coat and laid it flat across the narrow slats of the bench to create a makeshift card table. Katharine watched Ed expertly separate a deck of cards into two piles to shuffle for a game of gin rummy, the ornate blue design of the pack of Hoyle cards crisp and clear before he struck them all together in a clattering mess.

As she sat there, watching and listening, her mind wandered
back to the last time she'd had such rotten luck.

———

Twenty-one years earlier, in July 1934, Katharine had been looking for something besides motherhood to occupy her time when
on a hazy, hot evening the shrill ring of the telephone pierced the
air. She had been dozing in a chair in the study of the small, two-
story house in St. Paul, Minnesota, that had been home for her
and Ed and their now eight-month-old son, Sandy, for the past
several months. Sandy was a difficult baby who did not sleep well,
but she had finally gotten him down, and he currently lay asleep
nearby. She didn't want him to stir, so she sprinted the few feet to
the kitchen to pick up the telephone before it rang again.

On the other end, she heard Ed's voice clear and transac-
tional. The St. Paul police had just killed Homer Van Meter, John
Dillinger's right-hand man and the last living member of his gang,
in a storm of bullets on University Avenue. The FBI believed the
Dillinger gang was responsible for at least a dozen robberies across
several states, and they had been working with local law enforce-
ment to track down the gang over the past year. Ed was on dead-
line for another story he was doing for a radio show he hosted, and
he begged Katharine to go to the morgue to verify the story.

Katharine did more than that. When she filed the story for Ed
later that night, the write-up carried a unique detail: Van Meter's
money belt containing $52,000 was missing from the inventory of
his possessions in the police report. With this single fact, which
Ed broadcast on air, Katharine got Ed a career-changing scoop.

She also prevented the corrupt St. Paul police force from keeping a significant windfall by making the missing money a topic of public record, forcing the police officers involved to turn over the money.

The harassment began two days later. The phone calls came first, threatening the couple if they covered any more stories about the police force. Undeterred, Ed kept doing his job. But less than a month later, Katharine and Ed woke to the sound of car tires screeching on the road outside their house. Ed went downstairs to investigate, and when he opened the front door, he found their son's empty baby carriage ablaze on the front porch.

Katharine did the only sensible thing she could think of. She called her father, who was working at the War Department in Washington. Her father used his connections to contact the FBI. Several hours later a bright, shiny-eyed man in a dark suit from the FBI's local office knocked on the Clarks' door. When he left, he nodded to the two men sitting in a black sedan across the street. The Clarks were officially under round-the-clock protection.

An uneventful week passed before a phone call one morning interrupted their breakfast. The local FBI agent was on the other end of the line. He insisted that neither Ed nor Katharine leave their house until he arrived. An hour later, the agent pounded on the Clarks' front door. Instead of offering an explanation, he simply invited them out to their driveway where their Model A was parked. He pulled back the canvas top of the car to reveal hundreds of dollars in bonds stuffed inside. Katharine gasped. She had never seen so much money. The FBI agent told Ed and Katharine that the money was likely stolen, as there were two St. Paul police cars with two officers each currently parked around the corner from their home waiting to arrest the Clarks on a trumped-up robbery charge.

Dumbstruck, they decided to leave St. Paul. Ed submitted his resignation to *The St. Paul Daily News* the next day. In a week, he accepted a more family-friendly job covering crime in the courts of Alameda County in California, near where Ed's mother lived. Katharine begrudgingly gave in, but she vowed she would never surrender again.

The memory of this pledge echoed in her head as she heard Ed declare he had gin rummy It was quickly joined by another thought: Ed always got the lucky breaks.

At a quarter past midnight, almost sixteen hours after the trial began, Katharine and Ed sat inside their old, brown Peugeot wagon outside Belgrade's courthouse, waiting. They had stopped guessing when they might hear a verdict, replacing that game with trying to create different animals with their breath as it hit the frosty air.

Neither Katharine nor Ed had been able to learn much during the breaks in the trial throughout the day. The only development had been that by midmorning the court president had made the trial officially secret, because as the Communist press reported the next day, a public session would be the "detriment of good relations" between Yugoslavia and other countries. Otherwise, little trickled out of the room, including the two defendants who stayed inside even during an hour-long break between four and five.

Sixteen hours later the crowd from the morning had melted like the snow. The only people interested enough to still be outside were the other foreign correspondents alongside a handful of the defendants' relatives. Most sat scattered in parked cars on the quiet street under the veil of soft lamplight, but a few brave souls stood huddled together shivering in the night, waiting.

Katharine saw a tall shadow appear in the frame of the courthouse entrance. Bolting down the stairs, the man made his way to a dark sedan parked immediately in front of their car. He leaned into a rolled-down window to speak, and Katharine watched as three heads inside the car turned toward him. Katharine grabbed Ed's gloved hand, squeezing it in anticipation as she leaned forward, squinting in the hopes she could get a better look at what was going on. After a minute, the man stood up and opened the passenger door. A cane emerged first, followed by a hand and two long legs. Slowly, Milovan's mother stood and bent over the cane, grasping the man's offered forearm. Katharine watched the woman hobble to the base of the stairs, before turning to Ed. He was already exiting the car, and Katharine hastened to do the same.

The Clarks joined a small crowd of two dozen people forming at the base of the courthouse stairs just as another man appeared at the door carrying a large chrome camera. At the second to last step, he stopped and turned around, centering himself in front of the door and kneeling down to wait.

Moments later Milovan appeared wearing a wide grin. Steffie stood next to him clinging to his arm, exhaustion hanging heavily across her face and body. She had the same look Katharine had seen on soldiers who returned from battle alive but with their lives forever changed by what they had seen and experienced. The camera flash popped. The bright light blinded Katharine for a moment. Her eyes readjusted just in time to see Milovan, now at the base of the steps, leaning down to kiss his mother. He continued to ignore questions the reporters flung at him as he walked off into the cold night with his mother on one arm and his wife on the other.

Vlado appeared several minutes later wearing a smile so broad it rivaled the largesse of his shoulders, contrasting sharply with Vera's tear-stained cheeks, which now shimmered in the lamplight. They too stopped only for the cameraman and then proceeded to a waiting car. Vlado's limp was more prominent now, and ignoring the reporters, he leaned heavily on Vera to help steady his gait.

As Vlado closed the car door, members of the party press, who had gained admission to the trial, began to trickle outside. There was a somewhat artificial camaraderie among the foreign correspondents and the Communist newsmen. While the verdict was not clear from the expression on either Milovan's or Vlado's face, soon everyone in the small crowd on the stairs knew the details. Both defendants had been found guilty of hostile propaganda and sentenced to prison time, which had been immediately suspended.

Surprise crackled among the Western correspondents. Katharine turned to Ed, her mouth open to speak. He shook his head and nodded in the direction of their car. She knew he was right; there was nothing more they would learn, and speaking in the open, even as members of the Western press, was neither smart nor safe.

Katharine and Ed said their goodbyes quickly and walked to their car in silence. It was only after Ed turned the key in the ignition and let the engine run for a couple of minutes to warm it up

that he dared say to Katharine that this was simply another example that "Titoland often is a wonderland where anything but logic
applies." He added that the case reminded him of an old Balkan
saying Vlado had taught him right after the war: "All the cats satisfied and all the mice alive."

Yes. Everyone is satisfied, she thought. As Ed pulled the car out
into the slushy street toward home in the dark of night, he couldn't
see Katharine's wide grin.

The next morning, just before eight, Katharine joined Ed on Rade
Končara, the narrow cobblestone lane that ran in front of their
green, two-room house. An early morning storm had blanketed
the city with a thin layer of snow, giving literal meaning to the
English translation of Belgrade from the Serbian Beograd as "the
white city."

When Katharine wasn't concentrating on where she was walking, her eyes were drawn to the lone splashes of color poking out
from beneath the white lacquer. The sheen of copper rust that
peered through the edges of the old, weathered cars where the
snow and ice had not quite been able to land, the deep green of the
fir trees that lined the street in no apparent pattern, weighed down
by icicles that glistened in the sunlight shining down from the now
cloudless cerulean sky above.

At the end of the lane, they turned north toward the city center, walking along a wide avenue lined by tall buildings with balco-
nies that had once been fine and grand but that now sagged from
years of war and neglect. A single-car tram clattered down the

center of the avenue, while a dozen cars filled its lanes, engines roaring fiercely against the cold, weaving in between the horse-drawn wagons carrying people and goods, all taking cues from the large Cyrillic street signs marking the various intersections. A sour smell of diesel and cabbage competed with the sweetness of freshly baked bread. The shops were just opening their doors and windows, cranking their cloth awnings up toward the sky to let in the morning and the people. Dressed in colorless frocks covered by coats and scarves in various shades of black and gray, women with dour expressions and baskets were already out shopping for food from stores that had little to offer in variety and long lines to wait in, while men sat around tables inside smoky cafés drinking strong Turkish coffee, fiddling with their pipes, and waving their hands in passionate conversations about the smallest of issues.

A typical morning in Belgrade, Katharine thought.

After half an hour Katharine and Ed reached Terazije Square, the de facto city center. Jumbled together over centuries, the square put the city's patchwork past on display. Multistory buildings crafted in stone, brick, and metal ranging in style from Turkish to Renaissance and Socialist to Modern served as small homes, administrative offices, restaurants, and hotels. One didn't have to look too hard to see the bullet holes still marking many of these structures, a tangible reminder of the German occupation from the last World War. Color peeked out here too—pale yellow walls trimmed with white, red terra-cotta roofs, and green awnings covering the display windows of the bakeries and kafanas whose smell filled the air with the delicious aroma of fresh bread and pastries.

Standing on the sidewalk that ran along the park, Katharine

stopped to let a trolley car jangle in the street before them. As it passed, her eyes didn't follow the train. Instead her gaze continued higher up, taking in the majesty of the Hotel Moskva directly across the square from where she stood with Ed.

The hotel was the tallest building on the square. But it was what the eight-story building with its green and cream mosaicked facade reminded Katharine of that always made her stop to study it. Growing up, Katharine had dreamed of living in a Bavarian castle like the ones found in her favorite childhood fairy tales. She'd favored the original stories, the ones where the endings didn't always end in a happily ever after but instead showed how actions have consequences. Even as a girl she'd never understood the logic in telling untruths, glossing over reality. It was what made the propaganda from the local press even more infuriating to her. On this winter morning, most of the floral motifs that decorated the ceramic tilework were still visible—what little spots the snow's veneer latched on to sparkled in the morning sun, adding to the building's mystique instead of covering it up. Every time Katharine stood here, she couldn't quite believe Ed had an office inside.

Katharine and Ed entered the hotel's opulent lobby. In the present day, had there not been a charm about it that held her back, Katharine might have used the word *gaudy* to describe the hotel's long marble lobby that ran the length of the building. An oversize painting in the style of Botticelli commanded one's attention from the back wall. She was certain it was a reproduction; otherwise she assumed Tito or another party leader would have taken it for his own personal use long ago. A gold-leaf ornamental frame accented the scene of nymphs and women in various stages of undress while gold paint emphasized the nooks of the numerous columns and panels on the walls and ceiling. She had always been curious whether the frame had inspired the accents or the other way around.

Katharine turned to follow Ed toward the lift, her eyes locking on the only other art, an official photograph of Tito donning his full military dress resplendent with medals, ribbons, and ornate buttons. The splendor of a Communist leader dressed with so much flair struck Katharine as hypocritical.

They passed by the hotel's busy café known to serve the best coffee in the city. Katharine was tempted to suggest they stop for a cup when a loud noise caught her attention. She scanned the room for its source and noted four men with necks as wide as their chests looking unnatural and uncomfortable in stiff, blue serge suits, the uniform of Yugoslavia's secret police, the UDBA. Planted on the ground, an aproned waitress knelt near the men's thick black shoes, sweeping up a broken cup from the floor as the men leaned back against the bar studying the room.

Yugoslavia's secret police are not always so secret, Katharine thought as she stepped into the red-carpeted elevator and heard the heavy, ornate gold doors shut with a thud behind her. Ed and Katharine were alone in the car. Before she could say anything, knowing her so well, Ed reminded Katharine that the secret police in Yugoslavia had an unwritten rule not to touch Western journalists. As with many things under Titoism, the nationalist brand of communism the country had forged since 1948, Yugoslavia did things its own way.

The elevator dinged. They stepped out of the lift and continued down a long, red-carpeted corridor to the entrance to *Time's* office. The Associated Press and several other foreign papers also kept their offices in this grand hotel.

Inside *Time's* office, Katharine caught her breath a little as she took in the view. Out of one of the two large windows running the expanse of the wall before her, she saw the tree-filled Kalemegdan Park, whose footprint documented Belgrade's storied past. Since the third century, the park had been conquered, destroyed, and rebuilt more than forty times.

Katharine also noted the confluence of the Danube and Sava rivers beyond the park's edge. From this high up, the two distinct colors of the rivers, the Danube's teal and the Sava's gray, could be seen joining but not mixing, creating a single, blurred line where the two bodies of water met. It was a thing of natural beauty, made even more brilliant this morning by the sun shining down, illuminating the colors with a shimmering sheen. It struck Katharine that this confluence represented Yugoslavia itself, a country barely two decades old, one that knitted together many different ethnicities and religions with none of them quite mixing.

Katharine wondered how long the nation could last. If Tito had his way, ruling with an iron fist and via a single party, she thought perhaps a very long time. Tito was notorious for getting rid of his enemies. That was why it was so puzzling how lightly he had treated Vlado and Milovan.

Reminded why she was there, Katharine turned her gaze away from the window in search of the telex, a big, ugly tan machine that sent communications all around the world. Brimming with excitement, Katharine sat down and pulled her notebook out of her handbag. She opened to the page on which she'd written her report from the previous night in longhand and went through a mental checklist of all the quirks of sending a message by telex—the symbols she needed to use to signal capital letters and quotation marks, because those formatting luxuries did not exist on the machine. Then, she punched her report about the trial to her editors at the *Chicago Tribune* into the machine's thin, paper tape. The loud clattering of the keys overtook any other sound or thought, echoing off the walls around her.

After she'd written three paragraphs, she fed the paper through the machine, which would transmit her message across the Atlantic Ocean to the newsroom in Chicago. She waited a few minutes to receive confirmation the message had gone through before packing up her things and going to find Ed.

She found him sitting at his desk, typing. Telling him goodbye, Katharine hurried off. She had woken up with an idea that morning but needed more information to pull her plan together. She hoped her friend Joan Clark, the secretary to the U.S. ambassador, would help answer some of her questions.

TWO

BELGRADE

February 1955

On an exceptionally cold morning in February, Katharine awoke before the sun with a start. She had been dreaming about Milovan and the trial again. For the past several weeks it was all anyone in Belgrade had talked about.

The Communist Party press had focused its coverage on the Western press rather than the trial itself, accusing the newsmen of being agents of unidentified "western circles" who were trying to interfere with Yugoslavia's internal affairs and damage its reputation abroad.

But everyone else was focused on the mildness of the punishment for Milovan and Vlado. No one could understand it. As Ed wrote for *Time*, "even Communists in Belgrade appeared stupefied by the mildness of the punishment, and soon the rumor was all over town that Tito himself had sent word to go easy on his old comrades." Some felt the softer punishment had to do with the father-son-like relationship between Tito and Milovan. Others like Ed and Katharine believed it was more calculated, that Tito desired the "West to think of him as a warmhearted chap beneath all those medals and all that bluster."

Two facts informed Katharine and Ed's opinion. Yugoslavia had borrowed a half billion dollars from the United States in economic aid and one billion dollars in military aid since 1950. Tito had done this to ensure Yugoslavia's solo approach to communism could succeed. The second fact was Tito's strong reaction to a question Katharine had asked him about Milovan at a foreign correspondent dinner in February 1954. Over a dessert of Baked Alaska, Katharine requested comment on Milovan, whom the Yugoslavs had just removed from his office as vice president. With eyes narrowed and in a voice that was suddenly sober despite numerous martinis and wine, Tito answered Katharine: "Djilas is dead—politically." The dinner had ended shortly after.

Katharine thought about this exchange now, remembering how Tito had been uncharacteristically clumsy—spilling his glass of red wine on the crisp white tablecloth that covered his table on the elevated dais at one end of the room—as she looked up at the ceiling of their bedroom counting the cracks that ran across it, trying to calm her racing mind. But she couldn't stop the questions tumbling around inside her head. She could still see the crowd moving, spitting at Milovan, the scene vividly playing over and over. Her revulsion to it built inside her again as it had when she'd witnessed it that day.

She checked the time. Too early.

Ed snored loudly next to her. She turned her body away from him and sighed, her breath rustling the papers on the table next to her bedside. Only an empty glass with the remnants of last night's scotch prevented them from blowing off the table onto the dusty parquet floor below.

After several minutes Katharine gave up trying to fall back asleep. *No better time than the present to start on the plan,* she thought.

Katharine eased out from under the layers of blankets they used to keep warm during Yugoslavia's bitter winter months, topped by the patchwork quilt they'd purchased from a farm in upstate New York their first year of marriage. She stared down at the quilt remembering how she'd almost burned it when they had separated six years after they wed. But something about their split hadn't felt final, so she had packed the quilt away in a box. Listening to Ed's thunderous snoring, she acknowledged that while it hadn't been a smooth path, she was glad for her instinct. After the war, she and Ed had been able to settle in together again, and now the quilt brought much-needed color to an otherwise plain room.

As she sat up, Ed stirred slightly and pulled the covers closer to him. Katharine froze, not wanting to wake him and answer questions about why she was up so early.

When she heard Ed's snoring settle in more deeply, Katharine quickly felt around for her slippers on the floor. She pulled on her plaid flannel robe and shuffled the short distance across the bedroom floor, stepping into the bungalow's only other room and shutting the door to the bedroom silently behind her.

Sunlight was just beginning to creep through the main room's large, eastern-facing windows, producing a kaleidoscope of color across the furniture and fabrics. Katharine had never been up this early alone before, and she took in the room as if anew, marveling at it all.

At one end, the kitchen stood at attention waiting to be used. A large copper pot sat lonely on the tiny black stove—the only object that wouldn't fit into one of the drawers or cupboards. Next to it, a small white sink, spotted yellow with age and barely large enough to fit dishes from an intimate dinner party, sat empty. They were fastidious in cleaning it up each night to prevent rats.

At the room's opposite end, closest to the door, was the living area. A small sofa and two wing chairs—dulled by age and wear—were arranged face-to-face as if in conversation with each other. Their dog, Lucky, a glossy cocker spaniel, lay sleeping in the room's center near a mahogany table that served as both the place where they ate their meals and where Katharine worked.

A bookshelf that Ed built to house their many novels ran the length of the room against the windows. Katharine walked over to turn on the radio that rested on a central shelf next to their record player. She glanced down at the brown-and-red Shiraz rug that covered a large portion of the bungalow's parquet floor. She'd fallen in love with the geometric pattern of angular-shaped nightingales when she'd first seen it five years prior hanging in the open-air market in Tehran. But this morning, instead of thinking of the nightingale's symbol of happiness and contentment, she remembered her purchase of it—the lively negotiation with the old merchant who had been so impressed with Katharine's bargaining skills that he'd given her a small copper plate as a token of gratitude for the vigorous exchange. The memento now sat in a place of honor at the top of the bookshelf, directly above the radio. She glanced up at it for a moment dazzled at the light dancing off it as she turned the radio dial and heard the familiar crackle of the broadcast. She closed her eyes, lulled into her memories by the sound, traveling back to when she was fourteen and had experienced this wonder for the first time.

In the early hours of November 30, 1924, under the eaves of the open windows of the Officers Club on Corregidor Island in the Philippines, she had crouched, listening to the merriment inside. Around three o'clock in the morning, a hush had fallen over the crowded room, replaced by a faint whirring hum. Out of curiosity, she had raised her head so that her eyes just crested the window-sill. Her gaze fixated on the same thing captivating the attention of the hundred or so army officers inside the brightly lit room. No one could not take their eyes off the tawny man sitting on a dais at a table. He was dressed in white duck-cloth shorts and a thin white shirt, his hands alternating between fiddling with the knobs on a large brown box and taking a handkerchief from his back pocket to wipe the sweat from his forehead. For a brief period, it was as if every person was frozen. Then, an abrupt hiss followed by a deep male voice blasted the silence, crackling across each of the six speakers dispersed around the room, melting the moment away.

For the next two and a half hours, Katharine had stayed there under the eaves, captivated by it all. Eleven thousand miles away, in a Baltimore stadium, Army was playing Navy in front of a crowd of 78,000 in its annual football tradition. Yet here in this club room, a low, clear voice called the game live, play by play. In the background the sound of the crowd in Baltimore made it feel like she was there among the throngs cheering on Army. Katharine had gone to the Philippines for her father's posting expecting to be completely cut off from the United States and everything familiar to her. But a radio challenged that assumption. She was connected back home in one of the most freeing ways she'd ever experienced. And she was hooked.

Fifteen years later the military provided Katharine another adventure for the taking. When Ed left to join the Royal Navy in late 1939, wanting to join the war effort despite the fact the United States was not in it yet, she and her son, Sandy, had moved to live with her parents in the Panama Canal Zone, where her father was stationed leading the Pacific Coast Artillery Corps. With his thirty thousand troops spread across the jungle manning the antiaircraft artillery gun positions, her father had established two fifty-watt transmitters to support communication to the men. Katharine quickly volunteered to help the small team of men who helped entertain the troops with music and news, ensuring the soldiers stayed tuned to the radio so they heard the alerts for their work when they came across the airwaves.

The programming quickly became popular with the troops as well as civilians working for the Panama Canal Department. Though minor, the job gave Katharine a sense of purpose, unlocking skills that had been dormant since Minnesota. Later that summer, when the call came in from Powel Crosley, Jr., a businessman who owned the radio station WLW in Cincinnati, to her father looking for him to loan a man from his troops to WLW, Katharine had eagerly volunteered. She knew her father couldn't justify sending any of his men away, as the world was at war. With Katharine's mother's offer to care for Sandy in Katharine's absence, it was settled.

Katharine left and never looked back. After a year in Ohio, she caught the eye of Stan Broza, the head of programming at WCAU, the first CBS affiliate radio station, in Philadelphia. When Broza offered Katharine a job to announce for a new show, she pounced. Her father was now in command of the defense of the Eastern Seaboard in New York, but he had set up his wife, Sandy, and Katharine's sister, niece, and nephew in Philadelphia. The fact Katharine's family was in the same city was an afterthought, but she kept that to herself.

So it was that on September 30, 1942, shortly before 5:15 p.m. Katharine walked into WCAU's brand-new office on Chestnut Street for her first broadcast of *Today's News for Children*. She sat in a small radio booth before a microphone larger than her face and read from her script, reciting the sentiment that had been used in the ads taken out in the newspapers to promote the show. The world was in a rare period of history. Her aim was to "advance history lessons while history was in the making" by taking headline events and putting their history, geography, and ethnology in context for school-age listeners. Her pedigree from living and traveling extensively around the world as the daughter of an army general, who was now defending the Eastern Seaboard, was shared to give her authority. Over the fifteen-minute show, she spoke matter-of-factly and without much warmth, causing one reviewer to write that Katharine had come "to the microphone with plenty of authority but an air of condescension." But she was finding her voice.

Katharine had been adamant from the beginning that her program was not to be a conventional "kiddie" show. Although Broza was famous for creating *The Children's Hour* in 1927 with the slogan "Less work for mother dear whose gentle hands, lead us so kindly through little folk lands," that was not what Katharine wanted. She hoped to appeal to youth and adults. And she did. Katharine's show was so successful that Broza soon gave her another daily show to manage: a woman's news show that aired at 10:45 every morning.

Yet she could not quite overcome the limitations of her gender. Katharine was the only U.S. military-accredited female war news correspondent at a local station, but the woman's show was advertised as a mix of news analysis, helpful homemaking tips, and delicious recipes, perhaps partly because one of its main sponsors was a grocery store. Still, when Pat Kelly an executive at NBC claimed women couldn't make the grade as announcers as they possessed "neither the quality of voice nor the endurance," Katharine fired back, publicly. She detailed how in Cincinnati she had worked every day from 2 a.m. to 10 a.m., sometimes taking on a second shift at 6 p.m. as well for three different radio stations, serving as a radio engineer, member of the news staff, and announcer.

Despite the roadblocks—or perhaps because of them—Katharine was innovating everywhere. And so was WCAU. By 1943 she had penned a 1,000-word newsletter to help drive publicity. She had also lectured on radio at Penn Charter, one of the local private high schools. She'd been primarily behind the scenes or in Ed's shadow for so long. But at WCAU, she was the talent, the star.

While Katharine was still relegated to women's work, even that slowly changed. By 1945, Katharine had received national and local recognition for her work. In February, she received the award of merit from the *Afro-American*, a news weekly, for her "constant crusading for equal rights for minority groups." Katharine was singled out for the recognition because of her "unbiased, liberal and enlightened interpretation of the factors behind the recent transit strike" where employees walked out in protest that the Philadelphia Transit Company hired Black conductors and motormen.

And then there had been Berlin. When Katharine set sail in May 1945, she couldn't have imagined the history she would be part of making as one of the first journalists to make it into Allied-occupied Germany, *but that was another recollection for another time*, she thought as Lucky's licks on her ankles brought her back to the bungalow.

Awash with confidence from the memories of her accomplishments, Katharine went to the table and sat down in one of the high-backed chairs, gifts from the Dedijers when the Clarks had first moved to Belgrade. Although utilitarian, they were surprisingly comfortable, and Katharine thought of Vlado and Vera whenever she sat at the table.

Apart from the trial, the last time she'd seen Dedijer was during a dinner at this very table. It had been in early December 1954, the holidays were about to begin, and Dedijer had just been called before the party control board regarding his support for the articles Milovan had written. He had tried to explain to her the tangled web of Communist leadership and loyalty in the country by sharing a local belief: "There is a saying in the Balkans that behind every hero stands a traitor. The difficulty, of course, is to determine who is hero and who is traitor." It had stuck with her.

Now, unable to get this line out of her head, Katharine grabbed a pad of lined paper, turned to a new page, took the cap off a blue fountain pen, and began to write. She scrawled *The Djilas Plan* at the top of the page and underlined the three words with a loud stroke of ink from her pen. She sat back for a moment as she thought about the trial, Vlado, and Milovan. After a few minutes, she leaned forward and started writing, the blue ink covering page after page.

She needed to convince Milovan to talk to her. That she could help him. He had a story to tell, and she wanted to help break it. But she believed she needed someone to help her translate her appeal. Her Serbian was basic, and so, she believed, was Milovan's English. She made a list of who she could trust to help her before she turned her thoughts toward outlining how best to make contact with Milovan again.

She was still at the table working two hours later when Mica, the neighborhood woman who tended their house, arrived. Mica was a short, plain-looking woman, who, though she was Katharine's age, looked a decade older from the worry she wore permanently on her face.

Katharine was forever grateful to their landlady for her referral of Mica's service. Despite the smallness of the space, Katharine didn't want to cook or clean herself. And Mica did so much more than that for the Clarks.

Mica had helped Katharine and Ed assimilate into their life as the only foreigners in their neighborhood. Housing in Belgrade was scarce, but Ed's friend Stojan Bralovic helped them secure this rental after the landlady's husband, Tito's majordomo, was caught pilfering caviar and wine from Tito's personal stores. She'd needed to rent the house out when her husband went to jail.

Katharine remembered one morning after they'd first arrived. Mica was in her second week with them, and Ed had broken out into high-pitched whistling while putting on his shoes. After he left, Mica had turned to Katharine with grave concern, her eyes heavy with seriousness, and explained to Katharine that whistling attracted mice and rats. When Katharine told Ed about the exchange later that night, he'd laughed deeply. But Katharine noticed the next day, as Ed put on his shoes, that he didn't whistle.

Not wanting to be in Mica's way and also not wanting to risk what she'd been working on, Katharine quickly gathered up the papers fanned across the table, making sure to hide the title page. Although Katharine trusted Mica, and she wasn't sure Mica could even read English, now was not the time to put anything to the test.

Katharine stood up, excusing herself, and walked into the bedroom to dress, wondering what superstition Mica might offer if she knew what Katharine was up to.

THREE
BELGRADE

March 1955

Katharine walked into the Café Europa just off Terazije Square wearing her old camel hair coat and her favorite blue scarf. Twenty-one small square tables were haphazardly scattered across the black-and-white tiled floor with an eclectic mix of wooden chairs. Salvaged from different points in history, the chairs gave the place an approachability that made you want to sit and stay. It was just before lunch, but only about half of the tables lay empty waiting for diners, the greasy smell of fried potatoes and pork filling the air. So one barely noticed that the plaster on the dining room walls was yellowing here and there, the age spots mirroring the appearance of the café's owner.

The old Croatian proprietor rushed from the back to greet Katharine, kissing her warmly on both cheeks before showing her to her usual table. Katharine often frequented the café to write or meet sources, and she and the owner had struck up a friendship over a shared love of books and food. But today's visit wasn't about writing or meeting a source; she needed a favor.

Katharine scanned the diners as she followed the old man to the table in the back corner. She did not recognize anyone. More importantly, no one triggered her suspicion. Still, after she removed her scarf and coat and settled into her chair, she monitored the room and door. She'd arrived a full half hour earlier than she'd told her guest, to allow her time to assess the room. This was not the first time she'd held a sensitive conversation at this café, the clanking of plates and silverware providing the perfect loud cover. But today's lunch was different.

Thirty minutes later, Katharine watched as her friend Paul from the West German embassy entered the café, exactly on time. He took off his black fedora and coat, revealing a strong, angular jaw and wavy, dark brown hair. As he spoke to the owner, Katharine recognized the proper demeanor he used with anyone not familiar to him, the one she teased him as being so German. It was how he and Katharine had first interacted before they'd realized how much they had in common.

They had met more than a year ago, forging a bond over war stories and scotch, each one recognizing in the other a kindred spirit. Paul hailed from West Berlin. He had spent the entire war in his hometown city, caring for his invalid mother and, after her death, protecting his family's flat from looters and the Russian troops who rolled in immediately after the Nazis surrendered.

When he'd discovered Katharine had been one of the first journalists to enter Berlin in the war's immediate aftermath, and the first American woman to broadcast out of the city in early July 1945, he couldn't get enough. She was someone who understood what his city had felt like after the surrender. She had experienced what the photographs in the newspapers could not capture: the hunger on a little child's face as he scavenged in the rubble for crumbs, the struggle in the old woman's bend as she lowered to pass a bucket of debris along a long line of women attempting to clear the street, the pungent stench of dead bodies. They'd spent that night in deep reverie, establishing a great friendship.

Paul leaned down to give Katharine a kiss on the cheek before sitting down across from her. He nodded in approval at her glass of wine and ordered one for himself from the young waitress.

They caught up on work and gossip while they ate the daily special, stopping every now and then to toast their accomplishments. After the waitress cleared their lunch plates and was far enough away to be out of earshot, Paul leaned forward, his well-formed features tightened in seriousness. He looked Katharine directly in the eye and asked why she had really invited him to lunch.

The left side of Katharine's mouth edged up in a wry half smile. She should have known better. She leaned in to reply, mirroring Paul's stance and serious expression as she asked him to accompany her to Milovan Djilas's house the next morning. She tried to keep her tone casual, as if visiting an ostracized member of the public was something one regularly proposed.

Paul leaned back in his chair and inhaled deeply, his chest noticeably expanding and then contracting on the exhale. Yet he remained silent, his mouth a straight line.

Katharine continued speaking. She told Paul she needed a translator, as she wasn't sure how much English Milovan understood. She complimented Paul's flawless Serbian and shared how much she trusted him—subtle compliments to try to convince him to agree.

The tinkling of conversations from the other diners filled the quiet that now crowded the space between them. Neither of them said anything as the waitress returned with the check. Katharine withdrew several notes from her wallet, placing the money on the table and putting her water glass on top of the bills out of habit. Sensing he was still considering her proposal, Katharine stood and began to layer for the cold weather outside. Just as she buttoned the top of her coat, Paul told her he'd do it. She clapped her hands together, thrilled with the development.

Outside the café she hooked her arm in Paul's and told him her plan as they walked.

———

The next morning, Katharine blinked her eyes open to see a room full of yellow sunlight. She had slept more soundly than she had in months and felt refreshed.

She turned her head and saw Ed was already gone. She breathed a sigh of relief that she wouldn't have to lie to him that morning.

Katharine dressed in her favorite navy blue suit and pulled her shoulder-length hair back in a low chignon. Examining herself in the mirror, she felt something missing and grabbed a lightly used tube of red lipstick and applied it to her lips, smiling back at her reflection. *There.*

Still smiling with a skip in her step, Katharine went to the main room to grab her coat and scarf. Mica had already let herself in and was dusting the bookshelf. She turned around to greet Katharine and pointed at warm rolls on the table. Katharine grabbed one before she closed the door to the house behind her and joined the trickle of other pedestrians on the narrow street making their way to the city's center. Full of hope and determination, Katharine felt time pass quickly as she made her way to her destination.

At a quarter past eight, Katharine met Paul on the once cream-colored stone front steps of Parliament. Besides the building's baroque green cupola and intricate stone friezes, what Katharine loved most about it was the story behind it: that the interior designer had specified how the rooms should look by drawing watercolors instead of the technical blueprints. While this was her favorite building in the city, she had chosen it this morning for another reason.

Over a year earlier, Milovan had penned numerous articles in Communist Party papers and magazines exploring and challenging Communism. But it appeared to Katharine that it was only after Milovan wrote negatively about the wives of some of his colleagues that the real punishment came.[*] The government held a plenum where they stripped Milovan of all his posts—vice president of Yugoslavia and president of Parliament—and the trappings that went with them—a large house with a garden and a swimming pool, a car, a jeep, luggage, and a passport. Now Milovan and his family lived in a small flat in an apartment building just blocks away from the Parliament building where Katharine and Paul now stood.

---

[*]   *Anatomy of a Moral*, the article where Milovan attacked party members' wives, was not the primary reason for the plenum, but this was a widely held belief by Katharine and others who lived in Belgrade during the time and for years afterward.

The entrance to Ulica Palmotićeva was on the back side of Parliament. It looked like any other residential street in central Belgrade, lined with three-, four-, and five- story buildings whose tired facades were dulled from wear and inattention. In front of these buildings ran a narrow cobblestone street bordered by thin trees and parked cars. Paul and Katharine made their way to number 8 slowly, stopping often to duck between parked cars when vehicles rumbled past.

The stops and starts allowed Katharine to take in her surroundings. When they reached the gray, five-story pre-war building where the Djilases lived, her senses heightened. It was rumored that Yugoslavia's secret police monitored visitors to 8 Ulica Palmotićeva closely, although this morning, no one was in their immediate vicinity.

Katharine had already noticed the silhouette of a woman standing at a second-floor window staring at them from a building directly across the street from the Djilas home. Above the woman, on a small balcony, a man stood holding a camera now trained on her and Paul. She had expected this. Her friends at the American embassy had informed her that a family of secret police agents lived across the street from the Djilas flat, monitoring Milovan's movements around the clock and listening in on conversations in his apartment. Despite the fact her heart was racing, Katharine only just suppressed a temptation to wave at them. Instead, she turned and pushed open one of the heavy wooden-and-glass entrance doors as she muttered to Paul under her breath that the secret police had eyes across the street.

Katharine monitored Paul's reaction out of the corner of her eye, the only movement from his mouth to let out a low chuckle. Then he told Katharine not to worry, he knew all about them. *Of course he did*, she thought and sighed with relief as she walked inside.

On the third floor, Katharine knocked on the door of apartment six. Soon, a medium-built woman with a high forehead and freckled cheekbones flushed slightly with pink opened the door to the building. Katharine instantly recognized Steffie Djilas, Milovan's wife. Now, as she stood in the doorway, the contrast of the light and shadow between the apartment and the hallway made her appear like a sorrowful portrait figure. Steffie's faded black cardigan and skirt hung loosely off her, matching the limpness of the ash-blond hair that framed her pale face. Dark circles underlined her gray-blue eyes, sharpening the straightness of her nose, but when she looked up at Katharine and Paul, it was impossible to miss the warmth in her gaze.

Katharine found her voice, inquiring whether Milovan was available. When Steffie did not respond right away, Katharine looked at Paul, unsure of how to interpret her silence. He translated Katharine's greeting in Serbian and added something to the effect that Katharine was a friendly member of the Western media and would like just a few moments of her husband's time.

A smile erupted across Steffie's face. She stepped aside to let Katharine and Paul into the apartment. Milovan quickly materialized. He was wearing a frayed suede jacket and dark pants, the uniform she had heard he wore while he walked the city streets alone, reminding the world he was still alive.

After brief introductions, Milovan waved them into a cozy

room where a little tow-haired boy who looked about two sat playing with a small, furry white cat. Next to the toddler, Milovan's mother sat sleeping in a chair, an open book on her lap. Shelves surrounded them on nearly all sides brimming with books that Katharine realized at a quick glance appeared to be in at least three languages. At another time and place, she would have gone right up and examined the titles, making comments about ones she had read and asking questions about books that were new to her. But a small, white porcelain statue of Lenin in a position of honor on one of the shelves reminded Katharine why she was there.

She took a deep breath and turned to Milovan, asking him if he remembered her from the courthouse.

Milovan stared back at her blankly, furrowed lines wrinkling his forehead.

Katharine glanced at Paul, who quickly translated what she had said. As Paul spoke, Katharine could see her question now register on Milovan's face, the lines in his brow dissolving. He looked directly at Katharine and nodded, indicating with his hands that they should all sit.

As they did, Katharine told Milovan that she was a journalist for the *Chicago Tribune* and that her husband worked for *Time*. She added that Ed had been in Belgrade with United Press International (UPI) after the war in 1946, and he was a good friend of Vlado.

Milovan looked directly at her and responded in halting English that he knew Ed.

Katharine went on, surprised and encouraged. She told him she had come to reiterate her offer to help him, which she made at the courthouse.

Paul looked at Katharine quizzically before he translated her remarks.

This time Milovan responded at length in Serbian. He waited expressionlessly while Paul turned to Katharine and told her that Milovan was thanking them for the visit but that he wanted to make it clear that he was focused solely on his family at this time.

Katharine sat still, taking in the rejection. A feeling of desperation ran through her. *Was this really it?*

Seeing Paul finish speaking, Djilas nodded at Katharine and stood up.

Katharine grasped for something, anything as a thought popped into her head, and she opened up her handbag. She pulled out her notebook and pen and furiously scribbled her home address, 22 Rade Končara, across the page before ripping the leaf out of the book, the jagged line of the tear just missing the number of their home. She placed the paper on the table in front of the sofa and rose. As she put her pad and pen back in her bag, she pointed at the paper and told Milovan he knew where to find the Clarks before she thanked him.

Milovan nodded again before he turned to leave the room. Katharine and Paul followed him to the front door of the apartment. They shook hands again formally in farewell. And just like that, Katharine and Paul were back outside the flat.

Katharine glanced at Paul, raising her eyebrows at him and bringing her finger to her mouth to indicate they should be silent before she headed to the stairwell door. They walked down the stairs, out the building's door, and into the morning air in silence.

Once outside, Katharine looked at her watch. The entire affair had lasted no more than fifteen minutes. She wondered if she would see him again. She wasn't sure. Something compelled her to look again at the house across the street. The woman was no longer at the window, but the cameraman was still there on the balcony. But now instead of pointing at her, his lens hung from his neck recklessly, as if it too was finished with Katharine.

After Katharine and Paul put several blocks between the Djilases' home and themselves, Katharine leaned in to Paul and told him that the meeting had not gone as she had expected.

Paul tried to console her by telling her it would make a good story one day.

Nodding, Katharine turned to him and agreed, but she asked Paul if he would keep this particular tale to himself for now. She wasn't ready for Ed to hear it.

FOUR

BELGRADE

April–June 1955

A season of mud always followed Belgrade's long, harsh winters, the inches of snow melting, clinging to the thawing ground. Then as the temperatures rose, the mud caked in clumps before finally drying out, allowing flowers to emerge and blossom into the glory of spring.

Like the weather, Katharine's work for the *Chicago Tribune* had dried up. So she found she had plenty of time now to fill the small blue watering can that came with the house, carrying water from the kitchen sink outside to the bright geraniums and roses. She'd never had the time or inclination to care for flowers before, despite the fact her father could lose himself in his garden, painstakingly tending to his carnations and training his roses to grow up the trellises he had built by hand at each of his posts. But as at most homes in Belgrade, visitors entered the Clarks' home via an outer gate and passed through the yard to reach the front door, so she wanted it to look nice.

When Katharine was done with the garden, there were friends

to visit and books to read, both keeping her company while Ed traveled extensively for work. Usually Ed would have asked Vlado and Vera to check in on Katharine, but the two men were no longer speaking, at least not publicly. Immediately following the trial, Vlado had written a letter to *Time* that the magazine published in the February 14 edition. In the letter, Vlado claimed Ed's article, the one Vlado had begged Ed to write, "repeats statements made by me in The London Times, but also [makes] statements which I did not make." Ed knew this was a ploy Vlado was using to appease the Yugoslav government. He'd said as much to his editors, who had added the following to accompany Vlado's letter: "*Time* Correspondent Ed Clark, who has known Dedijer since wartime days, stands by his interview, but understands why Dedijer (since given six months suspended sentence for 'a criminal act of hostile propaganda') did not." Ed knew that although Vlado had received a light sentence, there were other, more private ways for the Communists to continue to punish his friend. Although Dedijer's life was not in danger, the government could take away his ability to teach or write or even put pressure on his wife and children. The result was that Ed and Vlado's relationship, at least in public, was over.

So when Ed returned from a two-week trip through Europe with his boss, James Bell, on a clear Saturday morning in the middle of May, he found Katharine on the couch reading in the warm sunshine, alone.

Katharine looked up to see Ed untuck a newspaper from under his arm and wave it in the air like the newspaper boys used to do in New York City when they sold the evening papers on the corner.

Ed bounded over to where she sat. She took in his grin as wide as a cartoon character, his eyes sparkling with excitement. She knew this look. He always got it when there was a juicy development in a story, or he had an exclusive scoop. Intrigued, Katharine reached her hand up for the newspaper. Her eyes caught a headline and her heart leapt, understanding Nikita Khrushchev and Nikolai Bulganin were coming to visit Tito in Belgrade in two weeks.

This was major news. Joseph Stalin's death two years before had created a new power dynamic in the Soviet Union and an opportunity for Yugoslavia and the Soviet Union to normalize relations that had been severed in 1948. Yugoslavia had left the Information Bureau of the Communist and Workers' Parties, the Cominform, an international organization of world communism, to pursue its own path toward Communism. At the time Stalin had said, "I will shake my little finger—and there will be no more Tito. It will fail." But that had not been the case. Tito had successfully navigated Yugoslavia's own path toward Communism, striking alliances with the West. And now two of the most powerful men in the Communist world—the leader of the Communist Party in the Soviet Union and the head of the Soviet Union's government—were deigning to visit Tito on his turf. Katharine suspected Khrushchev's agenda was to bring Yugoslavia closer to the Soviet Union if not fully back into its orbit. She mused on how Tito might respond.

For the first time in over a month, just for a moment, Katharine forgot about Milovan, who still hadn't replied to her offer of assistance. This visit was exactly the kind of story she had been looking to report. She couldn't wait to share it with her editors at the *Chicago Tribune*.

Katharine joined Ed on his walk to the office the following Monday. It was a warm spring morning, and everything seemed alive. Birds chirped in the trees along Rade Končara, their melodies soothing against the backfire of the half dozen old diesel cars that peppered their journey. The smell of flowers in bloom snuffed out the burning smell of exhaust smoke the vehicles left in their wake. On the main avenue the cafés had expanded their tables outside, and men congregated around the iron tables under colorful awnings drinking their coffees and smoking their pipes, the humming of their vigorous, passionate conversation drowned out by the cars and trolleys and horses. Even the water in the central fountain at Terazije Square was running. Katharine marveled at the architectural feat crafted centuries before to leverage the streams that still ran under the city to power its flow.

Inside *Time*'s office she beelined to the telex machine. But just as Katharine finished punching in her first line of copy, Ed interrupted with a telex message for her. Taking the thin, waxy paper from him, Katharine scanned the note. She immediately understood that her editors already knew about Khrushchev's and Bulganin's visit to Belgrade—they'd read about it in the U.S. papers over the weekend. They informed Katharine they were sending Larry Rue, the paper's veteran foreign correspondent, to cover the story.

She knew of Rue by reputation. He had made a name for himself covering the first World War, and then with the encouragement of the paper's owner, Rue had purchased a De Havilland Gipsy Moth airplane to chase down exotic news wherever he could fly.

She had never met him, but if newspaper jobs were rungs on a ladder, Rue's was at the top, while Katharine's was close to the bottom.

A heaviness pushed down on her, replaced quickly by a shroud of exasperation. It felt like anytime she got close to a big story, a man always swooped in and took away her opportunity.

She took a deep breath in to quiet the anger boiling within her. Exhaling, she crumpled the telex into a tight ball before throwing it into the rubbish bin next to the machine. She wiped her hands against her pants, reached up to brush a loose wisp of hair behind her ear, and stood up to leave, her jaw clenched. She didn't even bother saying goodbye to Ed. She'd seen the guilty look on his face when he delivered the message to her. He already knew she wouldn't be sending a note to her editors or covering the story in the way she had hoped.

———————

Just after 5 p.m. on May 26, Katharine sat alone in the living room of the bungalow, listening to the radio as a silver, two-engine Ilyushin Il-14 touched down on the single runway at Belgrade's Zemun Airport. On any given Thursday evening, the street outside the Clarks' home would be alive with workers returning home for the day, children being called in to dinner, and dogs getting walked. But that night, the street was loud with silence. It would have caught her attention if she weren't so singularly focused on the radio broadcast coming over the wire.

Despite the crackle, Katharine was able to imagine the scene thanks to the newsman's detailed play-by-play. The arrival of the plane. Khrushchev's descent down the stairs. The formal greeting

Tito provided the delegation, complete with lively, patriotic music, and, finally, Khrushchev's remarks in Russian, beginning with "Dear Comrade Tito."

Strange. This was supposed to be a state visit, not a Communist Party one, she thought.

Katharine waited for the customary translation of the speech from Russian to English to augment her rudimentary Russian, but it never came. And when Tito didn't follow Khrushchev with his own remarks as diplomatic courtesy dictated, she was left wondering.

It was hours later, after Ed returned home from his front-row seat at the arrival ceremony, when she received any further details. Ed had flown into their home brimming with news, beginning to talk even as he hung his dark coat and gray fedora on the hooks next to the door.

His boss, Jim Bell, followed Ed inside, apologizing for the dust he was wearing from the day. Katharine told him not to worry, pointing at the layer Ed was currently brushing off his pants, unaware he was the center of attention or of their exchange.

Katharine was fond of Bell, a man who was as cheerful interrogating a head of state as he was ordering dinner. He reminded her of a warmhearted professor rather than a hard-nosed editor. His bald head, chubby cheeks, and wire-rimmed spectacles contributed to this academic image even though she knew from Ed's interactions with him that Bell was not content with merely transcribing the facts. He pushed his writers constantly to bring deep and unique knowledge into their stories.

Bell thanked Katharine and, seeing the questions all over her face, asked her what she wanted to know as he greeted her with a hug.

Everything, Katharine thought. As the three of them sat down to eat the dinner Mica had prepared that morning, Katharine listened as he and Ed told her about the ceremony.

Bell would write later for *Time*'s cover story that Tito was "splendidly adorned—braided cap, sky-blue military blouse with ribbons, red-striped slacks" as he "sat in his open Rolls-Royce and puffed on his long cigarette holder," waiting for the Soviet delegation to arrive. Seven years before. the Russians had called Tito names like "traitor," "fascist," "spy and murder." Now Tito waited "unrepentant and unintimidated, master in his own land." When the plane door opened, "there, half as large as life, stood stubbly little Nikita Khrushchev," his thin hair flying in the wind, his light-blue suit wrinkled and ill-fitting about his hefty middle, "his arms up in a gesture which seemed to say 'Here I am, you lucky people.'"

As Tito walked up the red carpet to greet him, "Khrushchev happily skipped down the plane ramp, looking for all the world like a samovar salesman arriving at Minsk for the annual convention. He was all smiles and handshakes and pats on the back, and seemed to do a happy little dance. Beaming, Khrushchev said to Tito: 'Everything's going to be all right.'"

Bell had equally apt descriptions of the other men on the plane with Khrushchev: "Wistful and out of place in his distinctly subordinate role, goateed Nikolai Bulganin looked like a professor of geology who had suddenly been swept up in a reception for Danny Kaye." Anastas Mikoyan, first deputy premier, was "dark and sour, an Armenian rug merchant unsure of his sucker."

After the Russians had all greeted Tito, they turned to inspect the honor guard standing at attention. But Bell observed that Khrushchev was more focused on hopping "alongside his taller host, talking with his hands," barely giving the soldiers a sideways glance. Tito had frowned as the review ended at a microphone.

Khrushchev stepped up to the microphone and began the speech Katharine had heard on the radio. Over the course of the fourteen-minute speech, Khrushchev apologized to Yugoslavia for the country's ouster from the Cominform in 1948 and blamed everything on Lavrenty Beria, a former head of the Soviet Union's secret police and close associate of Stalin whom Khrushchev had tried and executed in the struggle for power following Stalin's death. Katharine now understood why she'd heard the crowd laugh partway through Khrushchev's speech: the allegation was absurd. Through it all, Bell observed, "Tito stood still, his hand thrust halfway down between the buttons into his blouse like Napoleon, his mouth pulled tight in a straight line for the duration of the speech." According to Bell, "It was the face of a stubborn, impassive Slav, determined that no man should read the thoughts which must have raced behind it."

As Khrushchev finished his speech and it became clear that Tito wasn't going to extend the courtesy with his own remarks, an awkwardness filled the air that you could slice with a knife. Finally, when the tension seemed untenable, Tito gestured to the men to make their way to the line of Rolls-Royces, Cadillacs, Packards, Buicks, and Mercedes-Benzes waiting to take them to their lodging. Along the route, crowds chanted, "Ti-to, Ti-to, Ti-to."

Ed concluded that she really had not missed much. But all

three of them knew she had. She felt a pang of longing listening to all of the details that Ed and Bell had given her, the things that weren't obvious through the airwaves. More than anything, she wished she had been there to see Khrushchev and Tito for herself.

———————

Two days later, in what felt like a consolation prize, the *Chicago Tribune* ran a story Katharine had written about the visit. Her editors had asked her to describe the palaces where the Russians were staying while in Belgrade. Next to her single-column piece was a half-page spread by Rue analyzing Khrushchev's speech. But soon the palaces would factor further into Katharine's destiny.

After two weeks in Yugoslavia, replete with diplomatic talks, trips to places like Tito's vacation island of Brioni, visits to factories in the countryside, and numerous parties, the Russian delegation prepared to attend the grandest fete of all—a farewell reception hosted by the Russian Ambassador in Belgrade, to which Ed and Katharine were invited.

At seven o'clock, Katharine, wearing a simple and elegant long black dress and her hair pulled back in a loose chignon, arrived with Ed at the grounds of the Obrenović dynasty's former royal compound. Built before the idea of world wars and Communist revolutions, the grounds contained two palaces and expansive gardens, which all provided spectacular views of Belgrade.

Katharine and Ed made their way past the manicured rows of roses to the pale, cream-colored palace ornately detailed with caryatids and Doric columns that would serve as the location for the evening's affair. On this clear night, the stars shined as brightly as the men and women walking the red carpet that ran up the wide entrance steps to the palace's front door, which was held open by tuxedoed men standing stiff as statues.

They showed their credentials and passed into a wonderland of splendor. The lemon-yellow walls of the grand reception room shone like the sun under the luster of three Venetian glass chandeliers dangling six feet from the high ceilings. The tinkling of conversation from diplomats, correspondents, and government officials danced around the hall. The marble floor was covered in a sea of glitter—men in uniforms bedecked with medals or showing hints of satin on fine suits, women in long silk gowns, many the latest off the runway from Paris, more than a few with deep décolletés to show off the jewels strung around their necks.

A liveried waiter carrying a tray laden with flutes of champagne passed before them. Ed grabbed two glasses and handed one to Katharine as he leaned in to whisper in her ear that it seemed like overkill to celebrate a joint declaration of friendship. Katharine allowed the sides of her mouth to turn up ever so slightly. She agreed with Ed's assessment.

The Russians had hoped to welcome the Yugoslavs back into their ideological fold during this trip, but instead, Tito had held his ground. Earlier that day, Bulganin, as the head of the Soviet Union government, and Tito had cosigned a document outlining principles of friendship, peace, and commitment to socialism, quite far from the Russian's initial hopes of having Yugoslavia align more closely with the Soviet Union. Right there in that room, seeing the opulence of the reception, Katharine fully understood the power

Tito was up against, and she admired him for a moment for resisting it all.

Katharine scanned the room. She was amazed at how many faces she didn't recognize. The Westerners stood out by the slimmer cuts of their suits and their less flashy dresses and jewelry. There were a lot of them. All the major publications and wires were here—most had flown in their European bureau heads. Rue had already departed, but Katharine's gaze landed on Bell nearby, and she pulled Ed toward his boss.

Bell was speaking to a tall man with a strong, square jaw and well-coiffed dark hair whom Katharine did not recognize. His well-cut suit lent him an air of importance, and Katharine guessed from his height and build that he must be American. Bell greeted Ed and Katharine warmly before he introduced them to his companion, Joseph Kingsbury-Smith, the head of the International News Service (INS), a US-based newswire founded by William Randolph Hearst in 1909.

The foursome fell into conversation easily, and Katharine and Kingsbury-Smith quickly learned they had many mutual friends. Bell and Ed carved off to discuss something for work while Kingsbury-Smith shared with Katharine the many gaffes he had witnessed throughout the officials' visit. How Khrushchev cracked inappropriate—and very bad—jokes, chugged lemonade like a thirsty sailor, and ate an orange with the voracity of a starving animal.

But the most embarrassing incident had occurred the week before when a flat tire on Khrushchev's chauffeured car prevented any further advancement along a country road. Not one to sit idle, the 61-year-old Khrushchev had challenged Mikoyan, his 59-year-old first deputy premier, to a wrestling match. While a mechanic changed the tire, the rest of the party looked on in disbelief as the two men tumbled in a roadside field, both of their faces red and shiny with sweat by the time the car was ready to drive again. According to Kingsbury-Smith, Khrushchev's favorite line was "Some time ago, every Russian was complaining: no butter, no bread, no meat, and always Mikoyan." He told Katharine that Khrushchev was always picking on his comrade.

Katharine was still laughing when U.S. Ambassador James Riddleberger, his wife, and Joan Clark—the ambassador's secretary—interrupted them. When Kingsbury-Smith recounted his story and the quote again, Riddleberger laughed in his warm way, the one that softened his sharp features and put even the lowliest ranking diplomat at ease. The ambassador then regaled the group with how he'd had his own trouble with Khrushchev at the welcome dinner.

He'd been seated next to Khruschev at dinner, and their conversation had covered a range of topics. When it came to the subject of the working class, Khrushchev argued Riddleberger had no sense of what it was or meant. The ambassador had replied that he'd been a farm boy, a bricklayer, and a house painter and guessed he had more contact with the working class than the Soviet leader. When the ambassador's wife chastised him for his bad manners, he told the rest of the group with a twinkle in his eyes that he had merely stated the facts.

They were all still laughing, imagining the scene, when seconds later, a loud voice interrupted their conversation with an announcement requesting that everyone move into the grand hall for a surprise. Kingsbury-Smith excused himself, but before he departed, he asked Katharine to stay in touch. Katharine was taken aback with surprise. She watched him go, hoping despite all the vodka and champagne flowing like water around the room that he would remember her and maybe even offer her a job.

The ambassador and his wife linked arms to oblige the announcement, while Katharine and Joan followed them into a large dining room outfitted with a stage. All the while Katharine scanned the crowd, looking for Khrushchev.

_____

Just past two in the morning, after a three-course buffet dinner and a performance from the Moscow Ballet, the troupe imported to Belgrade just for the occasion, Katharine found herself standing once again with Ed and Bell. This time Frank Kelley, head of the Rome bureau for the *New York Herald Tribune*, had joined their merry group, and the three men traded stories about the night. The rest of the foreign press corps and many Western diplomats stood in small clusters along the second-floor corridor doing the same.

The evening sparkled, the lavish detail and pomp so incongruous with the tenets of communism. Bell had just regaled them all with the conversation he'd overheard between Bulganin and Tito during the ballet performance. Apparently halfway through, not noticing Bell behind him or not caring, Tito had leaned into Bulganin and said, "A dancer is perhaps better looking than a negotiator."

To this Bulganin had replied, "Well, Khrushchev never had legs like these."

As the group stood laughing—only Katharine mostly from disgust—Tito and his beautiful young wife, Jovanka, ushered past. Katharine was always struck by the sight of them. Tito was already an imposing figure, which his tuxedo only sharpened. Jovanka was a mystery: a tall, dark beauty who tonight was in a long gown that dripped of money. But instead of being jealous, Katharine was simply curious. She studied Jovanka in the way women look at other women, before realizing that the appearance of Tito and his wife meant Khrushchev was likely nearby.

Katharine was still holding out hope of seeing the Soviet leader before the night ended. So far she had seen nothing more than a faraway glimpse of Khrushchev's shiny bald head. She knew Khrushchev and Tito had retired to a private room for dinner, but when she looked back at the direction from which Tito and Jovanka had come, she saw nothing.

She turned back to her group and watched as Tito stopped a little farther down the hall, seeming to have registered he was walking by group after group of journalists. Pausing, Tito took his cigarette pipe from his mouth to announce, more than ask, if the guests had enjoyed themselves. Katharine joined in with the others in nodding her head yes.

Someone closer to Tito asked, "How about you? Are you happy? You seem confident and pleased."

"I am satisfied," Tito replied. "Why not?"

Tito glanced back in the direction from which he'd come and leaned into his wife to say something to her before he walked back down the red-carpeted hall.

Several minutes later, Tito reappeared, this time with

Khrushchev in hand. Katharine's stomach flipped. *Finally*. As the two men approached, Katharine studied Khrushchev, taking in the buttons of his shirt straining against his belly, the bell bottom pants doing nothing to flatter his figure. His face was redder than the carpet on which his feet were lumbering in the slobbering walk of someone who was quite drunk. Katharine noted Tito's firm grip on Khrushchev's arm, guiding him down the hall to where Jovanka stood waiting.

As Tito and Khrushchev neared the group, Tito whispered to Khrushchev in Russian, "Journalists."

Khrushchev grinned so widely he could have passed as a living reproduction of a gargoyle rather than one of the more classical figures that graced the palace's many caryatids outside. His round face and bulbous nose stretched to their extremes, revealing an open mouth full of yellowing and gaping teeth. Katharine would have been disgusted if her attention weren't consumed by listening to Khrushchev slur in Russian to Tito, "Oh. They are very dangerous men."

Katharine turned to Ed and Bell, whom she could tell had seen and understood the remarks as well and were suppressing eye rolls. But she knew most of the group, including Frank Kelley, did not speak Russian.

She didn't have to worry, though, as someone in the group next to theirs asked Tito to translate to English.

Tito grinned as he explained.

Khrushchev raised his hands high, pulling out what was left of his tucked-in shirttail, and loudly announced in Russian, "The trouble is, you do not know the Russian people."

Again, Tito was asked to translate, and he did.

Kelley, who was standing next to Katharine, replied to Khrushchev in English, "That is because you keep us out of your country. You do not give us visas. We cannot get in."

By now an aide had come up next to Khrushchev and translated the remarks for him. Tito stepped back and took his wife's hand, taking in the scene before him as if watching a performance. His wife, however, looked as if she wanted to be anywhere but where she was.

Katharine turned her attention back to her immediate vicinity. Khrushchev had stumbled over to their group and was now standing next to her in front of Kelley. Khrushchev's translator had followed and stood behind him.

Khrushchev asked Kelley via the translator, "Is he English?"

"*Amerikanski*," Kelley replied with a grin.

Khrushchev was now so close that Katharine could smell the alcohol and tobacco on his breath. The scent mingling with his sweat was enough to cause her to turn her head to take a large gulp of fresh air. When she faced forward again, she saw she'd missed Khrushchev grabbing Kelley's hand in earnest. "You can come in any time you like," said Khrushchev. "You can come tomorrow." Then, as if realizing he had a captive audience for the first time, he let go of Kelley's hand and stepped back, almost falling, and spoke to the larger group with a giddiness that only those quite inebriated could effect. Waving his hands across a dozen or so of the crowd, he burbled again, "You can all come tomorrow."

Seemingly out of nowhere, Mikoyan, the deputy prime

minister, grabbed Khrushchev by the elbow and attempted to lead him away, saying, "Come on, let's go. Let's get out of here."

But Khrushchev shook him off. Katharine thought even sloppy-drunk Khrushchev could still best Mikoyan, before she caught movement out of her eye. Tito was swaying from side to side with an amused expression on his face. She turned back to Khrushchev as he repeated to everyone, "You can all come tomorrow!"

A German reporter identified his nationality before asking, "Can I come too?"

"Oh sure," said Khrushchev. "We are not afraid of the devil and you are not devils."

Mikoyan again tried to remove him, but Khrushchev wriggled free. He went on, loudly telling the reporters, "Our agreement with Yugoslavia contributes to peace and lessens international tensions."

"What did he say?" someone asked Tito. In all the jostling, Khrushchev seemed to have lost his translator.

Tito shook his head and said dryly, "He said peace," before moving toward Khrushchev.

"'Yes, yes," said Khrushchev happily, "peace, peace." He repeated this phrase, his hand outstretched.

As he stumbled again, Tito grabbed the tottering Khrushchev by the arm and led him downstairs, saying, "Come on, Khrushchev. These journalists will take you prisoner."

All the while, Khrushchev continued uttering, "Peace, peace."

Katharine watched, transfixed by the scene. She had come tonight to see the leader who it was rumored—and confirmed on this visit—to have replaced Stalin as the figurehead of the Soviet Union. But where Stalin had been ruthless, Khrushchev struck her as oafish. Now as she watched this drunk, rumpled man who was as tall as he was wide kiss every woman in sight, she was disgusted and at a loss for words.

Moments later, Katharine watched two men built so solidly that they had to be security guards flank Khrushchev. Each grabbed an elbow and lifted the Communist leader off the ground. As they carried him to his car, Khrushchev's feet still moved as if trying to walk through the air.

Generally speaking, Katharine viewed politics as a profession that required a certain refinement of character that was either evident at birth or acquired over time. But in Khrushchev, Katharine saw none of that. Katharine turned back to the group of correspondents, her mouth wide open from the spectacle she had just witnessed. There was no way President Eisenhower or the new British prime minister, Anthony Eden, would behave in that manner. As she listened to the men taking bets about whether Khrushchev would remember the exchange the following day, she shook her head and questioned if any of that even mattered.

———

Just after eight the next morning, at about the same time the Soviet delegation was leaving on the twin jet engine that had brought them to Belgrade two weeks earlier, Katharine woke to someone knocking loudly on the bedroom door.

At first Katharine thought she was dreaming. Then as she journeyed into consciousness, she told herself it was just her head pounding, a result from the evening before. Grasping her fore-head, she pushed down on it as she let out a small groan. She ran her dry tongue across her teeth, swallowing deeply and tasting the champagne and caviar along with the smoke and vodka from last night's reception.

But the knocking came again. They had only gone to bed four hours ago. *It must be important, or Mica wouldn't bother us,* she thought. Given the Clarks' occupations, visitors called on them at all hours of the day, mostly for Ed. But Katharine heard Ed snor-ing next to her as the knocking continued. *He always sleeps through things.*

Katharine sighed and willed herself to rise out of bed, standing up slowly to stave off the wave of nausea that threatened to over-come her, and staggered toward the door.

Katharine managed to croak out a question to Mica, asking her why she was knocking.

"There is a visitor at the outer door. A stranger," Mica replied.

Katharine indicated she would be right out and turned back toward the bed, where Ed was pulling a blue sweater over his head. He told her it was probably for him and suggested she go back to bed.

Too tired and hungover to argue, Katharine fell face-forward onto the bed, putting a pillow over her head to block out the light.

But moments later, Ed came back into the bedroom, closed the door behind him, and told Katharine that Milovan Djilas was outside to see *her.*

Katharine lifted the pillow from her head and turned to face Ed. She couldn't tell if the emphasis on the last word was surprise or jealousy. She realized she'd never told Ed about her visit to the Djilases' home.

Seeing Ed turn to go, she told him to wait and then blurted out the sketch of her visit to the Djilases' flat with her friend Paul from the West German embassy several months before. Ed stood listening quietly as she spoke. Still silent, he opened the door and walked out into the living room, closing the door firmly and loudly behind him.

The bang of the door galvanized Katharine. She slid off the bed and went straight to the dresser where they kept a bottle of aspirin. She caught a glance of herself in the mirror and decided she would dress first before dealing with the rest of her appearance. Katharine used the familiar motions of buttoning her blouse and pants to help keep pace with her mind, which was racing with thoughts and questions. *What was he doing here?* Her visit to Milovan's flat had been months ago. When she'd never heard from Milovan, Katharine had assumed the opportunity to learn more, to tell his story, was gone. But now, against her better judgment, she permitted herself to be hopeful about an opportunity once again.

She ran her fingers through her thick hair to rid it of the snarls, dipped a towel in what was left of the water in her glass to rub off the lipstick smudged on her right cheek, and pinched and stretched her face to flush the puffiness out a bit before making her way to greet her visitor.

Ed and Milovan were laughing when she entered the room, the two men sitting across from one another, relaxed and chatting like old friends. Ed was on the couch facing her and Milovan, who was in a chair with his back to Katharine.

She walked over to them, apologizing. When Milovan rose to greet her, she saw there was more of a warmth about him than there had been when she called at his apartment. *And is his English improved? Interesting*, she thought.

She quickly transformed into hostess. Seeing that Milovan still wore his suede jacket, she offered to take it before asking if anyone wanted coffee. Katharine hung up Milovan's coat and made her way to the kitchen, where she realized she had no idea where the coffee percolator was, as Mica normally made them coffee. She clattered around the few cupboards, finding it at last in the drawer beneath the oven. With a sigh of relief, Katharine measured out water and coffee, hoping she remembered the right ratio, and put it on the stove. She struck the match to start the fire and then leaned forward over the sink to wait for the water to boil.

As she stood there, she let her thoughts travel back to the last time she had made coffee like this, seven years earlier in 1948, in the hills outside of Athens. Under the belief that another war could heal the wounds that the second World War inflicted on their marriage, Ed had secured work with UPI for Katharine and himself. Their assignment was to cover the Greek civil war raging between the Communists and the Royalists.

The living conditions had been meager. Water was turned on only every third day, and fresh food was hard to come by. The perfect pot of coffee was a luxury. But in the grit, Katharine had found herself again, recovering from a broken heart and mending her relationship with Ed on her terms.

They'd been separated for almost a decade by then, follow-ing their own paths. Ed had enlisted in the Royal Navy in 1939 followed by a tour with the U.S. Army. After he was wounded, he began reporting for *Stars and Stripes*. She had eventually found her voice with radio, which sent her in May 1945 to Berlin. Her assignment from her boss had been clear: to uncover the human stories. After the Russians let the other allies into the city in July, two months after the German surrender, her life was consumed with her stories and the tiny attic room above press headquarters where she made her broadcasts.

As the days went by, more and more reporters joined the small group that had first entered the city, and Katharine fell in love with one of them. Affairs were a common part of war, but Katharine's had felt like so much more. Later, she would describe the soft-spoken Brit, a protégé of Edward R. Murrow's, as the love of her life. But weeks after she wrote Ed, telling him that she was leaving him for good, her lover had died in a car accident. Ed had offered to take her back. She'd accepted on one condition: she wanted to be equals, professionally. The success she'd had as a journalist during World War II wasn't something she was willing to give up again—not for motherhood or convention or patriotic duty to provide a man a job. Ed had obliged by finding them both jobs in Greece. Since then the arrangement had mostly worked out.

The spurting of the percolator interrupted her reverie, bringing her back to the present. She laid out a tray to carry the cups and the coffeepot over to the men. Milovan stood again as she returned to the sitting area and poured everyone a cup.

Her domestic chores taken care of, Katharine sat down next to Ed on the tattered love seat, full of hope and expectation.

There was no more small talk. Milovan jumped right in,

telling them he was there to formally reply to Katharine's offer. He detailed the many visits he'd received after his trial from members of the foreign media before he got to his main point. "My wife and I decided to go with the big, old woman," he said. Milovan's comment hung in the air for a moment. Katharine knew that though it was an accurate description of her, it was not meant seriously. Next to her, she felt Ed's smile before she saw it. Milovan shared that it was evident Katharine was not just looking for a story but that she really wanted to help. Hearing this, Katharine allowed the hope that she'd begun to feel the moment Ed came into the bedroom to announce that Milovan was in their home to grow inside her.

But her excitement very quickly stunted as Milovan said he was interested in doing a series of articles for *Life*. This meant he would be working with Ed, not Katharine, as *Life* was *Time*'s sister publication.

Next to her she felt Ed shift and lean in, recognizing the opportunity that had just been presented to him. She heard Ed start talking, but the sound was a dull echo in her mind as she turned inward. It was all she could do to focus her energy on keeping a straight face to mask her disappointment.

She chastised herself for having mentioned whom Ed worked for when she had visited Milovan. She shouldn't have gotten her hopes up.

This wasn't like all the times in those early years when she'd been so desperate to work that she'd been willing to help Ed source and confirm his stories, not caring if she didn't get credit. This time, she had seen an opportunity and gone for it. Yet the outcome would be the same. She knew it wasn't Ed's fault, but that didn't make it better.

She tuned back into the conversation as Ed was explaining he'd need to speak to *Life*'s editor-writer Jay Gould in New York before they could move forward. Ed reminded Milovan that Gould had helped Vlado write Tito's biography and recently worked on Winston Churchill's memoirs. Milovan nodded.

That was precisely why he chose the publication, Katharine realized.

Ed explained that given the sensitive nature of the request, he didn't want to send a cable while still in Yugoslavia; he would wait to send it from Trieste, the closest city just past the Yugoslav censor's reach, during his trip the following week. Milovan agreed to the arrangement.

Milovan radiated enthusiasm as he abruptly rose and excused himself. While Katharine fetched Milovan's coat, Ed met him at the door, and they agreed that Ed would come to the Djilases' flat when he had a response from Gould.

Nodding to them both, Milovan bade them farewell before he departed.

Ed shut the door behind Milovan and paused. He turned to Katharine and opened his mouth to speak, but Katharine got her words out first.

She unleashed her anger at Ed for once again getting a story that she had sourced. She had taken the initiative to seek Milovan out, yet Ed would get the scoop.

Ed stood silently until she stopped her tirade. But before he could speak, Katharine turned on her heels, strode to the bedroom, and slammed the door.

———————

A week later, as Ed told her he was leaving for Trieste, Katharine didn't look up from her book. Only when she heard the front door shut behind him followed by the loud squeak of the hinges of their outer gate opening and closing did she allow her gaze to rise and take in the empty room. She closed her eyes and leaned back against the cushions of the couch.

She wondered why she was acting like this.

Normally, she would have found the grace inside to move past it all. To speak rationally with Ed. To explain why she was so upset. It wasn't his fault he was a man or that he worked for a more prestigious publication than she did. Maybe she could have made him understand that for her, this was more than just a story. She had felt so helpless when the war started, but she had prevailed. When she and Ed reunited, both of them had changed. She wanted more, and he'd tried hard to get it for her. But now it was as if he was doing to her what everyone else had done after the war—setting her aside when she was no longer useful. She knew this wasn't exactly true, but that was how it made her feel. And it still hurt. She blinked back tears. She resolved to do what she always did—push through.

Ed returned the next afternoon to find Katharine arranging items on the bookshelf in their living room. She looked up at him as he held out a cable for her to read, trying to analyze what it said by studying his face. But there was no twinkle or frown to give her a clue, so she took the paper from him and scanned the two lines of copy. Gould had approved the series for *Life*, and he had offered a $700 advance—an unusually high amount for the magazine and an amount that would go far in Belgrade.

She handed the cable back to Ed and watched him leave the house again, on his way to give Milovan the good news.

———————

Katharine and Ed fell back into their routine. Summer was peaking, and to cool the bungalow down they opened every window in the house. But there were no screens on the windows, and often a bird or two found its way inside, which made Lucky bark.

One Saturday morning, about a month after Djilas called at their home, just as Ed had managed to shoo the third robin out of the house in as many days and he and Katharine were sitting down to a breakfast of fresh coffee and Mica's homemade pastries, they heard a man's voice call out for Ed.

Ed went outside to investigate. He came back inside a few minutes later holding about sixty sheets of typewritten pages in his hand and wearing the look he wore when he didn't know what to do. Ed waved the papers at Katharine and told her that Milovan had written his article in Serbian. Now she understood Ed's expression. For the next several minutes, they stood there discussing how to get the articles translated. Ed's assistant, though very good, was also a Communist Party member, so he was out of the question. Going to the U.S. embassy wasn't a guarantee of safety either. They had heard the stories about Madam Zhukov, who helped the foreign service officers as an interpreter. The embassy had only recently discovered that she had purposely mistranslated conversations and interfered with some of their visa cases.

Ed finally found someone he could trust and who wouldn't ask him any questions. But weeks turned into months, and Katharine had almost forgotten about the articles until three months later when Ed flashed the translations at her. They weren't quite raw, he told her, but they needed work.

When she told Ed that he should edit them before sending them to Gould, he had replied that wasn't what *Time* paid him for and that he already felt behind on his submission to Gould. Editing the articles would only extend the delay.

As Katharine watched him leave for Trieste to send the articles to New York, she held little hope Gould would accept them.

FIVE
BELGRADE

September–October 1955

The scent of fall was ripe in the air as Belgrade readied for a quiet evening under a starless sky in mid-September. Inside the Clarks' home, Katharine stood barefoot on the Shiraz rug with another cable in her hands, smelling Gould's rejection before she read it. Her eyes danced over the words, confirming her assumption.

In the cable, Gould explained his response, sharing how he'd had to pry the biography of Tito word for word from Vlado's lips, putting Vlado up in a New York hotel room for months on end in order to finish the project. The articles Ed had sent him needed too much work, Gould wrote. He wasn't interested in repeating the experience he'd had with Vlado ever again. Milovan could keep the advance, but Gould would not be running the articles that Ed had sent to him.

Katharine wasn't surprised by the message, but she felt unsettled. She continued to stare at the paper, turning over the words in her mind, processing her reaction to the cable as well as the ups and downs of the last several months.

After a few minutes she looked up and took in Ed. His face bore no marks of concern—no worry in his eyes, no crinkle in his brow, not even a slight frown was discernible on him. He was simply standing there with an air of indifference that conveyed to Katharine that he was as done with the topic as Gould. Something inside of her snapped, and she narrowed her eyes and leaned forward toward her husband. Still gripping the cable, she raised up her right hand and shook it before her as she unleashed all the emotion that had been building up inside her since Milovan's visit several months before. She had tried to repress those feelings, to push them aside while she watched Ed first take from her and then squander away an opportunity that she had created for him. Everything flashed before her in vivid color—her disappointment with *Life's* decision, her jealousy for losing the story to Ed in the first place, and her rancor at Ed's careless dismissal of it.

She pounced on him like a tigress. After several minutes, exhausted from her verbal tirade, Katharine balled up the cable and threw it at Ed. Not caring that she missed, she grabbed her coat and turned back to Ed, insisting that he share the news with Milovan before she slammed the door of the bungalow behind her.

Yet again, Katharine later learned, Ed did not listen to her.

Several weeks later, Milovan forced Ed's hand.

It was a crisp afternoon in early October, and Katharine and Ed were sitting in the main room of the bungalow. Ed read while Katharine wrote various editors she knew to inquire about jobs. The *Chicago Tribune* was shifting resources to other parts of the world, which meant Katharine's work, even as a stringer, was no longer needed. She had just finished a note to Kingsbury-Smith, the head of INS, whom she'd met at the Soviet reception, when Lucky barked.

Katharine looked up, first at the door and then at Ed. But he didn't budge. *It must be a good book*, she thought. She sighed with exasperation when the bell rang. She put down her pen, pushed back the chair, and went to the outer gate. When she opened it, Milovan's eager face greeted her.

Katharine almost laughed at his earnest expression but instead invited him inside.

Ed rose to meet him as Milovan walked to the sitting area.

They sat down in the mismatched chairs while Katharine returned to her letters at the table. She picked up her pen but made no move to use it. She couldn't concentrate and instead watched the men out of the corner of her eye, taking in their exchange.

Ed, lacking any diplomacy, blurted out that *Life* couldn't run his articles but that Milovan could keep his advance.

As the words poured out of Ed's mouth, Katharine shook her head slightly, embarrassed for him. *Why is he telling Milovan about the advance? Didn't he tell me just three weeks ago that Milovan didn't care about the money?* she thought. She studied Milovan and noticed his mouth turn down ever so slightly. His hands, which had been resting on his legs, moved together, and he clasped them into a fist on his lap. Without these small gestures, it might seem Milovan was okay with the developments. But as Ed kept speaking in his matter-of-fact tone, either not noticing the ticks that Katharine was tracking or disregarding them, his approach radiated insincerity. She felt anger bloom inside her again, rising like the water levels of the rivers in Belgrade when they swelled after a rainfall.

The men stood, and she bolted over to insert herself, offering to walk Milovan to the gate. She had started the chain reaction that had brought them to this moment, and she felt it her duty to see it through. Shaking Milovan's hand for what she expected would be the last time, Katharine lingered as the latch hooked in the gate and she watched Milovan walk down the street and out of view. As she stood there, she thought, here was a man who had something to say. Something people back home would want to hear. And yet, he had no way of delivering his message to them.

As she made her way back into the bungalow, a thought she had been suppressing for the past few months consumed her again. She closed the door behind her and walked over to where Ed sat on the couch reading. She leaned down and snatched the book out of his hand, looked him straight in the eyes, and demanded he bring her the articles immediately.

Ed sat there for a moment, stunned. He then rose and disappeared into the bedroom. He returned a few minutes later holding the articles in one hand and his well-worn brown leather briefcase in the other. He flung the sheaves of paper on the sofa's long cushion, just out of reach from where she stood. Whether he did this on purpose or not, Katharine didn't know or care. She stared at the pages, not moving until the front door of the Clarks' bungalow closed for the second time in less than ten minutes. She listened as Ed's footsteps faded before leaning forward to scoop up the slightly scattered papers and returning to the table to sort them before sitting down to read.

After an hour, Katharine put the first article down. She had read and reread the translation several times. The translator hadn't been exaggerating. Milovan's writing style was anything but easy. One sentence filled up half a page. His prose wound and curved around ideas and morals so dense they required even further exposition to explain themselves. But Katharine refused to give up. She read the contours of his arguments over and over until she felt she understood the point, until she found treasure. And it was there, buried deep in his writing: the devastating truth about Communism that would shake the world.

She had not read the translations before Ed submitted them to Gould, but the fact that Ed and his editors had not seen the finer points no longer mattered to her. Katharine decided she was going to find a way for these articles to be published, if Milovan would let her.

She was still working several hours later when Ed returned home. By then her emotions had settled enough to engage in a conversation without name-calling or yelling. When Ed walked in the door, she didn't look up at him. She simply stated, "I am going to work over these articles with Djilas—as you should have done—and make them what they should be."

On a cool morning in early October, Katharine set out for the Djilas flat full of hope and anticipation. Because fall usually brought storm clouds to Belgrade, she thought nothing of the cloud-filled, slate sky above.

She had taken more time than usual to dress that morning, zipping up her best black wool dress over new stockings whose line she'd made sure ran straight as a pin up her calf. She had stepped into her good black leather heels, the ones she saved for special occasions, and had slipped her camel wool coat on before sitting down in a chair to wait for Ed to finish getting ready. Closing her eyes, she had listened to the sound of the wind whipping the trees outside.

Now, halfway to her destination, she wished she'd been more practical about her outfit. The wind was a nuisance, gusting wildly and blowing her coat and the skirt of her dress every which way. *At least the ground is too wet to stir up clouds of leaves and dust,* she thought. This late in the month, most of the leaves had already fallen, leaving bare the branches up above and peppering the ground with verdant shades of pumpkin, ruby, and gold.

Katharine could feel the clumps of wet fallen leaves through the bottom of her shoes—soaking through the soles and slowing her down. She never understood why nicer shoes had such thin bottoms. But she didn't let it dampen her mood or distract her. Her thoughts focused solely on how to get Milovan outside of his flat so she could speak to him candidly without Yugoslavia's secret police listening in.

When she had told Ed she was going to visit Milovan to pitch him about working with her, Ed had insisted on accompanying her as a bodyguard. Ed had learned through friends that the government had increased pressure on Milovan and that he was under heightened surveillance. The secret police were harassing people on the street outside of the apartment building who might be associated with or visiting Milovan. Now she watched as Ed twirled a large umbrella with his wrist in tempo with his stride. One. Two. Three times. She hoped she wasn't dooming her pitch to Milovan by bringing Ed with her. She sighed and turned her eyes back forward.

About three blocks from the Djilases' apartment, the dark sky opened up. Ed unfolded the umbrella and hooked his arm with hers so they could both stay dry as rain pelted down on the city. But due to the wind, the slant of the raindrops outsmarted the umbrella, and when the two of them realized they were getting wet, they started to jog the remaining yards to reach number 8.

Katharine was so focused on arriving at their destination that she had almost forgotten why Ed had accompanied her until she saw the black sedan parked near the building's front door. The rain limited her visibility, but Katharine could still make out two figures in the front seats who were so hulking they made the vehicle look like a clown car. She would have smiled if there weren't something so unnatural about it all.

While she suppressed any emotion on her face, she couldn't control a cold chill that ran down her spine, making her shiver. Ed, who had dropped her arm to open the door, gave her a probing look, which she ignored.

Upstairs Steffie opened the door to the apartment, her eyes growing wide as she recognized both Katharine and Ed from earlier visits. She pulled them inside immediately, and Katharine was struck by the strength of her grip. Her gracious manner put them at ease, and she offered them tea before showing them into Milovan's study where he sat reading. Their two-and-a-half-year-old son,

Aleksa, sat on the floor with a picture book open before him. The tea kettle whinnied on the stove. Moments later Steffie returned with a tray for tea.

The group drank in the warmth in silence before Katharine, who had seen from the curtainless window that the rain had stopped, interrupted it to suggest the four of them go out for a walk. She knew it was the only way to talk freely. But as she heard herself talking, she knew she had made a mistake. Someone had to stay to watch Aleksa, as Milovan's mother was nowhere in sight. But it was too late; she had opened her mouth and needed to see it through. So Katharine wasn't surprised when somehow just she and Steffie ended up on the street.

Katharine asked Steffie which way she would prefer to walk as they exited the building and followed her guidance as they headed to the right, in the opposite direction from where the Clarks had approached. A big dark puddle blocked their path, and they stepped out into the cobblestone street between the gap of two parked cars.

Katharine caught their reflection in one of the car's side mirrors. She was struck by how she towered over Steffie by more than a head, but it didn't matter. Steffie easily matched Katharine's gait, which was slowed down by Katharine's still rain-soaked shoes. They fell into a steady rhythm as they put distance between themselves and the secret police.

Out of the corner of her eye, Katharine studied her companion. A weariness hung around her like an albatross, adding a heaviness that seemed too much for her tiny frame to hold. Not wanting to add to her burden, but having no other option, Katharine scanned their nearby surroundings one more time to make sure no one was following them or was within hearing distance before she began the appeal that she had been practicing for a week, shifting it slightly as she had planned to deliver it to Milovan.

Leaning down to whisper into Steffie's ear, Katharine told her how she wished to help Milovan's ideas get published. That she believed what he had to say was important. How she had read the translations of the articles he gave Ed for *Life* and thought they could be reworked for print in another outlet.

Steffie kept her eyes forward. The only recognition she showed was a small fumble with her feet. When Katharine caught her, Steffie looked up at her, smiling. She took Katharine's arm and linked it with her own.

Encouraged, Katharine went on to detail her proposal. She told Steffie she knew Milovan had wanted to publish in *Life*, but she was confident she could find a home in another publication. That she believed the best way to work was directly in English. Just as Gould had done with Vlado, Milovan could dictate his articles to Katharine, and she would write them down for him as he spoke. Katharine would also help edit the articles, molding and shaping the words to maximize their impact in English. Katharine knew that working at the Djilas flat was out of the question due to the listening devices the secret police had installed, so she offered up the Clarks' bungalow as a working office. And finally, the linchpin of her plan: the two couples would pretend to be social acquaintances. She and Ed could visit the Djilases at their flat often enough to keep the spies happy and busy, while the Djilases could visit the Clarks' home to work.

Steffie remained silent, but Katharine went on, determined. She knew Steffie would have to speak with her husband, so she outlined a way for Milovan to communicate his reply.

They reached an intersection, and Steffie told Katharine that she would talk to her husband. It was exactly the response that Katharine had wished for. Her heart beat a little faster as she allowed herself to wonder if there still was a chance.

Then, they both instinctively turned to each other to suggest they return to the apartment. They laughed at their shared recommendation, and as they began walking back to the building, they leaned into one another more fondly, talking about their families and lives as if they were dear old friends who had just run into each other on the street after too much time spent apart. Katharine recounted to Steffie a tale of how her son, Sandy, who was now a senior in high school, had gotten himself into trouble on a military base in Panama when he was the same age Aleksa was now.

As they continued up the street, the black sedan came into view again. Its silhouette was less menacing now but bestowed a semblance of urgency that caused Steffie to suddenly stop walking. She turned to look directly into Katharine's deep brown eyes, laying her hand on Katharine's arm. The two women, both mothers, stood smiling at one another for a moment, a look passing between them of respect based on mutual experience and resolve.

Once back inside the Djilas flat, they joined the men in the living room, where they were standing in front of the bookcase discussing some of Milovan's favorite books. Moments after entering, Katharine caught Ed's eye and winked at him. No one but she noticed Ed exhale loudly, understanding from their prearranged signal that all had gone well for Katharine on the walk. After a few more minutes of conversation, Katharine and Ed excused themselves, saying they needed to run an errand. They made polite goodbyes, mostly for the spies to hear, and Katharine crossed her fingers as she exited the flat, hopeful that she would be back.

As Katharine took Ed's arm, she looked up at the house across the street. The man with the camera was there again on the balcony, his lens up, pointed straight at her.

PART II
TRUTH

PART II

TRUTH

SIX
BELGRADE

October 1955

Katharine tried everything she could think of to distract herself while waiting for Milovan's response to her proposal. She pitched articles to her editors; went for long walks through the city's parks—actually taking time to listen to the propaganda that was being broadcast across the speakers that lined the walk; and even wrote several long letters home to her mother, sister, and son. Although she had vowed to keep in better touch with her family after her father had died the year before, like most of Katharine's promises to them, it had been easier to say than do. But none of these activities consumed her day or her attention for very long. So, when she started cataloguing their books and records with a system that would make a librarian jealous, Ed finally asked Katharine if everything was all right.

Now, on a balmy evening, nine days after her visit to the Djilas flat, Katharine stood in the small yard inside the Clarks' outer gate watching the street through the gaps in the ivy she had cut earlier in the day for just this purpose, willing the Djilases to appear.

A little before seven, two figures approached from the end of the lane walking arm in arm. The shorter one leaned in against the taller figure. Although Katharine still couldn't see them clearly, her stomach began to swirl with anticipation.

The Djilases had sent a signal to confirm they would be coming, but Katharine had learned after years of living behind the Iron Curtain not to count on anything until it transpired. Too much had been promised to her over the years that never quite materialized—people changed their minds, or things happened beyond people's control. But here they were, on the Clarks' street.

Shifting her gaze away from the road for the first time in an hour, Katharine walked back inside with a renewed sense of purpose in her step. She surveyed the room quickly. At the opposite end, dinner sat ready on the stove, the lid on the large copper pot holding Mica's sarma doing nothing to contain the sweet smell of the stew. The aroma made Katharine's mouth water. In the middle of the room the dinner table was set for four. Katharine had opted for a more formal setting, using the good china and silver from her mother, to show the Djilases respect. Two candles flickered brightly in the center of the table, softening the ambience and making the room feel cozier and more welcoming. Next to her, halfway down the wall of books, the smooth sound of Miles Davis floated from the record player, which sat on one of the middle shelves. After books, music was the Clarks' most prized possession, and jazz was their favorite genre. Katharine closed her eyes for a moment, taking in the music, then looked to the couch, where Ed sat drinking a scotch. She told him the Djilases would be arriving soon. Ed nodded in response.

Moments later, the bell at the outer gate rang. Katharine smoothed her hands down her plain black pants and stepped back outside. She pulled up on the latch to swing open the gate and found the Djilases standing next to each other holding hands and wearing wide smiles. She stepped aside to let them into the yard, following them to the front door of the bungalow, where Ed now stood.

In just a few minutes, the four of them sat awkwardly scattered across the huddle of the love seat and mismatched chairs that made up the Clarks' living area, not quite sure what to say. Ed finally initiated small talk, asking about their walk before the conversation finally turned to the Djilases' son, Aleksa. Soon the two couples were chatting about their children, talking as if they were lifelong friends.

After a bit, they moved to the dinner table. Katharine removed the cover from the tureen, unleashing into the room a savory smell of roast cabbage stuffed with ground beef, crispy bacon, and onions. A loaf of warm bread Mica had taken out of the oven right before she'd left lay nearby.

Silence set in as the group focused on the meal. When at last they came to dessert, they found their voices again.

Ed helped Katharine clear the table before asking Steffie if she played cards. She responded with a nod. Katharine had only met Steffie a handful of times, but beneath the shy and timid veneer Katharine suspected a card shark. She wondered if Ed knew what he was getting into as he offered Steffie his arm. The two of them walked over to the other side of the room, where a well-worn pack of blue Hoyle playing cards sat ready to be shuffled.

When Katharine heard the cards rustle against one another, she told Milovan she had to collect her typewriter for them to begin their work. Before Katharine came back to the room holding her 1929 Underwood No. 5, she turned on the water in the bathtub. She then turned on the tap at the kitchen sink. Ed had already turned up the volume on the record player to its highest level, and the sound of water gushing from two faucets now joined the record's brassy sound in a thunder of noise. Although Katharine was pretty sure their flat was not wired, she did not want to take any chances, and she had devised this plan with Ed the night before. They'd heard from enough of the embassy officials who really served as intelligence officers that running water and loud music was the best offense against listening devices.

Satisfied with the noise level, Katharine returned to the table and sat down, rolling a fresh, blank page into the typewriter before she met Milovan's eyes and asked him where they should start.

Milovan looked up at her with a glint in his eye and the edge of a grin on his face. He started at the beginning, with his family's history and his peasant childhood, and then went on to explain that his drive to find a better life for people in Montenegro was the reason he had left his homeland in 1929, seeking answers through his continued education at the university in Belgrade. In the capital of the newly formed Yugoslavia, Milovan had fallen in with an artistic crowd and was published widely in literary publications. But his first year of university coincided with the beginning of a royal dictatorship under which political parties were illegal, the press was silenced, and everything was controlled by an incompetent police organization. Milovan soon traded literature for politics and by 1932 had joined the Communist Party. A year later he began a three-year prison sentence for his activism against the king, eventually landing at Sremska Mitrovica, Yugoslavia's largest prison.

At Sremska Mitrovica, Milovan delved further into communism, reading books and discussing theories with other prisoners, many of whom now held leadership positions in Yugoslavia's Communist Party. When Milovan left the prison in 1936, he emerged more committed to the ideology.

Upon his release, he had married Mitra Mitrović, a woman and comrade he had met at university who had traveled diligently every Saturday at noon to stand on the bank of the Sava River near the prison donning a red sweater so he could recognize her through the bars of his cell, the last window on the right. They lived in Belgrade where Milovan led a thin group of Communists, waiting for and plotting further revolutionary activity.

Shortly after, Milovan traveled to Zagreb to meet Tito, a leader in the Yugoslav Communist Party who had been operating with the rest of the Central Committee outside of the country in Paris. Tito eventually set up a new Central Committee inside Yugoslavia—initially without the blessing of the Comintern,* the official international organization of Communist parties—and Milovan joined him in his efforts. In 1938 Tito appointed him to the Central Committee of the Communist Party of Yugoslavia and the next year to its Politburo.

---

* The Comintern was an international organization for Communism that preceded the Cominform.

War came suddenly to Yugoslavia. In April 1941, the Germans, Italians, and Hungarians invaded on all fronts. After just ten days, the Royal army surrendered. Like pieces of a puzzle, Yugoslavia was broken apart. Germany annexed most of Slovenia, Serbia, Croatia, and Bosnia and Herzegovina. Italy captured the balance of Slovenia, along with Kosovo and Montenegro. The Hungarians received some small principalities, and the Bulgarians assumed control over Macedonia a month later.

Two opposition forces quickly emerged in Yugoslavia: the primarily Serbian, nationalist Chetniks, led by Draža Mihailović, and the pan-Yugoslav Communist Partisans, led by Tito. While Mihailović pursued a greater Serbia, Tito, ever the opportunist, took advantage of the war to build his party. Tito framed the Partisan platform as a national one, hiding its real intention as a Communist revolution.

Milovan rose in the Partisan ranks, initially as a guerilla fighter before Tito removed him from the front lines and appointed him to head up *Borba*, the party's daily organ for propaganda in November 1941. Milovan spent the remainder of the war at Tito's side.

Tito selected Milovan to trek to Moscow to meet with Stalin in 1944 with orders to secure official recognition of the Partisans as the national government for Yugoslavia and to obtain $200,000 from the Russians to fund their movement. Tito also asked Milovan to inquire about the opinion of their Communist Party among the Comintern leaders and, if possible, with Stalin.

Milovan traveled by way of Italy, Tunis, Malta, Cairo, Tehran, and Baku, taking such a circuitous route to avoid the German bases on Crete and in Greece and to take advantage of aid from the British.

Milovan's first impression of Moscow was that it was "gloomy and somber and surprisingly full of low buildings." But Milovan had little time to consider his observation, as he was quickly whisked away to the Kremlin to meet with Stalin. There, after turning down several long, red-carpeted corridors where young men wearing the blue caps of the State Security saluted by clicking their heels, Milovan crossed the threshold into a long room devoid of any decoration save the portraits of Vladimir Lenin, Alexander Suvorov, and Mikhail Kutuzov, and greeted Stalin with a handshake. Milovan noted, "In his stance there was nothing artificial or posturing. This was not that majestic Stalin of the photographs or the newsreels—with the stiff, deliberate gait and posture." Milovan was also surprised at Stalin's "very small stature and ungainly build. His torso was short and narrow, while his legs and arms were too long." He was dressed simply in his marshal's uniform with only a golden star—the Order of Lenin, awarded to Heroes of the Soviet Union—on his left breast. He had a large belly, and on his head a few sparse hairs meant he was not completely bald. Stalin's face was white, with red cheeks; his teeth were black and crooked, and his yellow eyes had a "mixture of sternness and roguishness."

As they began to talk, Milovan observed that Stalin's accent was clearly not Russian and that he "was not quiet for a moment. He toyed with his pipe, which bore the white dot of the English firm Dunhill, or drew circles with a blue pencil around words indicating the main subjects for discussion, which he then crossed out with slanting lines as each part of the discussion was nearing an end, and he kept turning his head this way and that while he fidgeted in his seat."

When the conversation turned to the war effort and the recognition of Tito's government, Stalin asked his minister of foreign affairs, Vyacheslav Molotov, "Couldn't we somehow trick the English into recognizing Tito, who alone is fighting the Germans?"

Molotov smiled and replied, "No, that is impossible; they are perfectly aware of developments in Yugoslavia."

After an hour Milovan left the meeting with a sense of Stalin's determined intentions to support the Partisans and a hospitable reaction to the gifts Milovan had brought for him. Although Milovan felt the sandals and guns he presented to Stalin had "looked particularly primitive and wretched" after an hour of discourse with the marshal, Stalin had been civil with his reaction to them: "He in no way showed any disparagement. When he saw the peasant sandals, he exclaimed: 'Lapti!'—the Russian word for them. As for the rifle, he opened and shut it, hefted it, and remarked: 'Ours is lighter.'"

Afterward Milovan reflected, "I realized that it was by chance that I personally was the first Yugoslav Communist to be received by him." It was exciting, "the greatest possible recognition for heroism and suffering of our Partisan warriors and our people." He continued, "I felt a proud joy that I would be able to tell my comrades about this encounter and say something about it to the Yugoslav fighting men as well. Suddenly everything that had seemed unpleasant about the USSR disappeared." When Milovan left the Kremlin, he stepped outside into a violet-hued dusk shimmering with the northern lights and felt in his soul "a world of unreality more beautiful than the one in which we had been living."

Milovan met with many people in Moscow and even traveled

by plane to the Southwestern Front in Ukraine, where he met
with Red Army general and marshal of the Soviet Union Ivan
Stepanovich Konev, a "blonde, tall man of fifty, with a very ener-
getic bony face." A man of few words, Konev and his men had just
completed a campaign at Korsun'-Shevchenkovsky, which many
in the Soviet Union compared to the defense of Stalingrad. Konev
"sketched a picture of Germany's final catastrophe" for Milovan,
recounting with a smile how "refusing to surrender, some eighty
if not one hundred thousand Germans were forced into a narrow
space, then tanks shattered their heavy equipment and machinegun nests, while the Cossack cavalry finally finished them off.
'We let the Cossacks cut up as long as they wished. They even
hacked off the hands of those who raised them to surrender!'" Joy
at defeating the Nazis conflicted with the horror of the method-
ology within Milovan. Soon after, he steered the conversation to
other topics Milovan had interest in, about the military and some
of the Red Army's personalities. Before parting, Konev presented
Milovan with a pistol and he gave Milovan his own personal bin-
oculars to give to Tito as a gift.

Despite Milovan's rapture, kernels of doubt had been seeded.
After returning to Moscow, toward the end of his visit in the
Soviet Union, Milovan went to a dinner at Stalin's dacha outside
Moscow: "Such a dinner usually lasted six or more hours—from
ten at night till four or five in the morning. One ate and drank
slowly, during a rambling conversation which ranged from stories
and anecdotes to the most serious political and even philosophi-
cal subjects. Unofficially and in actual fact a significant part of the
Soviet policy was shaped at these dinners. Besides they were the

most frequent and most convenient entertainment and only luxury in Stalin's otherwise monotonous and somber life."

Over the course of the evening, Milovan and Stalin exchanged
conversation along a spectrum of topics including the dissolution of
the Comintern, Albania, news of the Allies' landing at Normandy
the next day received in an intercepted dispatch which he permitted Milovan to read, and another one that detailed internal relations
within Yugoslavia. Milovan summed up the evening later: "I might
conclude that Stalin was deliberately frightening the Yugoslav leaders in order to decrease their ties with the West, and at the same
time he tried to subordinate their policy to his interests and to his
relations with the Western states, primarily Great Britain. Thanks
to both ideology and methods, personal experience and historical
heritage, he regarded as sure only whatever he held in his fist, and
everyone beyond the control of his police was a potential enemy."
At the dinner's end Stalin presented Milovan with a sword for Tito.
Realizing he did not yet have a gift for Tito, on his return trip Milovan
purchased an ivory chess set in Cairo, noting that "even then there
existed inside of me, suppressed, a world different from Stalin's."

On taking his leave from Stalin, Milovan asked again if he had
any comments to make regarding the work of the Yugoslav party.

Stalin replied, "No, I do not. You yourselves know best what
is to be done."

When Milovan returned to Vis, where Tito had his Partisan
headquarters, he shared with Tito and the other leaders, "The
Comintern factually no longer exits, and we Yugoslav Communists
have to shift for ourselves. We have to depend primarily on our
own forces."

Several months later, the Red Army crossed the northeastern border of Yugoslavia in an advance that helped drive the Germans out of Yugoslavia for good. But in the Red Army's wake came reports of rape, murder, and looting. It was decided that Tito should speak with the chief of the Soviet mission, Nikolai Vasilevich Korneev, about the matter. Milovan, Kardelj, and Aleksandar Ranković, another top associate of Tito's who went on to head Yugoslavia's security agency, were present when Tito raised the problem with Korneev.

After Tito made his opening remarks, Milovan tried to explain further: "The problem lies in the fact, too, that our enemies are using this against us and are comparing the attacks by the Red Army's soldiers with the behavior of the English officers, who do not engage in such excesses."

Korneev shouted in reply, "I protest most sharply against the insult given to the Red Army by comparing it with the armies of capitalist countries."

The meeting ended with no result. Milovan's comments were generally viewed as "the cause of the first friction between the Yugoslav and Soviet leaders." These remarks would haunt Milovan in his subsequent meetings with Stalin.

Milovan embarked on his second visit to Moscow in April 1945 full of unease for what lay ahead. His comments to Korneev still clung to him like a dark shroud. As the plane carrying a delegation led by Tito to sign a treaty between Yugoslavia and the Soviet Union landed in Moscow, Milovan felt the rest of the passengers physically distancing themselves from him as they disembarked into the brisk Russian air.

While Stalin ignored Milovan initially, toward the end of the trip at a dinner at Stalin's dacha, he finally addressed Milovan, asking him about what he had said about the Red Army. Milovan tried to explain away his comment that he had not intended to insult the Red Army, but Stalin interrupted him. "You have, of course, read Dostoevsky? Do you see what a complicated thing is man's soul, man's psyche? Well then, imagine a man who has fought from Stalingrad to Belgrade—over thousands of kilometers of his own devastated land, across the dead bodies of his comrades and dearest ones! How can such a man react normally? And what is so awful in his having fun with a woman after such horrors. You have imagined the Red Army to be ideal. And it is not ideal, nor can it be... The important thing is that it fights Germans—and it is fighting them well, while the rest doesn't matter."

After several more lobs back and forth, each one a little lighter, Milovan felt the dispute over the Red Army resolved. But the seeds planted during his first visit had taken root. "In one little corner of my mind and of my moral being, I was awake and troubled."

After the delegation's three-day stopover in Ukraine, where Nikita Khrushchev served as the secretary of the Ukrainian Party and premier of the government, Milovan summarized, "The more I delved into the Soviet reality, the more my doubts multiplied. The reconciliation of that reality and my human conscience was becoming more and more hopeless."

From the way Milovan spoke, Katharine could tell there was more. But she had just looked at her watch, and it was almost eleven. The Djilases still had to walk the two miles home. Letting good sense override her curiosity, she interrupted him to suggest they conclude for the night. She glanced down at her typewriter as she pushed her chair back to stand. She took in the blank sheet of paper she had rolled into the machine several hours before. They hadn't started any work tonight, but his story was fascinating, and she sensed he was building to something important.

Katharine closed the door behind the Djilases and reflected on Milovan's journey. There was a certain inevitability to it, one preordained by geography as much as history. The Balkans had a storied past. Empires had come and gone: Illyrians, Byzantines, Goths, Huns, Ottomans, and Austrians. Some conquerors incited ethnic and religious differences while others temporarily calmed them across Slovenia, Croatia, Bosnia, Serbia, Macedonia, Montenegro, and beyond. Yet even within the region, Montenegro stood out as a country whose people refused to be wholly conquered in spirit. And Milovan, she felt, was no exception.

SEVEN
BELGRADE

November 1955

Katharine exited the Djilases' building for the fourth time in as
many weeks, her head tilted back and a peal of laughter rolling
out of her in response to something Ed had just whispered in her
ear. The two of them held hands, and as they stepped outside into
the late afternoon, Ed pulled her arm in closer, intertwining their
elbows for their walk back home.

Their visit had been especially happy today because Ed had
brought a toy for Aleksa that was small enough for the Djilases to
accept and big enough to delight the young boy. One of the other
foreign correspondents in Belgrade was moving back home and
had asked Ed if he wanted any of the items the family didn't want
to ship. When Ed saw the worn, two-foot-tall toy bear, its four legs
on wheels, he looked past the missing eyes and wobbling wheels
and spent a week patching and sprucing it up to present to the
little boy.

Aleksa was delighted. He had immediately climbed aboard the
bear and let Ed pull him around from room to room, whooping

the sounds he thought a cowboy might make. Katharine, Milovan, and Steffie had laughed loudly as they watched the charade, interrupting only to tell them to watch out for the cat.

Katharine thought about this scene again as they stepped into the cool autumn air. All her life Katharine had convinced herself she had never wanted to be a mother, had seen family as something that kept her from following her career. But after seeing Ed play with the Djilases' son, she questioned her perspective. Had it just been bad timing? Ed had missed out on most of Sandy's early years, and after 1948, so had she. Katharine knew she had lost out on that time with her son. Sandy was now twenty-two and almost done with the University of Pennsylvania.

Where did the time go? she thought as she took in early evening in Belgrade.

While they had been inside the Djilas flat, the sun had passed farther across the sky, drenching the sidewalk in shadows from the barren branches of the trees that lined the street. Katharine saw the dark sedan was still parked outside the Djilases' building. But the men inside were reading a newspaper instead of monitoring the street. *Odd.*

Suddenly, Ed called out loudly to someone named Dessa.

He leaned in quickly to whisper in Katharine's ear that Dessa allegedly worked for the UDBA. Katharine looked ahead of her in time to take in the short, thin, immaculately dressed woman approaching them on Palmotićeva Street. Despite her size she walked with a commanding air as if she owned the street.

Katharine knew of Dessa Bourne by reputation only. After the war, Dessa, whose father was Serbian and mother was Croatian, had married Eric Bourne, a British journalist who worked for *The Sunday Times* and was a good friend of Ed's from his postwar years in Belgrade. By the time the Clarks moved to Belgrade in the fall of 1953, Eric had divorced Dessa and returned to London, leaving Dessa his surname and a convenient cover as the Belgrade correspondent for *The Times* to hide her other rumored job assisting the Yugoslav secret police.

Seeing her up close and in person for the first time, Katharine pondered if Dessa had been the woman watching from the window of the house across the street during her first visit to the Djilases in the summer. Although slim and bony, where other women might appear frail or meek, Dessa commanded authority with a mix of elegance and steel. Her dark brown hair was styled meticulously in ringlets, not a single hair awry as it framed her plain, pointy-nosed, porcelain face, which reminded Katharine of a bird. Not the sweet kind like a robin or a magpie but like a crow or a vulture, the kind of bird that might poke your eye out or eat your young.

Dessa feigned surprise at running into Ed, although Katharine guessed if the rumors were to be believed that the meeting was purposeful and prearranged. She and Ed always spoke loudly about the details for their next visit to the Djilases in order to alert the monitors as to when they would return and to underscore the social friendship they used as a ruse to the real purpose of the couples' alliance. Dessa turned her gaze to Katharine but still addressed Ed, saying this must be the wife she had heard so much about. It was clearly a power move by commenting on Katharine to her face without really acknowledging her, as though she wasn't important enough to do so.

Ed realized this too, and he squeezed Katharine's hand hard to remind her to behave before letting go to kiss Dessa on the cheek. Katharine suppressed a wince from the pain, and she smiled thinly at Dessa as she shook the woman's cold, rakish hand, not trusting herself to speak.

After fifteen minutes of forced conversation, each having played his or her role, they parted ways. If it was true Dessa worked for the UDBA, Katharine realized this was the first time the secret police had interacted with Ed and her directly. She felt uneasiness weave its tangled web around her as she wondered what was next.

Several nights later, as Katharine and Milovan settled in for another conversation, she mentioned her run-in with Dessa, describing her as the woman who wrote for *The Times* but whom she'd suspiciously never seen at any press event in Belgrade.

Milovan threw his head back uncharacteristically, letting out a roar of laughter to rival the decibel of the blaring horns playing on the record player. Still chuckling, he told Katharine how, at the war's end, it was rumored Dessa's entire family joined the UDBA—her brother and both of her parents. And now Dessa's parents lived across the street from him.

When he finished laughing, Katharine changed the topic, urging him to continue where he'd left off last time. She reminded him he had been telling her how Stalin had discussed Dostoyevsky with him. She had not even bothered to set up her typewriter, expecting Milovan had more of his personal history to cover first.

Milovan picked up his story by telling her about his third trip to Moscow in January 1948. A military delegation accompanied him, and the group traveled by rail to Moscow, changing to another train that was sent for them from the Russians in Romania. The new train had big brass handles and a toilet so high that one's legs hung in mid-air while one was seated. The luxurious meals— caviar, hot cabbage soup with sour cream, and enormous entrées of fish and meat—served by white-coated waiters contrasted sharply with the frozen landscape passing by outside the window, peppered by burned-out buildings dark with char and half-starved women wrapped in shawls who worked to clear the track of ice and snow.

That first evening, halfway through a visit with the Yugoslav ambassador, Molotov called the embassy requesting Milovan visit the Kremlin that night. Milovan noted, "Such haste is unusual in Moscow, where foreign Communists have always waited long, so that a saying circulated among them: It is easy to get to Moscow but hard to get out again."

A little before nine that evening, a car transported Milovan to the yellow stucco building that housed Stalin's private office in the Kremlin. Stalin greeted Milovan and dove right in, telling him, "Members of the Central Committee in Albania are killing themselves over you!" Before Milovan could reply, Stalin went on, "We have no special interest in Albania. We agree to Yugoslavia swallowing Albania!" Stalin underscored this point by clenching his right hand into a fist and bringing it to his mouth as if to swallow it.

Although he tried to resist, Milovan developed a pit in his stomach, realizing nothing he said would sway Stalin's mind or comments. The Soviet Union had absorbed the Baltic countries. Were they trying to send a message that Yugoslavia was next? His discomfort grew further when Stalin ordered him to "personally write Tito a dispatch about this in the name of the Soviet Government and submit it to" him by the next day. This was an unusual request. Milovan deliberated what game Stalin was playing while the rest of the conversation meandered across topics like Tito's health and newspapers.

A lull in the conversation provided Milovan with his own opportunity for an unusual request: he asked for military supplies for the Yugoslav army. There had been challenges and difficulties acquiring supplies due to military secrets, but before Milovan could fully explain, Stalin went to his desk to call Bulganin, ordering into the phone, "The Yugoslavs are here, the Yugoslav delegation—they should be heard immediately."

After half an hour the conversation ended, and Milovan rode in Stalin's automobile to another lengthy evening at Stalin's dacha. The dinner began with a drinking game requiring each attendee—Stalin, Molotov and other prominent officials in Stalin's inner circle like, Georgy Malenkov, Lavrenty Beria, Andrey Zhdanov, and Nikolai Voznesensky—to guess how many degrees below zero it was outside and drinking as many glasses of vodka as the number of degrees guessed wrong. Not fond of drink, Milovan had fortunately looked at the thermometer at the hotel before leaving for the Kremlin and had made quick calculations to allow for further temperature drops since then, so that his answer was off by just one degree. Reflecting later he summarized, "This apportioning of the number of vodka glasses according to the temperature reading suddenly brought to my mind the confinement, the inanity and senselessness of the life these Soviet leaders were living gathered about their superannuated chief even as they played a role that was decisive for the human race. I recalled that the Russian tsar Peter the Great likewise held such suppers with his assistants at which they gorged and drank themselves into a stupor while ordaining the fate of Russia and the Russian people."

This thought ebbed and flowed in Milovan's consciousness throughout the evening as did his observations of Stalin's declining health, humor, and intellect. "Everyone paid court to him," he noted, "avoiding any expression of opinion before he expressed his, and then hastening to agree with him."

Although the men hopped across subjects and courses, by evening's end Milovan felt "there was truly nothing more to say after such a long session, at which everything had been discussed except the reason why the dinner had been held." There had been an undertone, something in the atmosphere "above and beyond the words" that was criticism of Tito and the Yugoslav Central Committee. Milovan resisted attempts to bring himself into an alliance with the Soviet leaders against Tito. The evening closed with a toast to Lenin, followed by Stalin trying to dance, encouraged by his ministers' claims that he was marvelous.

Although Milovan and the delegation presented their military requests to the General Staff, within days Soviet officials hinted about complications between Belgrade and Moscow. Suddenly Milovan and the military delegation found themselves with no business purpose in Moscow. To keep busy they became tourists, visiting museums and watching the ballet at the Bolshoi Theater. After they took in all the sights of Moscow, they asked to visit Leningrad. Everywhere they went, an officer from NKVD, the Russian secret police, escorted them.

A month later Milovan was making plans to return to Belgrade when he received a telegram from Tito informing him that Kardelj and Vladimir Bakaric, two senior Yugoslav government officials, were due to join the delegation in Moscow the next day. When Kardelj and Bakaric arrived, they discovered Milovan knew nothing beyond his suspicion that something was going on between Belgrade and Moscow. Knowing the rooms were wired, Milovan visited Kardelj's room that evening. While Kardelj's wife slept next to him and Kardelj himself lay in bed, Milovan whispered to him his impressions that Yugoslavia could not depend on the Soviets for resources and that he believed the Soviet Union was trying to diminish Yugoslavia to the level of other occupied Eastern European countries.

Two days later, Kardelj, Bakaric, and Milovan took a car across Red Square for another meeting with Stalin. This time Bulgarian prime minister Georgi Dimitrov and two other Bulgars were waiting in a large conference room. Over the course of an hour, the Soviets chastised Yugoslavia and Bulgaria for taking actions to announce an alliance between their two countries without the Kremlin's express permission or knowledge. When the two delegations presented facts that conflicted with this assertion, Stalin pushed back. "You didn't consult with us!" he shouted. "We learn about your doings in the newspapers! You chatter like women from the housetops whatever occurs to you, and then the newspapermen grab hold of it!"

The meeting concluded abruptly. There was no dinner at Stalin's dacha that night. Instead, Kardelj, Bakaric, and Milovan headed to the Yugoslav embassy to talk things over among

themselves without anyone listening in. They decided Stalin's primary objective was to absorb Yugoslavia into the Soviet Union. "A
dream was snuffed out on contact with reality," observed Milovan.
The men wanted to return to Belgrade as soon as possible to discuss the situation with Tito. The next day they told the Russians
they were being recalled. Milovan shared, "I was very happy when
I found they had given us a plane to go home in, because I knew
we were not so important they would waste blowing up a plane. If
it had been by train, I knew we were to have been killed. Even so
I did not draw a free breath until we landed."

Four months later, after a volley of correspondence between both
sides—with Milovan playing an enormous role for Yugoslavia by
helping Tito with his letters to Stalin and writing several pointed
articles—the Cominform expelled Yugoslavia from its membership. The date of the exit, June 28, was steeped in historical significance for Yugoslavia. On that day in 1389 Ottoman Turks defeated
the Serbs in the Battle of Kosovo. Over five centuries later, in
1914, it marked the date a Serbian nationalist group assassinated
Archduke Franz Ferdinand in Sarajevo, propelling the world into
the first world war. And then in 1921, it marked the proclamation
of Yugoslavia by King Alexander.

Milovan had returned to Belgrade a changed man. Travels
abroad—in 1949 to New York to represent his country at the
United Nations and in 1953 to London to attend Queen Elizabeth's
coronation, where he also met and befriended British Labor leaders Morgan Phillips and Aneurin Bevan—further expanded his

emerging perspective and fueled his thoughts. During this time, he also divorced his first wife and met and married Steffie.

Through it all, he wrote. In the fall of 1953, just after Ed and Katharine had arrived in Belgrade, Milovan started to publish his thinking. And by the end of the year, more than a dozen articles carried his ideas.

Katharine was familiar with this portion of Milovan's life. She and Ed had covered the articles, which began to publish almost immediately after they arrived in Belgrade along with the subsequent plenum. "When Djilas' heretical words first broke into print," Ed wrote for *Time*, "the Red world gasped." Ed detailed, "Most sensational of the fires Djilas built was a bitter, spicy article attacking wives of big shots in the Communist hierarchy for their snobbery and rudeness toward a pretty young actress.... But more basic was a series of articles he published in *Borba*, the official party daily, criticizing the theories and techniques of the Yugoslav party." In one Milovan wrote, "When a revolution has been successful the next logical step is a turn toward democracy...There is and can be no other way out but more democracy, more free discussion, freer elections of social, government and economic organs, more adherence to law."

Ed went on to summarize what most Westerners in Belgrade believed: "Djilas' attack came at a moment when Yugoslavia was a stir with cold cross winds. Since Stalin's death, there has been a guarded renewal of relations between Belgrade and some Cominform capitals. Yugoslavia has renewed full diplomatic relations with Russia. Might Tito, the black-sheep Communist, return to the fold now that there was a change of shepherds?"

Eventually the old Communists in Tito's ranks demanded a showdown, and Tito called a plenum. One hundred and eight Central Committee members convened at three in the afternoon on a cold January 1954 afternoon in a onetime bank replete with marble columns and bronze grillwork to arraign Milovan on charges of heresy. "I arrived feeling numb, bodiless," Milovan recalled. "Though I knew that the verdict had already been reached, I had no way of knowing the nature or severity of my punishment."

Tito began the plenum with a speech that was "a piece of bitingly intolerant demagoguery. The reckoning it defined and articulated was not with an adversary who had simply gone astray or been disloyal in their eyes, but with one who had betrayed principle itself." Kardelj went next, disparaging "ideas that till yesterday had been his as well." Other former colleagues and friends spoke against him. Milovan later wrote, "The longer the plenum went on with its monotonous drumbeat of dogma, hatred, and resentment, the more conscious I became of the utter lack of open-minded, principled argument. It was a Stalinist show trial pure and simple. Bloodless it may have been, but no less Stalinist in every other dimension—intellectual, moral, and political."

Tito saw it too, but through a different lens. The next day, while deliberating the proposed punishment, which was one step short of expulsion, Tito stepped in to temper grumblings, saying, "He should not be expelled, or the foreign press will write that we are behaving like Stalinists!"

In the end, Milovan was removed from his position as vice president and head of Parliament, a position to which he had been elected just days before. They'd allowed him to keep his membership in the Communist Party, but Milovan turned his membership card in several months later; "to remain a party member in such circumstances would have been ignominious." He withdrew into an isolated albeit principled life.

Katharine, sobered by his experience even though she had witnessed and reported on it, sat staring at Milovan. In that moment she understood that the split between Moscow and Belgrade was a turning point for Milovan as much as for Yugoslavia. The country had pursued its own path to communism and so had Milovan. The exchange with the Russians started him down a new path of thought. And soon thereafter, she thought, his unchecked thinking had led him to question the very principles of Communism itself.

———————

Several weeks later, Milovan continued talking as he paced across the parquet floor. He had finished sharing his story with Katharine, and they had moved on to their work together. Milovan would speak out loud what he wanted to say in a mix of French, English, and Serbian, while Katharine wrote his ideas in English. This eliminated the need for a translator and allowed her to help him edit and shape his thoughts and arguments.

Katharine stopped tapping her fingers against the white glass keys of her typewriter. She was sure he had just said something incredible. She wanted to make sure she had heard correctly. She unrolled the sheet of paper from the machine and began reading. She scanned the text and felt a flutter of excitement as her mind processed the words she had just transcribed. Could this be true?

She raised her head and looked squarely at Milovan's pacing

figure, interrupting him mid-sentence to say, "But, Milovan, if you say that, you can no longer be a communist."

Immediately, everything else in the room stilled. Katharine sat rigid in her chair, her eyes fixed on Milovan, who had stopped pacing and whose head was now bowed in thought. From the corner of her eye she saw that Steffie and Ed had laid their cards down before them and were also looking at Milovan expectantly.

A spectrum of emotions passed over Milovan's face. Finally, a peaceful expression came over him, and he replied with a steady confidence, "Well, I guess I no longer am."

Katharine was stunned. With these seven words, Milovan wiped out a large part of his past. Communism had been something he had believed in so much and for so long. He had sacrificed so much for it. He'd gone to war and jail for his beliefs. Although Milovan had handed in his Communist Party card eight months earlier, that had struck Katharine as a mere protest. It had occurred before she had spent time with Milovan and understood him as a person. This statement, this admission, was more definite, more final.

Katharine broke the thick silence that hung in the air like a heavy fog, suggesting their work was done for the evening.

Milovan nodded in agreement. He and Steffie collected their coats, and Katharine walked them out to the gate. The stars were bright in the clear sky above. One of them blinked at Katharine, making her feel even more that she was floating in a dream. Katharine kissed them both on the cheeks and watched them walk toward their home before shutting the outer gate against them and the night.

Back in the bungalow, Katharine leaned back against the

front door to collect herself. After a moment, Ed interrupted her thoughts, telling her something she had never thought she would hear. He confessed to her that she had been right about Milovan. Katharine's eyes grew bigger under raised eyebrows as a wave of shock flowed across her body. She couldn't remember a single time in her entire life where Ed had ever admitted fault.

Katharine started to open her mouth, but Ed interrupted, telling her he was proud of her. She had been right to pursue Milovan. Ed had thought Milovan was just a reluctant participant playing the role of Communist Party reject who felt it his duty to continue his theoretical explorations of communism as a hobby. But tonight, Ed told her, he realized that he had misjudged Milovan.

As Ed lifted his drink to toast her, Katharine stood there speechless, staring at her husband. Eventually, she mustered a quiet thank you. She was grateful for Ed's appreciation, but even more, she was glad that her instincts had been right. She had known Milovan's cause was important, but that evening, watching his realization and the transformation it meant for him, she felt gratitude to be able to bear witness to his journey and to help him along it in some small way.

Their work had evolved beyond just the articles. Their relationship too had shifted. *Is he a friend?* she wondered. She knew better than to become too close to her sources or her causes, but this felt like so much more than that. She put these thoughts aside as she joined Ed on the couch. He had already turned the water off and put the cards away, and the topic turned to planning their trip to Paris for the holidays.

During the last week of November, a blizzard besieged Belgrade. The Košava, a fierce northeastern wind that began in the Carpathian Mountains and followed the Danube northwest to Belgrade, was to blame. Temperatures dipped well below zero, cold even by winter norms. The storm blanketed the city with snow literally as high as eyeballs in some places. No cars or buses could move. People who had to get out struggled through the drifts on foot. On the outskirts of the city, wolves howled, the sound mean and hungry. Even Lucky didn't want to go outside.

Because of the weather, Milovan and Katharine were behind on their work, but Milovan wanted to make more progress on their four article series so they could submit it for publication.

A little after seven in the evening, Katharine opened the door and saw Milovan covered in snow from his shoulders to his boots. Her maternal instincts kicked in. She pulled him inside, insisting he give her everything to dry, while she asked Ed to pour him some freshly made tea. Despite the weather and the likelihood that the secret police would be home in front of their fires instead of surveilling Milovan, Katharine still took precautions, turning on the water and the record like always, before she handed Milovan the final drafts of the articles she'd edited.

Four hours of extensive work later, they both reached their limit and stopped. Milovan asked Katharine if the pieces were developed enough for her to start pitching publications. Katharine hesitated. She had been putting off this topic until she'd received her job offer from INS. But fortunately that had recently come in, and emboldened by the question and the state of the series, Katharine offered to pitch the articles to her new employer.

Milovan told her he thought that sounded like a good idea and that he trusted her instincts.

Ed, who had been reading while they worked, offered to walk Milovan home.

The two men set out just before midnight. Several hours later, Ed returned home, wet and weary. Katharine, who had stayed up reading on the couch to make sure Ed made it back safely, waited for him to take his winter gear off before she asked him what had taken so long.

Ed began talking as he poured himself a drink and told Katharine that the snow had slowed them down. Before they turned down his street, Milovan had stopped under a streetlight and pulled a small, flat object wrapped in a handkerchief from inside his coat pocket. He handed it to Ed, who was surprised at its weight. He unwrapped it to find a pistol, a chrome Mauser 7.65, the one Milovan had told them that Konev gave him on his first trip back from Moscow in 1944. Although the light from the street lamp was dim, Ed had been able to read the inscription: "to Milovan Djilas from Ivan Konev, Marshal of Soviet Armies." Milovan had tried to give it to Ed.

Katharine cried out, interrupting him to share her hope that he had not taken the gun.

Ed assured her that he had not. He told Katharine that Milovan had been quite insistent, saying that the Clarks needed the weapon more than he did. But even if that had been the case, Ed said to Katharine, the gun's association with a Communist general went against every principle he had. So Ed had wrapped up the gun and handed it back to Milovan. Milovan simply stated, "Well, if you don't take it, they will, eventually."

Katharine sat back, processing. Milovan really was shedding his past. When the party stripped him of his titles, they'd taken his passport and his luggage. Then he'd turned in his own party card. But this gun. She knew how sentimental it was. It represented part of his role in helping his country chart its own course. This pistol had meant a lot to him. Even with his fall from power, it was a memory of the role he had played.

But as she thought about it further, more than anything, she hoped Milovan's prediction that the Yugoslav government would eventually take the gun would not come to pass. For she knew if it did, it would mean something terrible had happened to Milovan.

EIGHT
BELGRADE

January–May 1956

On New Year's Day 1956, Ed spontaneously purchased a parrot from a man peddling them in the shadow of the Eiffel Tower. Ed and Katharine had not been able to return to the United States for the holidays, so they had elected to visit the City of Lights. He had returned to their hotel room with croissants in one hand and the bird in the other. With a solemn bow he introduced Katharine to Joey, having decided to name the bird after Joe DiMaggio. Ed told her that the bird would be keeping him company while her new job with INS took her all over Europe. Katharine simply shook her head. She suggested that if the bird was going to serve as her replacement, she would have to teach him how to say "Goddammit, Ed"—something Katharine said to him often. Moments later when Joey squawked *Goddammit*, they both fell onto the floor in fits of laughter.

Back in Belgrade, Katharine could tell that Mica, who had never warmed to Lucky, really didn't know what to do with Joey. Katharine noticed that Mica completed her work even faster than usual, finding excuses to leave the house for errands or bringing food she had prepared at home instead of making it at the Clarks' as she had previously done. But Katharine had barely been at home since the new year either. Ed joked that she now traveled more than he did, and it was true. In the last month, INS had sent her on trips to Hungary and Romania. As a result, she was behind on her extracurricular work for Milovan's series.

One late morning in early April, Katharine found herself alone at home. She had just returned from another week in Hungary where she'd been investigating the role of religion in a supposedly secular Communist country. She sat before her typewriter staring at a blank piece of paper, the keys beneath her quiet fingers cool and smooth.

Thirty minutes later she had finished her mailers about the trip. Three articles now lay in a pile next to the typewriter waiting for her to send to Allen Dodd, the editor in London to whom Kingsbury-Smith had assigned her when he'd offered her the position. But there was one more thing Katharine had left to do. She rolled fresh paper into the machine and stared at it for five long minutes. Where should she begin? There were so many pieces of information she needed to convey. Most of all, she hoped it wasn't too early in her tenure with INS to send this note.

Katharine closed her eyes and took a deep breath to calm her thoughts, taking in the sweet smell of the honeysuckle bush in new bloom just outside the window. She had opened it to let in the fresh spring air, wanting to replace the staleness built up during the week while she'd been away. Squawks from a flock of low-flying herons migrating north startled her. She blinked her eyes open and saw her jumpiness had marred the paper in the machine with random letters. Sighing, she pulled the paper out of the typewriter and rolled a clean sheet in again. She returned her hands to the keyboard and began to type, translating her thoughts into words on paper without any more concern or delay:

April 7, 1956

Dear Mr. Dodd,

We arrived back in Belgrade late the night of April 5. Mailers and a letter about the general working set-up in Budapest are on their way.

This letter however is about a different subject and is being carried to Trieste by a friend who will mail it from there April 9th.

Would INS be interested in a series of articles by Milovan Djilas, the former vice-president of Yugoslavia (and President of Parliament) who was purged last year? Milovan was the chief agit-prop Yugoslav communist. He travelled to Moscow as head of the Yugoslav delegation asking military aid during the war; he also headed delegation to cominform meetings.

He is a good friend of mine and I have in fact helped him with some writings. I thought INS might like at this time a series by him interpreting the communist new look, warning—or not—about the forthcoming Khrushchev, Bulganin visit to London, and some personal remarks about the new boys at the top. I will see to it that there is not too much "gobbledygook" of communism in the articles.

As a matter of fact, I could write the articles for him if I drag out of him a little more of the personal remarks. I know his views on the dangers of present-day communism and why communists can denounce Stalin with so little embarrassment.

Payment for such a series would be very nominal. I have not talked to him about payment but I am certain money is not the prime objective in his view. I would personally suggest that what payment INS made should be held for him in either England, Germany or America.

There is only one point about which I should caution you. If we use his series it will make foreign correspondents and especially INS very unpopular in Belgrade for awhile. I have weathered such a storm before, however, and understand how much the Yugoslavs want to keep correspondents here—no matter what we write. It would mean that for a time Yugoslav "reporters" would write snide stories about interfering foreign reporters. I do not think it would hurt INS business although at this stage I have not mentioned it to Mio. I am certain he would not want to know in advance.

I am certain I do not have to impress upon you that it would be wrong to mention Milovan's name in letters. When you answer this one, please refer to him simply as "your friend." Once we get the articles and they are printed, he will not be in any danger because then the regime will know all the press here will be watching like a hawk to see what does happen. But if the regime got wind in advance that something was planned, Milovan might be hauled in for questioning (of several months) or banished out of Belgrade to a village.

I am enclosing a copy of this letter so you can send it to

Kingsbury-Smith. I do not want to ask my friend to mail more than one letter. I would appreciate a note saying when this arrives and of course I would like a decision as soon as possible.

I have not said anything definite as yet to Milovan but have explored the subject enough to know we can go ahead. Also, since I think he wants to talk we better move in before he turns to some other correspondent.

Most sincerely,
Katharine Clark

When she was done, Katharine held two and a quarter single-spaced, typewritten pages in her hands. As she reread it, she was proud of every word.

Katharine folded the paper, put it in an envelope, and addressed it to Dodd care of INS's offices in London. She put the envelope in her large purse and readied to walk to the U.S. embassy to hand deliver the note for Joan Clark, who would pass it to the embassy official traveling to Trieste that week. She looked down at her watch and saw it was almost noon. If she walked fast, she might be able to convince Joan to join her for lunch.

————

A week later, as Katharine rolled a new sheet of paper into her typewriter, a squeal erupted from Steffie. Katharine looked over to where she and Ed sat playing cards. Steffie turned to Milovan and Katharine, sharing that she had won a new game Ed had taught her, the gleam of victory evident in her face and voice. Katharine laughed as Ed told Steffie they should play the best two out of three, before turning her attention back to the table where she saw Milovan wearing a wide smile on his narrow face. There was a mischievous look in his eyes.

Sliding several handwritten pages across the table to her, Milovan leaned in and whispered to Katharine that he needed her help getting a letter to the West. As she looked down, Katharine saw the writing was in Serbian, but she could make out the salutation. It was a note to Morgan Phillips. She bit the inside of her lower lip as she collected her thoughts. She was curious what Milovan was writing to the head of the British Labour Party. She hadn't done anything like this before for Milovan. But she knew his mail was monitored, the secret police read everything received or sent, and sometimes prevented delivery all together. She knew for Milovan to correspond with Phillips there would be no other way than by pigeoning it out of the country by hand through a courier. Katharine looked over at Ed. He was laughing, his attention engrossed in the game in front of him. Turning her eyes back to Milovan, she took the paper from where it lay on the table and slipped it into her nearby handbag, not having to say anything else to indicate she would help.

On April 16, Ed and Katharine were in the middle of dinner with their friend Richard "Dickie" Williams from the BBC when a loud knock on the door interrupted the boisterous laughter that had filled the room. Dickie had just been recounting one of his harrowing tales from the war, which was made all the more enter-taining by his thick Welsh accent.

Not knowing who it might be, Ed went to the door and opened it, his eyes still focused on Katharine and Dickie. But when Ed saw both their faces suddenly become serious, he turned to take in Milovan standing in the frame, pale as a ghost.

Katharine was by Ed's side immediately, and she ushered Milovan into the room. She steered Milovan to the sofa while she looked back at Ed and pointed her head toward their bar. Katharine knew Milovan didn't like to drink much, but she thought tonight might be an exception.

She turned back to Milovan and tried to take his coat. Ed tried to offer him a vodka, but Milovan held up his hand to both of them, telling them he wouldn't be there long enough to take his coat off or to have a drink, but that he had not known where else to go. With Katharine, Ed, and Dickie now gathered around him, he sat down and began to talk.

Steffie had left for her job as a bookkeeper at the bank that morning as she usually did. Everything had been fine. Normal. But early in the afternoon, Milovan had received a harried call from her, asking him to come at once to escort her home. He obliged, still not understanding.

At home he convinced Steffie to go to bed, and at her bed-side she finally told him what had transpired. Steffie had finished paperwork before she took her lunch break. She planned to run an errand during her break, but after she'd taken just a few steps outside, a strange young woman whom Steffie didn't recognize ran up to her. Milovan told Ed, Dickie, and Katharine, "A woman grabbed my wife publicly and screamed to bystanders that she was my mistress." Beseeching Steffie to give Milovan a divorce, she accused Steffie of stealing Milovan from her and called her a bad woman who would pay for her crimes. It was very busy outside the bank, and many pedestrians stopped to stare. As the crowd grew, the police arrived. And although Steffie never said a word, the police charged both women with creating a public disturbance, which meant that Steffie would have to go on trial.

"My wife had never seen the woman before and did not answer her but ran back into the bank where she works and telephone me."

Milovan paused before he told them it had all been his fault. He had understood from a friend that the UDBA would be increasing attacks on him by any means necessary but had not thought it would be in this way. He told them this was "part of a campaign to destroy me politically by discrediting me morally." He believed this same woman had been writing him and telephoning him since January. And worse, a friend of his had recently been fired on the grounds that his friendship "gave Mr. Djilas moral support."

Discomfort settled in the room. Katharine, Ed, and Dickie sat stunned.

Finally, as Milovan stood to go, Dickie blurted out, it sounded like a "frameup of the worst sort."

Dickie's comment triggered something in Katharine, and she rose from her seat and said they would help however they could as she walked him to the door.

Milovan nodded and thanked her before he bade them all a good evening and walked out.

Hearing the gate close, Katharine turned back to Ed and Dickie, a look of unshakable resolve settling on her face. She told them she wanted to make a list of all the newsmen in Belgrade, in order of whom they could ask to attend Steffie's trial.

Four days later, when Steffie appeared at a private hearing before an examining magistrate, Ed, Katharine, Dickie, and Sydney Gruson, the new reporter for the *New York Times* in Belgrade, sat directly behind Steffie. The magistrate sat at a table beneath an official portrait of Tito in his full military dress and regalia, his head looming large on his thick neck. It was the only decoration in the dreary room.

The magistrate took in the quartet of foreign correspondents before he turned his gaze to Steffie. During the proceedings, while the magistrate asked questions and Steffie replied, the reporters, based on Katharine's careful instructions beforehand, made a grand show of recording notes in notebooks or whispering loudly to one another. All the while the old magistrate kept looking at them. After just fifteen minutes, he dismissed the case and assessed the female provocateur a fine.

Nothing about Steffie's trial was carried in the local press, a fact that Gruson included in a story in the *New York Times* the next day. Under the headline "Ex-Aide of Tito Sees New Smear," Gruson included the same quote Milovan had made to Katharine, Ed, and Dickie at the Clarks' house that the trial against Steffie was "part of a campaign to destroy him politically by discrediting him morally." Katharine knew Tito would be incensed at the coverage. She smiled with satisfaction, although she knew that it was only a small victory in a longer war.

Toward the end of April, Katharine received a letter from
Kingsbury-Smith. As she read it she realized Allen Dodd had
shared her letter with him as she had requested, and Kingsbury-
Smith was writing in reply to her pitch about Milovan.

April 24, 1956

Dear Katharine,

With reference to your April 7th note to Mr. Dodd, I would
certainly be interested in a series of about four articles which
could be carried under the signature of your friend providing you
thought the material was really newsworthy. We might be able
to pay a few hundred dollars for such a series, but, of course,
we would like to have a look at the material first if you could
possibly arrange it. I am inclined to rely on your judgment and
if you felt the material would be newsworthy, the chances are we
would take it.

The most recent developments, including the dissolution of
the Cominform, should make interesting subjects for comment.
But most interesting of all, would be the interpretation of just
what the new tactics mean, who is the boss, and the role that
these new people, especially the two top ones, played under the old
regime. It could be a very interesting series.

I hope you can persuade your friend to go ahead with it. If
you do succeed, please have the articles sent to me personally.

Perhaps one of our friends will be leaving Belgrade about the time
the articles are ready, and you could send them to me that way.

With kindest regards.

Most sincerely yours,
Kingsbury-Smith

Katharine let out a small yelp of joy. The note gave Katharine
hope and confidence in her new employer as well as in Kingsbury-
Smith himself. More than that, it was real. She had done it. She had
found a home for Milovan's articles. She couldn't wait to share the
news with him after she returned from her trip through Hungary
and Czechoslovakia that she was setting out on the next day.

On May 15, Katharine opened the door to welcome the
Djilases inside, expecting to celebrate, but instead she took in the
sour expression on Milovan's face. Katharine paused, taken aback
for a moment. With a look of puzzlement on her face, she turned
to Steffie, who told her he had been that way all day.

Katharine ignored Milovan during dinner, wanting to let him
share why he was clearly in such a bad mood. But when he still
wore a brooding expression as she offered him Mica's decadent
chocolate dessert, she finally asked him if his mood was related to
the article in *Borba*, the Yugoslav Communist Party daily paper.
That morning *Borba*'s editor had written a public reply to a private
letter that Morgan Phillips, who led the British Labour Party, had
sent to Tito. Katharine imagined Phillips's letter to Tito had been
prompted by the letter Milovan had written Phillips the month

before, as *Borba* claimed Phillips was interfering in Yugoslav affairs and mentioned Djilas by name. But Milovan simply shook his head in response to her question, and everyone ate dessert in silence.

As Katharine cleared the dishes, just as she was wondering whether she and Milovan would work that night, he asked her to get her typewriter.

Taking his cue, Ed asked Steffie what game she wanted to play as he went to the bookshelf to get the well-worn pack of Hoyle cards and turn up the music.

Katharine emerged from the bedroom carrying her typewriter. Before she had even set it down on the table, Milovan told her he needed her help with another letter—but to help write it, not just send it. Clenching his hands together in a tight fist, he began to explain. He told her how that morning Srpska Knjizevna Zadruga, a local publisher, had informed him they were not going to publish a book he had submitted to them—his autobiography. When he had given it to the editor several weeks ago, the editor was thrilled. But that morning the same man told Milovan that his book was below standard. Milovan paused and looked at Katharine, conveying with his glance that this lie had gravely insulted him. He told Katharine that writing was all he had left.

She stared at him in disbelief. The government kept doing the most absurd things against Milovan. A second later, full of purpose, she asked to whom they were writing. When Milovan responded he wanted to write to the editors of the *New York Times*, she thought dryly, *Of course.*

Katharine sat down in front of her typewriter as Milovan got up from his chair and started to pace, dictating what he wanted to say as he walked.

"Dear Sirs," he began. "I would be grateful to you if you will publish this letter, especially because I cannot publish in my own country."

Katharine typed quickly, her fingers flying over the keyboard to keep up with his animated speech.

"May 15th it was said to me by a publication enterprise," he went on as Katharine added in parentheses that it was a Serbian literary cooperative, "that my manuscript, which I sent them over a month ago, will not be published. They gave as a reason that the book is 'autobiographical and might provoke discussion.' The real reason is, however, to prevent me having any publication. This enterprise publishes autobiographies, but even so my book is not essentially autobiographical."

Milovan continued: "I stress that Mr. Zivanovic told me that none of the editors actually read the book." Then he added, "This prevention of publishing was done at order of political factions. In February 1954, Marshal Tito told correspondents that literary activities would be permitted to me. By this it is impossible for me to earn a living for my family in the only manner which I can."

He stopped and asked her to read it back to him. When she finished, she looked up and saw the tight smile on his face. The letter was pointed and splendid, and he knew it. Katharine placed the letter to the side. She knew she'd have to find someone to take it to the West before she left for Bulgaria, where she was going to be the first news agency reporter to visit the country since the Cold War had begun over a decade earlier.

But before that, Katharine wanted to prepare Milovan for the interview with Ed's boss, James Bell, who was making the trip to Belgrade to do a story on Milovan for *Time*.

NINE

SOFIA AND BELGRADE

June 1956

As Katharine walked on the yellow bricks paving the roads in Bulgaria's capital, she felt like she had been transported to Frank L. Baum's Oz. On the broad avenues, cleaned every day by the government—first swept and then vacuumed—people with pleasant, almost friendly faces moved in an orderly fashion, not milling in the street like in Belgrade. At night, new fluorescent streetlights shone brightly in the city center, nothing like the creepy shadows formed by the weak light of Belgrade's lampposts. It was a "pleasant shock," she wrote in her first article about the trip, like no other Balkan capital she had yet experienced. "A thaw is taking place in Communist Bulgarian communism," she wrote, "but patches of snow are still visible."

Katharine had returned to Sofia after travels across the country where she had seen the contradictions of progress and stagnation firsthand. Kingsbury-Smith had been so pleased when he obtained a visa for her to visit Bulgaria that she vowed to take full advantage of her access to travel widely.

She had visited a cooperative farm in Vratsa in the northwest of the country. Agriculture was a significant part of Bulgaria's economy, and Katharine heard there was a stark "difference between communist plans and communist reality." Joining the collective—which required a farmer to give up his land save for one-half hectare (1.2 acres) that he could farm for himself and almost all of his equipment and livestock—was positioned as elective. But the reality was the peasants were "compelled to join the cooperative." Only a handful "held out against the pressures of ostracism, and sudden huge increases of taxes on their property." But those who joined the collective were taxed too—assessed by local government officials who seized "the amount of produce they believe represents the tax." The farmers weren't paid for rent on the land they contributed to the cooperative; for working the land, they instead received a daily wage of two leva, which amounted to about thirty-two cents. As one man told Katharine, "What we really get is just enough to keep alive." This was a far cry from the promise of increased production and livelihood due to collectivizing.

In contrast, Katharine drove east to a tiny village on the Black Sea where an oil field had recently been discovered, representing "a step toward the industrialization which was one aim of the Communist revolution." She observed: "standing on a derrick talking to the crew it was hard to realize I was not in New Jersey. The look of the land, the smell of the oil were just the same."

And in Sofia, she had observed the government's failed attempts to have its citizens eat preserved food. Instead of opting for the cans of tomato paste, glass jars of beans and peas, and cans of fish displayed under large posters of Lenin and Stalin, the longest line at the market was at the butcher's, where tripe was selling for a bargain price.

Now, Katharine was about to open the door to leave her room at the Hotel Bulgaria for a bowl of strawberries in the dining room—the fruit was in season, and she had never tasted anything quite so sweet. She had another day of investigation ahead of her, but she stopped when a bellboy slipped a white envelope under the door. Leaning down, she tore the envelope open before she even stood back up and found a telegram from Kingsbury-Smith: "articles splendid / releasing starting sunday / writing concerning special bonus for you and other financial aspects / kingsmith +/+"

Katharine couldn't believe that all their work would finally be in print. Then she jumped with a start realizing that Sunday was just three days away. Katharine had wanted to be in Belgrade when the articles ran. Although the pieces wouldn't be published directly in Yugoslavia, she knew the content would make its way into the city and circulate more quickly than if they dominated the front page of their local papers. Katharine faced a dilemma, as she was supposed to be in Bulgaria for another week on a visa that had been hard to come by. Hesitating for only a moment, she began to pack. When she was done, she surveyed the room one more time to make sure she had not left anything, before she headed for the front desk to check out.

An hour later, as she pulled onto the road that would take her north toward Belgrade, Katharine wondered with anticipation about what the reaction to Milovan's articles would be.

She didn't have to wait long. By Monday, one day after the first article ran in the United States with the title "A Top Communist Exposes the New Kremlin Danger," she heard people talking about it in whispers in the bookstore she visited and in hushed conversations at the cafés that lined the avenue as she walked to keep herself busy while Ed was in Moscow. By Wednesday, two more articles had run. Although the articles were not published in Yugoslavia, their contents circulated widely in the city. *Borba* was forced to respond.

Kingsbury-Smith had been pleased with the series. He wrote Katharine a letter, sharing, "I think respect for him will be greatly enhanced." He had also asked Katharine if there were other topics Milovan might want to write about. The information Milovan possessed from being an insider was more valuable than anything the Central Intelligence Agency could acquire, try as they might. Milovan had laid bare, in plain and simple terms for anyone in the West to read, who was in charge in Moscow and what they were like.

But as Katharine approached Terazije Square, her thoughts weren't on additional topics for Milovan to write; they were on Ed. The media storm around Djilas had turned into a hurricane as these articles fed swirl that had started several weeks before. While Katharine was in Bulgaria, the *New York Times* had run the majority of Milovan's letter to the editors. And *Time* had run Bell's profile on Milovan under the title "The Unyielding Man." Combined with the series, Katharine now feared possible retaliation against Ed, who was currently in Russia covering Tito's first trip there in years. It was widely known that she worked for INS and that Ed was her husband. Katharine knew the Russians were not as concerned with Western opinion as the Yugoslavs were. The men Milovan had written about "came to power through Stalin...[and] were held down and firmly controlled by Stalin;" with the Russian leader now dead, they were "enjoying a field day" and would have no trouble taking action against a reporter if they deemed it necessary.

Katharine entered the lobby of the Hotel Moskva and walked directly to the elevator. After all her years abroad, she still found it strange that the only way to get an update on a travelling spouse while he or she was traveling was through the editor. She waved at one of the hotel staff walking toward her who raised his hand to reciprocate, causing him to drop the papers he carried. Katharine stopped to help pick them up, and when she turned around to carry some of the items to the front desk, she saw two large men in blue serge suits enter the hotel and look straight at her.

Am I being followed? Her stomach turned. She walked quickly to the elevator, feeling a renewed sense of urgency to learn about Ed.

Upstairs in *Time*'s office, she sat down at the telex. She had written a recap for Bell of the press reaction to his story about Milovan in *Time* as well as the other pieces. She pulled her notes out and wrote the shorthand to establish the connection with the Bonn office where Bell worked: "time life gdsbg* pls. eye got copy for you from katty clark." Once the confirmation came through,

---

*   gdsbg was the code for *Time*'s Bonn bureau, located in Bad Godesberg, a municipal district of Bonn.

Katharine typed out her report in the shorthand required of the medium. She told Bell that the reactions in the local press had the "same theme." All the recent press coverage and Milovan's series were part of "a campaign organized by reactionary american [sic] circles against peaceful, independent policy of yugoslavia [sic] timed when Tito is on great mission of peace and friendship to moscow [sic]." She then gave Bell a series of detailed quotes from the two magazines before she wrote, "jim am worried about eddie please notify when learn his whereabouts."

After a minute, Bell's reply came in: "everything fine."

She sighed with relief.

With her job done, she left. Downstairs she walked by the café and saw the two men in serge suits eating pastries and drinking coffee. Neither of them even glanced at her. *I'm becoming paranoid*, she thought.

_____

Several days later Ed returned from his two-week trip to the Soviet Union with the heady mix of exhaustion and excitement that comes from covering history in the making. He was brimming with stories, but so was Katharine. The two of them stayed up well into the morning catching up.

Ed told Katharine how a crowd of two hundred thousand in Moscow broke through security at a rally and tumbled Tito, his wife, and all the reporters and cameramen against their automobiles soon after they had appeared. Khrushchev had barely escaped. Then in Sochi, Tito and his wife toured lemon gardens and palm groves full of statues of Communist leaders dressed in bathing costumes, where Tito played his favorite parlor trick: he picked a leaf from a nearby shrub and then, holding it flat in his left fist, smacked it hard with his right hand, producing a sound like the bursting of a blown-up paper bag. Katharine shook her head, appalled at these childish antics from a country's leader. When Ed finished talking, Katharine told him about the response to Milovan's series and the other news coverage in Belgrade. She showed him the wall of cartoons she had tacked up to the inside of the armoire from the local party papers—the first ones ever done of her. In the lampoons she was depicted as the evil reporter from the West trying to spread falsehoods about Milovan to undermine Yugoslavia at a pivotal moment.

While Ed laughed at the pictures depicting her as a large giant of a woman, he also told her he was proud of her. Katharine beamed. They fell asleep, laughing and happy.

———

The next day, as Katharine took Lucky outside, she noticed a black car out front filled with four men straining against the sedan's small silhouette. She came back inside and announced to Ed that they had tails.

He looked up from his breakfast, taking in her calm expression, and asked her if she was sure.

She sighed in response, telling him to look for himself if he didn't believe her.

While Ed rose to look, Katharine thought about the four men in the car across from their house. The last time she'd been in a situation like this had been decades earlier. Just before her family had left the Philippines to return to America, her mother, sister, and she had traveled extensively through Asia. On the last leg of the trip, they had taken a train through China. It had been the fall of 1926, and a civil war was brewing in China between the Kuomintang-led government of the Republic of China and the Communist Party of China. The girls and their mother had been advised to stay in their compartments, leaving only to eat in the dining car, telling anyone who asked that they were diplomatique. On the last day of the trip, Katharine had convinced her little sister to have some fun by talking about their fellow diners with each other in a language no one else would likely understand, pig Latin.

All had seemed well as the train steamed into the station in Shanghai. They greeted their father on the platform, and then Katharine and her sister had run ahead of their parents to collect their trunks. But before they reached them, a train window squeaked open. A white-coated waiter poked his upper body out to catch the attention of two nearby policemen, gesticulating wildly as he pointed at Katharine and her sister. Seconds later, the two girls were escorted away by the officers, her sister screaming, "I want my mother," while Katharine held her head high, not uttering a word. Hours later, an embassy officer helped secure their release, and the family discovered the waiter had thought Katharine and her sister were Communist spies. Following the guidance of the embassy official, her father had taken them all to the ship and locked them in their room until it set sail. When policemen arrived at the boat to attempt to re-arrest the girls, they were refused entry, and soon after Katharine and her family set sail for the United States.

Now, as Katharine thought about the car idling in front of their house, she felt the same thrill and trepidation. Except this time, it wasn't a silly teenager's game, and her father wasn't there to rescue her. It brought home for Katharine the real impact of her association with Milovan.

This was unusual. They were the only Western journalists with secret police tails.

This meant something. And it was dangerous.

TEN
POZNAN

July 1956

Katharine woke before dawn to the sound of gunfire, a light layer of sweat already dampening her tanned brow. She didn't flinch as another spray of bullets went off, echoing loudly through the otherwise quiet predawn hours. She'd already grown accustomed to the sound, which had dominated the early mornings of the past several days. As she lay on her back, splayed out across a thin, lumpy bed in one of the only vacant hotel rooms in Poznan, Poland, Katharine could not turn off her thoughts. When the next rounds deployed, she pulled a musty-smelling pillowcase over her head in the hopes of drowning out the noise.

She'd arrived in Communist Poland on the last day of June to cover the anti-Communist protests that had broken out a few days before on the morning of June 28. Now, several days later, tanks patrolled outside and inside the city, including on the street outside her hotel. Katharine was told semiofficially that the troops were stationed on the roads to Poznan because the riots were a great shock to the nation and the troops were needed in the event the rioting evolved into a revolution. To help prevent this, the government rounded up alleged activists and sympathizers in the early morning hours. As Katharine listened to the gunfire, she wondered who had fallen victim this time, imagining their faces full of anguish and determination for their cause, their families crying as a husband, father, or brother was ripped out of bed and taken to prison.

Sighing, she continued to lie there for an hour. At five she rose. The room was dark, so Katharine felt her way from the bed to the small table and chair she had set up as a makeshift desk. There was a lamp with a light, so dull she could barely see the scrawl of her handwriting on her notepad. But she didn't need to read. All her notes and observations had the same theme: death.

For the past two days, everywhere Katharine went, she found people eager to discuss their lives in Poland and share their opinions with her. Many of them were questioning communism, echoing the comments she'd been hearing from Milovan for the last few months. But these were the human stories that her editors always charged her to seek out. And in each of them she saw evidence to support Milovan's theories.

There was a little man at the café who shared his experience of Buchenwald, a Nazi concentration camp. A desolate mother whose son had been arrested during the riots and who now waited outside the police building hoping for news of him. And an old man who simply wanted to ride in Katharine's car; he had come up to her while she was examining a map, figuring out where to drive to next, and told her, "Before the war, my dear, I had four cars."

Everyone had been eager to discuss the details. Some believed the protests started because the post-Stalin liberalization in Poland was moving too slowly, while others held the view that the Polish people were fed up with their living conditions and the economy's extreme inflation. The protest had started with workers asking for higher wages and lower food prices. Women and children had joined the cause, the crowd quickly growing into the thousands as it descended from the factories to the city center.

No one Katharine encountered could explain why the protests had turned deadly, but when shots were fired, the chaos had ensued for several days. The article Katharine filed the night before by phone to Berlin had been matter-of-fact. Her lead read: "This correspondent estimates that at least 400 persons were killed in the two-day anti-Communist workers' revolt in Poznan." Although the Polish government's official death toll was just 48, Katharine had done her own calculations by visiting eleven hospitals across the city. A kind, exhausted doctor at the civilian hospital closest to the protests estimated that they had tended to 200 wounded and that 50 people had already died. Officials and nurses at the other ten hospitals had similar stories to share. Katharine was appalled at the discrepancy.

But this morning, she had moved on to a bigger story. Yesterday, her last source had told her the first person killed in the protests had been a child. The man encouraged Katharine to visit the city's cemeteries to see the tombstones of newly dug graves for herself. As he was speaking, a group of army officers sat down at a nearby table. The man abruptly changed the subject and said, "Oh, you know how it is," before quickly standing up to leave. Katharine did not need to ask why. She remained at the table, finishing her coffee before paying the bill and exiting the café, resolving to act on the man's tip the next day.

Now, Katharine pulled out the map of Poznan she'd received from the hotel when she'd checked in and put an X on each cemetery she wanted to visit. She also put a circle near the location of the military checkpoints she had encountered while touring the city earlier. She knew the placement of checkpoints might change, but she hoped to minimize the time spent showing papers and fake smiling at the Polish officers to ensure she could visit all seven graveyards.

Katharine turned on her car a little after six. Outside, the sun was just beginning to rise, casting a warmth across a city still scarred from the activities of the last few days. Given the early hour and so close on the heels of the police raids, the streets were empty of pedestrians and other drivers. She drove past overturned cars and trucks that littered the streets and first-floor storefronts still boarded up. When would it all return to normal? How long would it take for the citizens of Poznan to resume their lives?

Despite her planning, Katharine found herself at a checkpoint in no time at all. A large green tank was positioned diagonally to block two-way traffic, the twin guns of the vehicle seemingly pointed right at her. Katharine saw two men inside, their heads just visible, one in each turret, laughing about something. Against her will and despite the warmth in the air, goose bumps formed on her arms. She hoped the officer walking toward her wouldn't notice. Katharine handed the young man her papers, smiling up at him and squinting at the sun, which was breaking through a scattered skyline of clouds above. He briefly glanced at her papers and waved her through.

Katharine put her foot back on the accelerator and soon arrived at the first church. There was nothing remarkable about the one-story, white wood building with a short, fat bell tower, but it had been the place her source had mentioned explicitly by name, and she felt it right to start her day there.

At this time in the morning, Katharine expected to be the only person in the cemetery, although from the newly dug graves and numerous bouquets of fresh, colorful flowers, she knew that it had recently been busy. So Katharine was surprised to see someone else in the graveyard. A man stood before a modest, simple cream-colored headstone, his shoulders heaving. At first, Katharine left him alone. But as she walked among tombstones and noted the names and dates of births and deaths, she eventually found herself upon him. The man turned toward her as she approached, tears on his cheeks and fear in his eyes.

Katharine identified herself as an American. His grief resumed full-time residence on his face, washing away all other emotions. Still looking at Katharine, he pointed at the tomb-stone. "My son was killed by my own countrymen," he said. Katharine shifted her gaze from the man's eyes to the tombstone before him. As she took in the name and date of birth, her mind calculated that his son was just a teenager. Katharine pulled a camera out of her bag, pointed at it and then at the grave marker, asking for permission without saying a word. The man simply nodded at her, and Katharine snapped a photo, evidence for her story and for herself. She thanked the man and left him to his mourning.

Katharine walked back to her car and sat in the driver's seat for a long moment collecting her thoughts before she turned the ignition and drove away.

After she had visited more cemeteries, she returned to her hotel room, exhausted not only from the heat but also from the despair that she had encountered at each resting place. Although she was not the model mother, she could not even begin to imagine a parent's grief at losing a child. With no emotion left inside her to give to the story, Katharine sat down at her desk and wrote the facts.

"How old is a child?" she began. Then she added: "The Polish government said no children were killed in the Poznan uprising. I visited three municipal and three church cemeteries out of a total of seven in Poznan. I found the grave of a teenage boy. It was being tended by the youngster's father, who told me: 'My son was killed by my own countrymen.' I saw the records and visited the graves of Bozdan Novak, 19, Janusz Skora, 16, and Andrezej Hoppe, 18, who, according to the records, died during the uprising. There was no way of telling exactly how they died. I found the graves of Leon Kalz, 15, Jerszy Jankowski, 15, Wieslaw Kuznicki, 16, and Roman Struzalkowski. Roman was born March 20,1943. By any mathematical system, he was only 13 when he died during the uprising June 28."

Was it enough to show the hypocrisy? She hoped her editors wouldn't change a word.

As she turned to leave her room to call in the story, her eyes caught on the headline of the Communist Party newspaper *Trybuna Lubu*. Katharine remembered the paper had stated that the Polish government didn't shoot the working class. *Outrageous,* she thought. She returned to her desk and wove this into her narrative. Satisfied, she went to the hotel operator to get help connecting to Berlin to dispatch her story.

The next day she drove twelve hours home to Belgrade via Czechoslovakia. At the Polish-Czech border, Czech guards spent more time than usual inspecting her baggage and car. When they found the unexposed camera film inside her toiletries bag, the guards held her while they phoned Prague to obtain permission to let her through with the film as Katharine insisted they do. She was furious with the guards and with herself. She should have guessed there would be anxiety about preventing pictures from Poznan circulating inside Czechoslovakia.

As she sat there waiting for the person on the other end to determine whether the officers would permit her to keep the film, Katharine knew she wouldn't need to develop the pictures to remember what she had seen in Poznan. It would haunt her memory.

_____

The next night after Katharine returned from her travels, she and Ed hosted a party. At the end of the night, Ed walked U.S. Ambassador Riddleberger to his car. Riddleberger typically drove his own car instead of using a chauffeur-driven government car as a way to keep some control over part of his former life prior to becoming an ambassador. He did this no matter the occasion.

But when Ed and the ambassador reached Riddleberger's car, they met an unexpected sight. All of the glass on the ambassador's car—the windshield, the windows, and even the mirrors—had been smeared with mud. The men rubbed their eyes to make sure it was not the night playing tricks on them. When it was clear what had happened, they located some tools and water and proceeded to remove as much mud as possible to allow Riddleberger to drive home.

The next morning when Katharine took Lucky out, their normally reticent neighbors told Katharine that they had seen the perpetrators who had placed the mud on the ambassador's car. Katharine's suspicion that it had been the UDBA was correct. The secret police had mistaken the ambassador's car for the Clarks'. It was yet another reminder of the risk she and Ed were taking in working with Milovan.

And it wasn't the only one they would receive over the next several days.

The next morning at 10 a.m. exactly, Ed and Katharine picked up Milovan, Steffie, and Aleksa to drive to the countryside for some much-needed relaxation. Despite the barks from Lucky in the back, Katharine couldn't take her eyes off the reflection of the black sedan in the rearview mirror. It was following their every move. If Ed turned left, so did the black sedan. If Ed sped up, the black sedan did as well. There was never any other car in between the Clarks' car and the black sedan. Ed even took a little detour through the city to confirm they were being followed. The driver of the black sedan made no attempt to remain discreet. *So much for taking the secret police seriously,* Katharine thought from where she sat in the back seat with Steffie and Aleksa.

Ed eventually turned onto the road that led to the highway out of the city. After about a half hour's drive, Avala, a small mountain with a war memorial, came into view, its forested peak verdant with life against the white fluffy clouds that flooded the sky. As they approached the turnoff, the different hues of green came into clearer focus, showing the diversity of the flora and fauna that populated the mountain. Ed turned the car off the main road and parked.

As they laid out several blankets and set baskets of food down, the four men from the black sedan took up position in a wooded area about fifty feet away. They ignored the men as best they could: Milovan and Ed took Aleksa to look for birds, while Katharine and Steffie set up their lunch.

As they ate, Katharine told Milovan about Poznan. She started from the beginning and told him what she'd experienced: the protests, the gunshots, the fallen bodies, and most of all the contradictions between what she had physically seen with her own eyes and what was reported in the newspapers. As she spoke, she watched his face brighten. He told her that her intelligence was encouraging and was making him rethink parts of a book he had just finished writing. Surprised, Katharine joked that she had been away a long time if he had managed to write a book in her absence.

The men from the secret police whiled away the time with a soccer ball, their game continuing through lunch. More than a half dozen times the black-and-white checked ball bounced into the group's picnic area. Every time Ed or Milovan returned the ball, the men responded with polite thank-yous.

Just after two, satiated and happy, the Clarks and Djilases

packed up their picnic and headed back to the car. The secret police trailed closely behind, continuing to follow them like a pack of hyenas stalking prey. On the drive home, Katharine hoped it was only her active imagination that made it seem as if the car was speeding up to close in on them.

ELEVEN

BELGRADE

July–August 1956

Katharine pushed her foot almost flat against the car's accelerator
as she sped toward Belgrade. She had rolled down the windows
to let in the wind, hoping it would cool the July heat. Tendrils of
her thick hair whipped against her cheeks as she passed the long,
brown stretches of fields occasionally colored by a small town or
lone, red-kerchiefed woman bent over working in a field.

She was returning from another trip to Poland. She'd gone to
find more stories about the aftermath of the protests in Poznan,
but she'd found much more. Across the country, everywhere she
went she discovered a deep awareness of the events in Poznan.
The Polish people understood how to read between the lines of
the official reports. After eleven years of living as part of the USSR,
they were tired of the lies and the abysmal standard of living.

Katharine had witnessed a hotel porter refuse a $25 tip, opt-
ing instead for two cigarettes—literal proof Poland had become a
"cigarette economy," where money was less valuable than goods.
To help bring this to life, Katharine wrote an article in which she

tallied the cost of food and basic items to give her readers a sense of what the Polish people were going through: "The average Pole must work four hours to buy a dozen eggs (average pay is considered 700 zloty a month), 21 days to buy a pair of shoes, 6 days for his wife's cotton dress, 22 days for a woman's rayon suit, one week's work for a shirt, 18 days for a sweater and four and half days for his baby's pair of shoes. If he dreams of a second-hand wrist watch he must spend three month's pay." And all of this depended on whether the items were actually for sale. She added, "Frequently one sees long lines in front of a shop here. Those lines mean the shop actually has for sale the goods which are displayed in the windows."

Everyone Katharine met talked about the difference between Communist plans and reality, and in their stories, she heard proof of Milovan's ideas. In the south of Poland in a small town called Katowice in the Silesian region, under a sky as black as the coal mined beneath it, one miner told Katharine, "We don't think any worker in this country—whether he is here in the mines or in a factory at Warsaw—is paid enough to exist—much less to live decently. Our standards are a thousand percent lower than the miners of France." Another miner said, "We do a lot of work for the USSR. And Polish miners do not like that." In Krakow she talked to numerous people who spoke openly of Russians who were in the Polish secret police.

But the story that haunted Katharine the most involved a little girl in Wrocław. Construction across Poland stood in various stages, most of it halted because raw materials were scarce. In Wrocław, Katharine described a city of 350 thousand that looked "as it did when the last bomb fell. There is the raw jagged look of buildings with only one wall standing. Bricks and plaster are scattered throughout the city covered with the dust and trash of eleven years. There is even the stagnant fearful odor of the unburied conveyed no doubt by imagination because it is impossible to believe local gossip that corpses remain in the rubble." She went on, "For ten years this ghost of a once great and beautiful city has been in darkness. Now a few street lights are strung which sharpen the shadows and make more eerie this unbelievable and frightening place." In the half-light Katharine asked a pedestrian walking by to comment on the lack of construction in the area, and the man's eleven-year-old daughter had answered, "No one builds anything because we don't know if we are German or Polish." Katharine realized the girl had never known anything else. Unsure how to respond, Katharine instead helped the girl make a playhouse using the bricks that lay around them. When the girl laughed, Katharine was reminded that the child was real, whole, despite her country's confusion over their identity.

Over a decade before, Katharine had witnessed the Potsdam Agreement, which turned the German city of Breslau into the Polish city of Wrocław overnight. Eleven years later, a broken skeleton of a city laid forth clear evidence that nothing had been resolved to make the twelve islands that composed the city or the many buildings damaged in the war whole. When Katharine talked to the diplomats in Warsaw, they told Katharine Wrocław was "at the bottom of the repair list." It is not certain whether Poland will keep this Western territory and the cities being reconstructed are the ones the Polish government is sure of maintaining.

Her mind on geography and luck, Katharine slowed down as the Belgrade skyline came into view. She thought about how much this city had seen over centuries of war and power shifts and wondered what its future held.

Katharine passed the familiar black car of the secret police sitting outside their bungalow as she parked down the street. Ed must be home. She was grateful that the UDBA hadn't followed her out of Yugoslavia.

Inside the bungalow Katharine found Ed waiting for her on the sofa with a smile. Her body tensed, sensing something unnatural, out of place. It took her a moment to register the water running in the tub and the sink and Etta James's crooning on the record player. She glanced around the room but found no one else. She set down her worn suitcase and turned her eyes back on Ed as he blurted out that *Time* was transferring him to Vienna. He told Katharine that his boss James Bell felt important things were about to happen elsewhere in Eastern Europe, and he wanted Ed to be able to move more freely across the region than was possible from Belgrade.

When Katharine asked how much of the move had to do with the secret police, Ed was silent for a long time before he confirmed that it played a significant role. He reminded Katharine what she already knew—that it was unusual for foreign correspondents to be followed by the secret police. He then asked her what Kingsbury-Smith thought of the fact the secret police were tailing her. Katharine felt sheepish. She still had not told Kingsbury-Smith about the development. She hadn't wanted to give her editor any reason to get rid of her. Working with Milovan was a risk she'd been willing to take, but she hadn't thought about the impact it would have on Ed. She should have known that even though Ed had nothing to do with what Milovan and she were working on, no one else was willing to believe Katharine was working alone. They couldn't believe Katharine—a woman—was capable of doing what she had done. In another time and place, the whole thing might have been funny or at least ironic. And while she had known their situation with the secret police would accelerate their departure from Yugoslavia eventually, it all seemed so sudden.

Ed told her that Bell wanted him in Vienna by the end of the month. There was no discussion of whether Katharine would accompany Ed. She was already scanning the house with a new eye, studying and assessing the items that would have to be moved. *It won't be too bad. We can probably fit most of it into our car,* she thought. But as her analysis moved from her brain to her heart, Katharine felt a burst of sadness. Moving was part of the job of a foreign correspondent, and she and Ed had already made Athens and Tehran temporary stops. However, Belgrade had come to feel like something more permanent, almost like a home, in large part due to Milovan and Steffie. She was not looking forward to breaking the news to them.

_____

Two nights later, Katharine felt a heaviness cloak the air in the bungalow after Ed announced the news of their move to Vienna to the Djilases. No one spoke. Katharine added they would visit Belgrade often. But it felt like second place. They all knew it wouldn't be the same. They drank in the silence, each one of them trying to start up a conversation again, but any attempts to talk about something, anything other than the Clarks' impending move, felt like flat, stilting babble and nothing moved forward.

Eventually when Ed rose to change the record to a more upbeat jazz album as he did every time he and Steffie broke off from the foursome to play cards, a transformation happened. Steffie leaned over to Katharine and whispered in her ear that she would miss her, before she stood to walk over to the card game Ed already was dealing out cards for. Then, Milovan leaned forward to tell her he had news as well. He'd received several letters from publishers in the United States offering to publish his books in response to his letter to the *New York Times*. Milovan asked Katharine to help him investigate the publishing outfits, to tell him if they were legitimate and whether they aligned with his beliefs. She knew nothing about the publishing world. But she'd never let something like that stop her before. She promised to investigate both publishers for him.

Milovan nodded his gratitude as he opened up his knapsack. He set two sheaves of papers on the table between them as he now asked if she would also help get his books to the West. He told her that he had brought his autobiography with him in the hopes she could pigeon it to the West. In that moment, Katharine did not hesitate, although she knew how much was at risk. She told him they would have to use their visits wisely—to collect as many of his papers as possible for her to take to the West.

Katharine took the manuscript from him and placed it on the bookshelf, where she retrieved the four marked-up articles they had been working on for his second series for INS. Given everything that had happened that night, she didn't have the heart to tell him she didn't think they were as good as his first ones. As he eagerly leaned forward over the pages, Katharine couldn't help but smile, thinking about how much she would miss these sessions after she and Ed moved to Vienna. She took a mental photograph to hold on to for her memory.

TWELVE
BELGRADE AND VIENNA

August–October 1956

As the Clarks' departure from Belgrade neared, Katharine went into overdrive. Although moving was part of the lifestyle of a foreign correspondent, this time was different. Beyond simply packing up their apartment in boxes and suitcases, saying goodbye to friends, and driving off in a car to a ship, plane, or her new home, she had the Djilases to consider.

Katharine stood in the middle of the living area of their house and reviewed her list of items to do before they left. She was almost done and felt a sense of satisfaction in their completion. The first item pertained to Milovan's new articles for INS. Katharine had sent the second series off to INS in New York via a friend who was traveling to Switzerland. In a cover note she wrote to Kingsbury-Smith, she shared, "I don't find these as interesting as the first batch but maybe I'm getting used to them." She then added specific instructions for each article, telling Kingsbury-Smith to perhaps eliminate the first one entirely and just use it as an introduction to the series and, for the fourth article, begging Kingsbury-Smith "to be careful and not let anything be changed." She added that this is "the first time he [Milovan] has mentioned his own country and I expect the fur will fly locally. I have checked each of these articles with him and his main point is to keep it 'communist <u>leaders</u>' whenever he uses that phrase and not just 'communists.'"

In addition to *Land Without Justice*, Milovan had given Katharine part of *The New Class*, the new book he'd written, and other important papers—ones he told her he'd be killed for if found in his possession—so she could pack them in her belongings for Vienna. She put everything except the portion of *The New Class* in two separate piles at the bottom of her trunks, covering them with clothing and household items like linens, china, and curtains.

Katharine had a different plan for *The New Class*. She hadn't read it yet, but given what little Milovan had told her about the book, she felt it best to carry it out of the country on someone. She was also still holding out hope that Milovan would finish the part he was reworking to account for what had occurred in Poznan before she left.

Katharine also had found a way to care for the Djilases as if she were still in Belgrade.* The government had stopped providing Milovan his pension, so the family subsisted on Steffie's salary from the bank. Katharine often brought the Djilases items from the U.S. embassy's commissary, and since she would no longer be able to do this once she left for Vienna, she arranged with Robert Meyer, the chief of mission from CARE (Cooperative

---

*   In *Rise and Fall* Milovan outlines that he rejected assistance offered to him but in numerous letters over several years Katharine references attempts to assist the Djilases.

for American Remittances), an international nonprofit with an office in Belgrade, to send food and clothing to the Djilases from abroad. The channel also provided Katharine with a way to track Steffie's security as well. Meyer assured Katharine he understood her instructions to only give the packages Katharine sent to Steffie and to report to Katharine immediately if Steffie didn't come in to claim her package. Katharine hoped this would never happen, but she knew freedom wasn't certain in a Communist state. And she had witnessed with the Djilases and numerous others how the secret police used phone and mail privileges against citizens to punish them. Katharine wanted insurance—to have a way to communicate with the Djilases and monitor them even if she couldn't speak with them directly.

Last, there was the topic of money. While Milovan was being paid for his writing, getting the money to him was complicated. The banks in Yugoslavia would track the money back to its source and either take a cut or leak the figure to the authorities. This information would likely be used by the government in their efforts to undercut Milovan. They would either claim Milovan had sold out to the West or that the West had not paid Milovan enough. But more challenging still, Milovan didn't want it. He had written Katharine a handwritten letter on June 17 in which he stated "that all such money should be given for the humanitarian aid of Socialist emigrants from East European countries." Katharine appealed to Kingsbury-Smith asking for his help, writing, "I'm sorry if it makes your side of the problem even worse. Undoubtedly, some socialists will ask what disposal has been made of the money. There is also the problem of <u>which</u> socialists? Turning it over to a general fund of the socialist international is perhaps the best way. If it went, for example, to a specific Yugoslav emigre there might be hell to pay in the local press here."

Kingsbury-Smith had responded, "I will try to find some way of handling the matter on the basis which your friend would consider fair."

He had lived up to his word, Katharine thought, on this and every other detail related to the man whom Kingsbury-Smith still called only "your friend" in his correspondence with her following her instructions from months before.

Just before Ed and Katharine were to depart Belgrade, Joan Clark hosted a dinner party in their honor. As they left the bungalow for this one last soiree, Ed raised his eyebrows at Katharine as she grabbed her work bag on their way out the door. When they arrived at Joan's apartment, Katharine discreetly set the bag down on the floor and continued into the party. Ten minutes later, making sure no one was looking, their host, Joan, picked the bag up, disappeared into her bedroom for two minutes, then returned, placing the bag where she had found it. Katharine watched it all out of the corner of her eye and felt victorious that Joan, though she didn't know it, now had the first portion of the manuscript for *The New Class* packaged up to be carried outside of the country.

Katharine and Ed settled into the evening, the sparkle of the crystal no match for the laughter and tears that ran more freely than the alcohol. After dinner, Ed and Katharine sipped their cocktails as they moved more intimately around the guests, diplomats and journalists from multiple countries. No one in their circles believed in goodbyes as their paths were likely to cross again, but the Clarks had been a social anchor for so many of them, hosting parties at their small house and always taking time to help. They would be sorely missed in Belgrade's expatriate life.

Toward the end of the night, Katharine found herself alone with Joan. Her friend nodded at the new political officer from the embassy and told Katharine that he was the one heading to Trieste the day after next. Although the officer didn't know it yet, he would be the one to send the package Joan had taken out of Katharine's bag earlier in the night, the one addressed to Katharine's attention at *Time*'s office in Berlin. When Joan had told her of this new officer and his trip to Trieste the week before, Katharine had known instantly this would be how she would get *The New Class* out of Yugoslavia. Katharine smiled to herself as she thought about how the first half of Milovan's politically charged book would be out of the country in less than forty-eight hours. She knew she would have to get the remainder out eventually. Milovan had not finished it. But she would deal with that when the time came.

———————

Three days later, Katharine and Ed drove out of Belgrade just before nine in the morning in a car stuffed with their luggage, their cocker spaniel, Lucky, and Ed's parrot, Joey, in his cage. They set out west on a road Katharine and Ed had traveled many times before. And for the first time in several months, a black car did not tail them. Ed had let it drop to some of his contacts earlier in the month that they were leaving, and the next day the car had disappeared as if it had never existed. Still, Katharine wouldn't let her guard down until the papers were outside of Yugoslavia.

Belgrade's jagged skyline and coal-polluted air disappeared behind them. Katharine stared out her window as the landscape opened up. Tiny villages with thatched roofs scattered across the open fields broke up the repeated scenery of crops being harvested by black-hatted men and kerchiefed women who worked the land on either side and often dashed across the road, not realizing the speed of an approaching car.

They encountered very few vehicles—an occasional bus, a handful of cars sporting both foreign and local plates, several military jeeps. But there was an abundance of animals. Peasants walked their cows, geese waddled down the center of the road, and storks and magpies flapped their wings in companionship just outside the car's window. As Ed swerved to avoid a stray cow, he expressed concern and worry that a recent psittacosis scare resulting in the quarantine of animals meant to stave off the spread of the disease could potentially prevent Lucky and Joey's entry to Austria. Katharine assured him everything would be fine. She couldn't tell him that they had more serious things to worry about if the guards did a search of their car.

As the Alps appeared in the distance, the scenery grew more dense, oak and pine trees craning upward toward the mountains' snow-capped peaks. Katharine felt her senses heighten with every foot they climbed up the steep, narrow, unpaved road to the Loibl Pass, one of the border crossings between Yugoslavia and Austria. The hairpin turns provided amazing views, but Katharine barely noticed. She couldn't think of anything except making sure she kept Milovan's papers safe.

When they reached the top and approached the checkpoint on the Yugoslav side of the border, Katharine's hands were wet with sweat. She wiped them on her pants as she squinted into the sun to see a tall border guard peering in the window at her. She tried to smile, but she feared that her face showed nothing but guilt, that he could hear her thundering heart through the glass. She turned when she heard Ed speak, watching him hand their passports to another guard. His baby face had a dour expression. *He looks younger than our son,* she thought. *Is this a good sign, or a bad one, or no sign at all?*

Before she had time to think any further, Lucky let out a sudden loud volley of barks and leaped into the front of the car to sit in Ed's lap. He took a quick sniff of the air before he leaned forward and started licking the hand of the customs officer, who still had one hand on their car, his long fingers curving over the open window. As if on cue Joey started sharing his limited range of vocabulary: "Goddammit. You're hilarious. Good morning." The guard let out a peal of laughter, a sound Katharine couldn't imagine possible from someone who looked so humorless. He stamped their passports and stepped back from the car without so much as a question, waving to the man at the crossing gate to crank up the barrier.

After a brief stop with the guards on the Austrian side of the border, they were on their way, the car turning and switching a slow descent down the mountain into a lush, green valley. By the time they were at the base, Katharine had fallen asleep.

Ed shook her gently awake several hours later as they arrived in Vienna. Night had fallen some hours before, and the city lights glimmered against the cloudless midnight sky as they drove over a low bridge that connected the two banks of the Danube. Katharine had visited Vienna many times before, but it wasn't until they pulled up to an old, white three-story building on Sternwartestrasse, a tree-lined street with a patch of grass dividing the sidewalk from the road, that it dawned on her that this city was now her home.

––––––––––

Vienna agreed with Katharine in every way except for the distance she now felt between herself and the Djilases. She tried to make up for it by sending Milovan's books to the publishers in the United States. The letters Milovan received came from two men: Frederick Praeger and Felix Morrow. Katharine's inquiries, via Kingsbury-Smith, into both men and their publishing outfits had checked out.

Instead of choosing one, Milovan wanted to work with both. As the two of them discussed before the Clarks departed Belgrade, Katharine was to provide *The New Class* to Praeger and *Land Without Justice* to Morrow. So when Ed came home with the large manila envelope that had the first page of *The New Class* inside and she had last seen in her purse at Joan's apartment, Katharine thanked him and immediately addressed a new packet to the attention of Frederick Praeger, stuffing what she had of *The New Class* inside before she sealed it to take to the post office. She also wrote a quick note to Milovan and Steffie to let them know what she had done. She planned to mail *Land Without Justice* once it was unpacked.

A week later, Katharine was happy to receive a handwritten note from Steffie and Milovan in reply to the coded update she'd sent them. "You can imagine how we were pleased with your letter," they wrote, confirming they had understood her update.

With Milovan's work settled, Katharine turned her attention to her own work. She had not assumed she would be able to remain with INS after their move to Vienna, but she had written Kingsbury-Smith soon after Ed shared the news of Bell's desire to move Ed to Vienna and had asked if there was any way she could continue. INS not only kept her, they gave her a promotion, and she felt obliged to live up to her new role. Her first assignment was to cover the trials stemming from the aftermath of the Poznan riots. First scheduled for August, the trials of twenty-three individuals were delayed first until September and then pushed to early October. Katharine learned the delays were due to the Polish government's attempts to resist Soviet pressure to use the trials to blame the Poznan protests on the West. Instead of this falsified propaganda, the Polish government wanted to focus on the economic causes of the workers' discontent and protests. Except for Yugoslavia in 1948, Katharine was unaware of any previous example of a Communist country refusing to follow a Soviet directive.

But in order to cover the trial, she needed a visa to enter Poland. This was proving troublesome. She shared her frustration with Kingsbury-Smith: "There is no answer yet from the Poles. We will telephone the Polish foreign office the first of this coming week and see if our so-called friends there can be prodded. I think they did not like our coverage of Poznan so it may take a bit of doing. The London TIMES' [sic] Preston told me yesterday the Poles had said off the record that only he and the New York Times would get visas." *In an odd way the Poles' reaction is a compliment*, she realized. Her reporting of the protests had been in-depth and truthful. The protests had loosened controls on the censors as they had been focused on other things, but she suspected the government wanted to control the trial coverage more tightly. Despite their resistance to Soviet pressure, Poland was still in Communist hands. She was determined now more than ever to get into the country.

Her efforts didn't pay off. Katharine was relegated to reading about the trials along with the rest of the world, noting their significance from afar. These were not the typical show trials behind the Iron Curtain where the defendants pled guilty and the sentence was preordained. Instead as one editorial summarized, "at Poznan men have tried to tell the truth and judges had tried to assess it."

The publication of Milovan's second series with INS coincided with the trial. In one of the articles, Milovan concluded, "Communism today has lost its soul. What holds it together now is less and less ideals and more and more power and the selfish interests of a new class—party bureaucracy created in the course of Communism's rise to power. The strength of modern communism is more and more physical and not spiritual."

As Katharine read the articles again in the wake of the Poznan trials, she thought about the nationalism that was starting to emerge within the Soviet bloc and the deep rifts in Communist countries between the workers and their leaders. She wondered how much more rebellion the Soviet Union would tolerate.

———

On the morning of October 23, after a two-week trip to Belgrade and Budapest, where Katharine had covered escalating tension among Russia, Yugoslavia, and Hungary, she sat at her type-writer to write a letter to Morrow to accompany the *Land Without Justice* manuscript she had just packaged up to send him. Ed had unpacked the trunks containing the papers while she'd been gone, telling Katharine he had fallen to his knees in prayer when he found them, seeing they were written in Serbian, guessing what they were, glad he hadn't known about them while navigating the Loibl Pass.

Following the instructions Milovan had given her before she left, Katharine typed:

October 23, 1956

Dear Sir,

I am sending you under separate cover a book by Milovan Djilas in which you have expressed interest.

Mr. Djilas has asked that any questions about this book be sent to me because his mail is opened and/or kept from him.

I presume you have a translator for Serbo-Croat because Mr. Djilas did not ask me to have it translated here. If you do have any difficulty with it, however, please let me know and we will see what can be done.

I have helped Mr. Djilas by rewriting some of his articles so it is possible that once translated you will need help on rewrite. His style is difficult in Serbian so it comes out very labored in English. But it is always worth the work.

Sincerely,

Katharine Clark

Rereading the letter one last time before she sealed the envelope, she nodded in agreement with her final statement: it was always worth the work.

THIRTEEN
BUDAPEST AND VIENNA

October 1956

One hundred fifty miles southwest of Vienna, under the cloak of a light fog, hundreds of angry students gathered in groups at universities across Budapest. They had been organizing for the past week, and they now had a list of sixteen demands, among them the release of imprisoned Cardinal József Mindszenty, the leader of the Catholic Church in Hungary; a demand for freedom of the press, free speech, and free elections; and a public trial for the former Communist Party secretary Mátyás Rákosi, whose ruthlessness was often compared to that of Stalin. But their plans to march peacefully toward the Polish embassy to express solidarity with the Polish government, which had recently stood up to Khrushchev by refusing his directive to not recognize Yugoslavia, were suddenly retracted. Instead, they were marching "ten abreast along the wide Danube quays to Petőfi Square" where a bronze statue of Sándor Petőfi, one of Hungary's most famous poets, generally credited with starting Hungary's 1848 revolution against the Hapsburg empire, stood at attention. As the students walked, others joined their advance. By the time the crowd reached the square, it numbered 200,000. A young man stood next to the poet's statue and repeated the words Petőfi had uttered over a hundred years before: "By the God of our Hungary, we shall be slaves never more!"

The crowd roared.

News of the gathering spread quickly throughout the city's 1.75 million inhabitants, and so did its spirit. Workers, housewives, and even children took to the streets fanning out in pockets across the city. A small group of students took over a printing press and turned out pamphlets declaring "Russians go home!" Demonstrators tore out the red star of the Soviet Union from national flags hanging on public buildings. Students and workers headed along Stalin Boulevard toward the most reviled object in the city—a twenty-five-foot bronze statue of Joseph Stalin—with blowtorches, ladders, and wire. They cut the statue down so that only Stalin's boots remained and placed the flag of Hungary on a pole sticking up from the boots flying high above the decapitated head that lay among the tram lines in the street below.

As news of these events trickled outside the country by radio and wire, Hungary's Communist Party secretary Ernő Gerő condemned the demonstration and hinted at the use of Soviet force.

Later that day, enraged students tried to take over the radio station to broadcast their demands. But the AVH, Hungary's secret police, arrested them. The AVH launched tear gas on the crowd and fired upon them, killing a student outside the Radio Free Europe building. The crowd wrapped the body in a flag and held it up as a symbol. If Poznan had sounded the first note, the uprising in Hungary was a symphony. What had begun as a student rally became a revolution.

Upon hearing of the developments in her office in Vienna, Katharine first thought of the young Hungarian intellectual she had met the week before in Budapest. He had been a source for a story she was investigating on writers across the satellites. They had met in a café where he had explained to Katharine how the writers and intellectuals had begun to meet. "We are Communists, but we intend to be free Communists," he told her. "Our poets and writers get credit for opening our minds, and for our loyalty to Hungary. They began the first criticisms of our terrible economic conditions, and of the fact our country signed trade agreements harmful to the nation. Our poets and writers had a meeting to which 6,000 persons came—so many that the Army loaned a club for more meetings and it was an easy move from criticism of economic problems to discussion of the problems of the truth and lies we were getting."

Katharine's second thought was how to get into Hungary, as she had just used her visa and would need a new one to return. This proved difficult, however, so for the next week, she leveraged her network of sources and listened to Eger radio to report on the developments transpiring inside Hungary. On October 24 she wrote, "The anti-Communist Hungarian underground reportedly revolted in the mountains along the Romanian border today as the Reds claimed Soviet troops put down the Budapest rebellion with hundreds of casualties. An authoritative diplomatic source in East Berlin said Soviet divisions were battling the underground band in the rugged Transylvanian Mountains and that Soviet jet planes were bombing the rebel strongholds."

The next day, she wrote, "A Swiss businessman returning to Vienna from Budapest said heavy machine gun and tank fire continued to rock the Hungarian capital this morning before he left. He said the shooting came from the direction of Gellert Hill where students and workers Wednesday tried to destroy a monument honoring Russia. Other travelers reported that parts of Budapest were in flames, including the National Museum. One said he watched Hungarian soldiers tear the badges from their caps and join the freedom demonstrators." Other travelers reported the rebellion had spread far beyond the capital.

In the early hours of October 28, Imre Nagy, the man whom the protestors had reinstated as the leader of Hungary, delivered the speech of his life. In a radio address, he called for a cease-fire, promising amnesty to those who took part in the uprising and signaling a willingness to negotiate with the revolution's leaders. He also stated the revolution was a legitimate, democratic uprising, not—as the Soviets painted—a counterrevolutionary act. He went on to promise a long list of changes: wage increases, the dissolution of the AVH, and the immediate removal of Soviet troops from Hungary. Fighting stopped, and a shaky cease-fire set in.

The next day, a week after the revolution had started, in the late evening of October 29, Katharine finally reached the Hotel Duna in Pest on the east bank of the Danube River, and fell into the lumpy bed of her third-floor room. She fell asleep almost immediately. Next to her Ed did the same. They had decided to take their chances without a visa, and Katharine had successfully talked their way across the border earlier that day without one. It had been an exhausting eight-hour drive, taking twice as long as usual because of the numerous checkpoints they encountered along the way and the exodus of pedestrians and traffic leaving Hungary.

The next morning, as the sun poked through the thin fabric of the drawn curtains, she awoke to the sound of French, Dutch, and German in the hall and guessed that other reporters had also arrived in the city. She was curious to see who else had made it in so she reached over to shake Ed awake.

After they changed and freshened up, they ventured down to see about breakfast. In the hotel's ground-floor restaurant, they found a strong cup of coffee and many old friends. There was Michael Rougier, a photographer from *Time*, and Elie Abel, the *New York Times* man now in Belgrade. Ilona and Endre Marton, husband-and-wife reporters for UPI and the Associated Press, who had recently been released from a Hungarian prison after being convicted the year before by a secret Hungarian court for spying for the United States, were also there. They lived in Budapest and had been covering the events since they started. Everyone exchanged tips about how to survive walking the streets of Budapest, how to duck into doorways, and how to spot sniper areas to avoid altogether.

An hour later, despite the danger lurking in the streets, Katharine and Ed ventured out in search of stories. They had been warned to hug the buildings, to shuffle from doorway to doorway down the street to protect themselves from being hit by stray bullets. All the starts and stops gave Katharine ample time to survey the city.

When they had arrived the night before, she had only been able to make out the boxy silhouette of the Soviet tanks looming above them, still standing guard on most streets, although if Nagy was to be believed, the Soviet troops and their tanks would be withdrawing that day. In the brutal morning light, she could see that Budapest lay in ruins. Trees were uprooted and pavement stones were missing. Tramlines were turned over, and burnt-out cars and trucks cluttered the streets of most blocks. Leafless branches from trees rustled across what was left of the cobblestones and sidewalks, reminding Katharine of tumbleweed blowing in the desert. And up above, in the sturdier branches, still connected to their trunks, corpses hung, swinging like pendulums in search of equilibrium. There were signs pinned to many bodies indicating the ones who were known and suspected members of the Hungarian secret police.

But the bodies weren't just relegated to the trees. Everywhere Katharine looked, she saw death. Dead civilians and Russian soldiers littered the ground. Where possible Hungarian citizens covered the corpses with blankets and sprinkled them with lime to hide the smell of decomposition until the bodies could be carried away. But the city was overwhelmed, and the smell of the decaying bodies clung to the wind anyway, wafting in and out of what remained of the city's buildings.

As Katharine took it all in, she didn't have the energy left inside her to react. She was already so numb to the smell and sights that when a Hungarian man near her suddenly fell dead, she stepped around him. "Oh excuse me," she exclaimed when she slipped on some of his blood. She only realized the absurdity of her reaction later that night when she wrote about her day for INS, trying to make sense of the emotional journey through her words.

After the man had been shot dead before her, she rounded a corner and came upon a boy who looked to be about seventeen. He was giving instructions to a teenage girl dressed in ski pants and a heavy woolen coat: "The trick in knocking out a tank is to get close enough. It's always a problem of getting close enough so you can throw your cocktail and make it pay," she heard the boy tell the girl. The cocktail was a wine bottle filled with gasoline and rags. Katharine soon learned that "[a]fter as little as 10 minutes' instruction in handling a gasoline incendiary bomb, a grenade or a machinegun, girls like this one went out to do battle with Soviet army tanks. Many were cut down or torn apart by Russian machinegun or 100-millimeter tank gun fire."

Fortunately, later that same day, as Nagy had promised, the Soviet troops withdrew from Hungary. They didn't go far—only to the border—putting them in a perfect position to reinvade if necessary.

With the Soviet withdrawal, Cardinal Mindszenty, the Catholic prelate imprisoned since 1949 for treason, was freed, a significant win for the revolutionaries.

That afternoon, as Katharine approached Cardinal Mindszenty's house for a press conference, she saw three tanks now manned by Hungarians guarding the cardinal from danger. Rebels with tommy guns at the ready and belts of grenades stood guard in front of the double wooden entrance and on the roof. The sixty-four-year-old cardinal told reporters he had been released the night before from house arrest in another location by forty freedom fighters in the three tanks that now stood guard in the street at Felsopeteny. They had driven him to his home in Budapest. Wearing a red skull cap of his office and a red sash, along with a small Hungarian tricolor pin, he removed a fur-lined coat before saying, "I have been sick for many years, but with this great news I feel fine." Katharine noticed his hollow cheeks and red-rimmed brown eyes as he welcomed young priests and walked around the room for photographers.

Despite the positive developments, the rebels were still at it. As Katharine toured the city, she saw the kind of "'mopping up' that is the heritage of every revolution." Although the Hungarian soldiers attempted to maintain order, "rebel bands roaming the streets halted vehicles and pedestrians and, unless the persons questioned could identify themselves satisfactorily, they were shot to death on the spot" as suspected members of the secret police. "Each Hungarian has his own particular private fight with the Russians," she observed, detailing how Hungarians, including thousands of youths now in the police force, were not only searching for members of the secret police but also for Communists. One young man told her, "We are only temporary police. I will be an engineer some day. But now I have my gun and more ammunition than anyone knows. Even when they disband our group I am keeping my gun. I will keep it until the last Russian is gone—and maybe until the last Communist is dead."

On the fourth floor of the Hotel Duna, Ed, Katharine, and other reporters sent out their write-ups. The Communists had lost control of the borders and the censorship of the press. The minders were busy with other work, and the spies focused on other things. As a result, a balanced, honest, and accurate account of the details was able to make it out of the country and alert the rest of the world what had happened.

———

On November 1, Katharine and Ed ate dinner in the dining room of the Hotel Duna when three nineteen-year-old boys approached their table and asked Katharine, "What do you think of our war?" But it was clear the boys did not want an answer; they simply wanted to talk. Until then, they had not been able to speak freely in their country.

While Katharine and Ed sat chatting with the teenagers, a cook approached the table and said, "Excuse me, Madam, but this is one day we are going to listen to the Voice of America in public." He walked past their table and plunked himself down in front of the hotel radio with other members of the kitchen staff. The group settled in and turned the volume up so that Katharine's conversation with the boys was drowned out.

Katharine smiled. Earlier in the day, she had come upon a bitter, violent fight between young rebels and members of the AVH. She had stood watching the exchange of gunfire between the two opponents, part mesmerized, part fearful that she would be struck by a stray bullet. When the spray of gunfire turned especially vicious, she broke from her inert state and looked around for somewhere to hide. She saw an ambulance nearby and ducked behind it, crouching down before analyzing which way to go next.

She ran off toward the corner of the street, stopping only when an old man reached out his hand toward her. She had her mouth open to ask how she could help him when he started to bow from his waist as he said to her, "Madam, please let me thank you as a representative of the now free Hungarian people." Katharine hadn't known how to respond, unsure what he was thanking her for, but she had stopped running.

Every Hungarian was proud. Soon after this, Katharine sat down in a private room with Cardinal Mindszenty. She was the first reporter to secure a one-on-one interview with him. During their conversation, the churchman told her, "The thing which no one in the world—not even the big powers—dared do was done by small, forlorn Hungary."

But it was not to last.

While Katharine had been interviewing the cardinal, Nagy had gone on Radio Budapest and indicated he was rejecting the Warsaw Pact, a treaty signed by the Soviet Union and its satellites that provided for a combined military command under General Ivan Konev. By rejecting participation, Nagy was rejecting Russia's military control over Hungary.

Unaware of this development, Katharine was shocked at how empty the Hotel Duna seemed upon her return. She was even more surprised to see a serious-faced representative from the U.S. delegation in the lobby of the hotel. He told Katharine about Nagy's radio address and asked if she and Ed wanted to join a convoy leaving shortly. Recognizing the reality of the situation and knowing the Soviet tanks were just beyond the northern, western, and southern borders, Katharine walked up to their third-floor hotel room to tell Ed to pack. Their convoy left at 12:45 p.m. but met a roadblock where they were turned back to Budapest by Soviet tanks. In Budapest members of the U.S. Legation called on Soviet Ambassador Yury Andropov who did not understand how the group had been turned back, and he "promised to settle the matter."

At 9 a.m. the next day, large flakes of heavy snow were beginning to fall as the convoy again headed out of Budapest. Carrying a letter of safe passage from the Soviet embassy, they "made fine progress" despite encountering Russian tanks and scout cars along their drive. They had no trouble until they were within 600 feet of the Austrian border. There, two Soviet tanks blocked the way, one pointed at them and the other pointed at Austria. The soldiers waved at them, indicating they should recede. Captain Thomas Gleason, the assistant military attaché at the U.S. legation in Budapest, tried to show the soldiers a piece of paper. He had told them it was a letter from Andropov, meant to ensure their safe passage. Katharine rolled her window down as she saw the guards refuse to look at the paper. One of the soldiers yelled at Gleason, "Go back or I shoot." Soon the convoy had turned around and was returning to Magyarovar, the last town they'd driven through.

It was midafternoon when the line of cars rolled into the town. Katharine caught sight of the telephone exchange and jumped out of the car when Ed stopped to let several pedestrians pass before it. She told Ed she was going to try to get through to James Bell, telling Ed to wait.

Inside, Katharine dialed *Time*'s Bonn bureau and was in the middle of telling Bell about the Soviets and the border when the connection dropped. She tried to dial him back, but there was no tone. The lines had been cut, she realized. Banging the receiver down in frustration, she exited the building to find Ed.

A Russian soldier grabbed her and pulled her roughly to the back of a waiting wagon. From the Russian he was speaking to his colleague, Katharine understood he had mistaken her for a local. This was not unusual. Her plain dress, high cheekbones, and other sharp features helped support this impression. She usually found this mistake an asset, but not today, especially when she further understood that the other women in the back with her had been segregated because they were thought to have an infectious disease. The guards took the women to a house and locked them into a back room with nothing on the floor but hay. Katharine looked around and sighed. She leaned back against one of the walls and slowly worked her way down to as comfortable a seated position as she could to wait for release.

An hour later, she heard knocking and loud English cries toward the front of the house. Katharine smiled, relieved. Ed had found her. As she listened to him talk in stilted Russian, she shouted in English at the top of her lungs that she was there, in the back.

Moments later, a guard came and called her name. Katharine raised her hand, and he motioned for her to follow him. He stood waiting as she stood up slowly, stiff from sitting on a hard floor for so long. They walked down a dark hallway to the front room where Katharine found Ed wearing a goofy smile to cover the worry that blanketed the rest of his face. Ed thanked the guards and they quickly left.

As they got back into their car to find the convoy, Katharine asked Ed where he had gone. He explained that an armored car had come up behind him, forcing him to move. He'd pulled over a little ways up the street to wait but grew worried when she hadn't yet appeared. He knew how often she was mistaken for a local so he had doubled back and an old man had confirmed that a woman matching her description had been taken by the Russians. The man told him the direction the truck had gone, so Ed started pounding on doors. After knocking on two dozen doors and getting told "*nyet*" over and over, he'd finally found her.

Katharine leaned over and squeezed his hand as they drove toward the city center, unable to find words for her gratitude.

In front of the town council building, they saw the other cars from the convoy. Katharine could just make out Robert Clark, one of the foreign service officers from the U.S. delegation who had been part of their group, standing near other members she recognized. They pulled up alongside them and learned that the council had agreed to billet them at the boarding school for young boys across the street until they could figure out how to proceed. Ed parked their car with the rest of the group's vehicles, and he and Katharine joined everyone as they made their way inside the building.

After a nice dinner of goulash, the correspondents gathered around an old Hungarian porcelain stove with a bottle of scotch someone had had the foresight to pack. Just then a boy of about seventeen approached the group and said, "I am a minor in a major situation, and I need a drink."

Someone in the group laughed and responded that if he could

get the fire started, they would happily give him a glass. The boy was successful, and the captives went to sleep with a fire roaring in the stove and under heavy blankets supplied by the school to protect against the cold, believing that "all would be well in the morning."

But in the predawn hours of Sunday November 4, at the same time Russian tanks rolled into Budapest, Russians soldiers invaded the school. They entered and searched every room—even the women and children's rooms, which were in one long dormitory separate from the men's rooms. Katharine was surprised when she woke in the room she shared with two Danish women to find a Russian guard looming over her, his long, bushy black mustache hovering just inches over her head, a machine gun pointed straight at her. Katharine pushed the gun to the side so she could sit up. As she rose from her bed, she told the guard in fractured Russian that she needed to use the bathroom. The guard said nothing and left.

Out in the hallway she found more soldiers, including two stationed in front of the bathroom doors down the corridor. At first they refused her entry, but then a group of children barreled past them and Katharine followed.

As the members of the convoy assessed their situation, they huddled with members of other delegations in the school with them—Danes, Swedes, Italians, French, Dutch, and Brits—who had also been turned back from the border. Soon, the diplomatic leaders were collectively negotiating with the Russians, who wanted the building for a military headquarters and were trying to push the groups even farther into Hungary to a place called Gyor.

Everything was a negotiation. They were told they were not

allowed downstairs. But the guards relented, and they were able to have a breakfast of tea and bread. A Red Cross worker found some powdered milk for the smaller children. But despite all their entreaties, they were not permitted outside to walk the courtyard. A guard told them, "If you want fresh air, open the windows." Katharine later wrote, at this "[W]e all began to think terms of long internment." The day passed slowly.

The next morning, in the midst of hot tea orders, several soldiers came into the room, shouting, "[G]et upstairs with your passports." Following the order, upstairs they found two Russian officers seated at a long table, checking off numbers of the nationals of each group and noting their cars before announcing they were all free to leave.

They all filed into their cars and formed a convoy similar to the one they'd been in several days before. This time an armored Soviet car accompanied them to make sure they made it across the border. As the group rolled away to comfort and security, Hungarians, who felt this group was the last they expected to see of the West, stood weeping. Two old women stood at the window of Ed and Katharine's car. "Won't you help us?" they asked. "Send us arms, not leaflets. Send us ammunition, not food."

But it was a teenage boy who pulled at Katharine's heartstrings the most when he bowed at the waist and said, "[I]n the name of a betrayed Hungary, I ask you to come back."

As they drove away, she thought to herself, *I will*, before she quickly replaced this thought with another: *What would Milovan make of the events in Hungary?*

FOURTEEN
BELGRADE

November 1956

The drive back to Vienna passed like a dream. Once there, Katharine learned about what had transpired in Budapest while they were captives. Reports out of the city were difficult to find, but it appeared that by the early hours of November 4, the capital was surrounded and the Soviets had seized control of all communication points. The Russian troops were led by Konev, the military leader who had led the Soviet troops into Berlin during the last stage of World War II and also commanded the Warsaw Pact troops. Konev was also the man who had given Milovan a pistol in 1944 when they met at the Southwestern Front. That morning the Soviets had rolled their tanks back into Budapest, and by the time the insurgents woke, it was too late. Nagy delivered an impassioned radio address that morning before he fled to the Yugoslav embassy and then seemingly disappeared. The Russians quickly replaced Nagy with a more Soviet friendly ruler named János Kádár.

Katharine focused on how to get back in to Hungary to cover

the aftermath of the Soviet invasion. In Vienna, the lights of the beautiful old building that housed the Hungarian embassy in Vienna were dark, the building completely empty except for care-takers. Inquiries around the city revealed the Hungarian embassy in Yugoslavia was still open, so Katharine convinced Ed to drive to Belgrade to see if they could get visas there.

They checked into their favorite hotel before the Hungarian consulate quickly denied them both visas. Not wanting to waste the trip, they called on old sources for information. Katharine's conversation with a government official was fruitful. He told her that "the atmosphere is very much like it was in 1948. The Kremlin blames Yugoslavia for the loss of control in Hungary." The overall sentiment in Yugoslavia was that despite "Khrushchev's line that there are many roads to socialism" due to the events in Poland and Hungary "he must now revert to the Stalin theory of central con-trol over all the Communist parties." When Katharine asked this same official why Yugoslav troops were moving closer to the bor-der with Hungary, he told her the soldiers' movement was "purely normal." Katharine knew better. She could feel the tension in the city. Everything felt more on edge.

Initially, Tito had backed the Hungarian revolution, thinking it was similar to the one he had led in Yugoslavia after the war to create another national Communist state. On November 11, Tito had delivered a speech calling the Soviet bloody invasion "a fatal mistake." But when it was clear the revolution in Hungary had tones of anti-communism, Tito had pivoted his position back to support the Soviets.

Katharine knew Milovan well enough to know that he wouldn't

have been able to keep silent about Yugoslavia's flip-flopping concerning the Hungarians. And he had not. Milovan had written in an article published in *The New Leader* on November 15 in New York that "the revolution in Hungary means the beginning of the end of communism generally."

After calling in an article summarizing the conversation with her source, she telephoned the Djilases to check in on them and arrange a time to visit. Steffie picked up and in a frightened voice implored Katharine to "come to the flat at once." Katharine barely hung up the phone before she grabbed her coat and bag. She scrawled a quick note to Ed telling him where she was going before she raced down the two flights of stairs, having no patience for the hotel's old, slow elevator, and ran out into the rain. She had a bad feeling about what awaited her at 8 Ulica Palmotićeva.

Steffie opened the door visibly shaking, her eyes puffy above her tear-stained cheeks. Katharine enveloped her friend in a hug and felt her crumple—whatever had happened had emotionally and physically drained her. Steffie whispered in Katharine's ear that Milovan had been arrested by a judge and four men from the secret police. The quintet had searched the apartment from top to bottom for four hours. Katharine let go of her friend and held her at arm's length to study her, not quite believing what she had said. Steffie broke the spell, motioning with her hand for Katharine to follow her.

Inside, if Katharine hadn't known better, she would have thought the home had been burglarized. Drawers stood wide open, books were scattered all over the floor, and Milovan's desk was a mess. She immediately saw that his typewriter was missing.

She would later learn that the "police had searched the apartment so thoroughly that they found some long-lost nail scissors and several stray cartridges." In addition they'd seized a camera and the pistol Milovan had received from Konev.

Steffie used hand signals to tell Katharine that she had something for her. Katharine followed Steffie into a bedroom, where Milovan's mother lay on a cot. The old woman turned to look at Katharine and smiled before reaching down into her bodice and pulling out a thick sheaf of typewritten papers. Milovan would later write that he had "purposely left lying around" a copy of *The New Class* for the police to confiscate, but they had ignored it. Milovan's mother motioned for Katharine to come toward her. As Katharine leaned down, Milovan's mother handed the document to her and said in a raspy whisper, "They didn't get this."

Katharine, expecting the secret police was listening still and wanting a cover, loudly asked how everyone was doing as she stuffed the sheaf of papers into the large purse she always carried with her. When she turned back to Steffie, her friend mouthed to tell her it was the book, and Katharine instantly knew she was holding the rest of *The New Class*. Steffie matched Katharine's volume to reply to her that everyone was well. Then she motioned for Katharine to go. Katharine hugged Steffie and made her excuse to leave, although it was the last thing she wanted to do.

Katharine walked downstairs by herself, taking a deep breath as she reached for the door. She stepped out onto the cobblestone street in the direction of the hotel, not allowing herself to look at the house across the street where the secret police lived. Although only a few blocks away, Katharine anticipated she had to run the gamut of the secret police eyes as well as those of plainclothes policemen who always lurked around a place where someone had recently been arrested. She also knew because of all the heightened political tensions that the spies would be looking for Westerners. But just like the Russians had mistaken her for a Hungarian woman the month before, she knew most Yugoslavs thought she was Slavic, and she hoped she could leverage this to blend in enough for the next few blocks. Almost immediately, however, she heard heavy feet behind her.

As the footsteps on the cobblestones behind her grew louder, she willed herself not to turn around. Her only chance now was to blend in, to make everyone believe she was a local. She knew no one from Belgrade would dare look back to see if the secret police were in pursuit.

She wanted to run, but she forced herself to slow her gait, shivering a little despite her sensible wool coat. She tried to count to three between each footstep the way her mother had taught her so many years before in preparation for her wedding.

Luckily, the steady drizzle that had been falling since morning had stopped. She was grateful it was still a few degrees above freezing so the wet streets had yet to turn to ice. But she knew that wouldn't last. The weather forecast for this cold afternoon called for a blizzard. As if to confirm her thoughts, a strong gale of wind whipped up and stung her cheeks like a sharp, frosty wasp. No matter. Biting her lips together, with her head forward, she tilted her face down and leaned into it, the angle also allowing her to avoid eye contact that might attract suspicion.

A minute later, she walked by the window of a brightly lit

dress shop, stopped, and lifted her gaze, pretending to examine the boldly colored frocks on display. She knew enough from her years living in a Communist country that inside there would be nothing for sale like what was advertised in the window. The same was true at every store like this. Only when there was a line wrapping outside of the shop and around the corner like a trail of bread crumbs was there anything to buy inside.

But shopping wasn't her aim. She studied the reflection of the pedestrians behind her. A handful of men and women carrying umbrellas under their arms and shopping bags in their hands shuffled by.

The footsteps were closing in on her. Clenching her jaw and forming tight fists with her gloved hands, she readied herself. A moment later, a fat, middle-aged man with an ushanka—the traditional bushy fur hat with ear flaps for warmth imported from the Soviet Union—and a long, dark coat that strained against his girth appeared in the reflection. Quickly he was upon her. But he passed where she stood, hurrying on his way, the footsteps echoing loud in his wake.

She let out a shallow exhale.

Nothing out of the ordinary, she thought.

Still, she knew she wasn't safe.

Not yet.

She squeezed the handbag she was carrying over her right shoulder tightly against her ribs, patting it to make sure everything was still inside. Grabbing the collar of her coat and drawing it in closer, she began to walk again, allowing herself to move faster now along the remaining two blocks to her hotel.

As she hurried, she thought about what was next. She needed to get out of the country. She had to deliver on her promise.

Everything depended on it.

Inside the hotel lobby, the white-haired manager smiled warmly at Katharine as he informed her that Ed was already in the room. Katharine thanked him before she ran up the short flights of stairs to tell her husband what had happened.

He turned as she barreled into the room. Taking in her nervous energy, his eyes searched hers for what was wrong.

Katharine glanced around the room. Not trusting anything anymore, she went over to the desk and scribbled quickly on the bottom of a piece of paper. Her note shared that Milovan had been arrested, Steffie was OK, and that they needed to leave for Vienna immediately. Then she went to the dresser and started to take her things out to pack.

———————

Half an hour later, a light snow had begun to fall from the darkening sky, the snowflakes small and dainty in the air. Katharine and Ed sat in their car waiting for an opening in the traffic. She studied her husband, taking in his strong jaw, which was clenched tightly as he analyzed the oncoming cars. She turned her head to look out her window, and the uneven edges of the papers she'd hidden in her bra for safekeeping poked sharply against her flesh. Her mouth tightened into a thin, straight line as she considered her secret.

When they turned onto the *autoput* leading northwest to Zagreb, night was falling and the snow, which had given some signs of stopping, started falling more heavily. The only light came from their headlights and the occasional car passing them on the other side of the road heading toward Belgrade.

After they had driven for forty miles, one of the snow chains Ed had put on the car before they left Belgrade broke loose. The car swerved a little as Ed navigated it to the side of the road. He quickly patched the broken chain with a spare link, and after warming his hands for a few minutes against the stale, dry heat blowing at full blast from the car's vents, he pulled the car back onto the autoput. But a few miles farther, the other chain snapped, and Ed had to hold firm to keep the car straight this time. When he got out to investigate, he came and sat back in the car with a grave expression. He told Katharine this time the chain had wrapped itself around the axle, and they didn't have enough spare links to repair it.

Katharine remained silent. After a moment Ed decided he was going to take both chains off and take the air out of the rear tires so they could keep driving. Katharine got out to help, and ten minutes later they started out again.

It was slow going. After five hours, close to ten at night, they pulled into a gasoline and restaurant stop at Slovenski Brod. Ed turned to her and asked if she thought they should stop and get a room for the night. Without hesitating, Katharine said they should continue to Zagreb. She didn't tell him her reason was that she wanted to get as close to the border as possible.

Ed sighed but relented. He asked her to fill up the car with petrol while he went inside to drink a slug of rakija. Katharine shuddered. She had never understood Ed's affinity for the fruity brandy characteristic of the region.

After Brod, their car was the only vehicle on the road, which meant there were no more tracks for Ed to follow. Fortunately, the German POWs, who had largely built the autoput at the war's end, had made most of it straight as an arrow, and the few curves that were there, Ed knew by heart since he had driven it over a hundred times. Nevertheless, the lack of tracks became a real issue as they began to run into snow drifts. Several times Ed had to back out and charge forward again. The last time Ed had to do this, he got out of the car and scuffed through the snow to make sure that the road was below—he was worried they had left it completely.

It was after one in the morning when they finally drove into Zagreb. They pulled the car up to the hotel they liked to stay at near the railroad station, and Katharine saw the whites in Ed's knuckles disappear for the first time in hours. She went to the trunk to collect their bags. When Ed still hadn't gotten out, she went over to the driver's side door and opened it. Ed told her he didn't think he could make it to the room. He couldn't move his legs—he'd used up all his adrenaline on the drive.

Katharine went inside the hotel. She greeted the manager warmly and asked him for a favor. Several minutes later two men from the hotel staff pulled Ed out of the car. They carried him up to a room, one holding his arms and the other his legs and helped Katharine strip Ed and put him in the bathtub, where Katharine began drawing a hot bath.

The next morning, although the snow had changed to rain, Katharine told Ed to take a different route to Vienna to avoid the Loibl Pass, as the autoput was still covered with snow and ice and the pass was harrowing even in good weather.

Several hours later they arrived at the border crossing between Yugoslavia and Austria. As their car moved closer to the gate, Katharine clenched her hands into fists so tightly that her knuckles turned white. Although no one could see her, she didn't dare touch the papers that were still lodged in her bra. She hadn't even taken them out to sleep the night before. Her breathing became heavier, and Ed looked over at her.

He asked her if she was upset about Milovan's arrest. Then, without waiting for her answer, he told her it would be alright. Katharine let him believe that was her preoccupation. Nothing could be left to chance. There was too much at stake. But this time there were no trunks, no dog, no parrot to distract the attention of the border agents.

She shifted her weight slightly in the seat, and as she did, the sheath of papers hidden in her bodice chafed against her ribs.

When it was their turn at the border crossing, a patrol guard waved them forward to conduct a check. Ed advanced the car, opened the window, and handed over their papers to one officer while another patrolman began examining around and inside their car.

When the second guard got to the back of their vehicle, he opened up the trunk and started going through their luggage. Katharine could see most of what he was doing in the side mirror. She inferred the rest with her ears. So when she heard him make lewd comments to his fellow guards as he waved one of her bras around, her indignation overcame her nervousness and good sense. Before she knew what she was doing, and before Ed could stop her, she threw open her car door and jumped out onto the snowy road. She smoothed down her pants and stood up to her full height before she strode to the back of the car and, in the sternest schoolmistress voice she could muster, asked him exactly what he thought he was doing.

As she watched the reddening face of the officer, who she now saw looked no older than a teenager, she had to tell her inner self not to lose her nerve by feeling sorry for him. Without making eye contact with Katharine, he sheepishly gave her the bra and turned to walk to the guardhouse. Katharine watched him go before she turned to the suitcase and closed it shut. As she walked back to the passenger seat, she let out an exhale. The contents of the bags had all been riffled through. How lucky that she had not put the papers in with her luggage this time. It took all the restraint she could muster not to feel her chest to make sure the papers were still there. She got back in the car as elegantly as possible, still holding the bra in her hand.

From the side, she saw Ed look at it. She asked if everything was okay, and he said they'd been cleared to cross the border.

Not trusting her voice, she simply nodded. The first officer raised his hand to the man at the crank, and the white crossing gate began to rise. Ed hit the accelerator a bit harder than he'd planned, and as they exited Yugoslavia, dark, sooty gray snow flew up all around them.

Some three hundred yards later, at the checkpoint to gain entry into Austria, the Austrian border guards looked at their passports and press credentials and welcomed them back to the country.

As Ed continued the drive toward Vienna, Katharine closed her eyes. She had just snuck the rest of *The New Class* out of

Yugoslavia. She felt victorious and sad. The book could be published, but Milovan would be unable to participate. Katharine vowed to see it through. She would soon learn how challenging that job would be.

FIFTEEN
VIENNA

December 1956

Katharine stood before one of the tall arched windows that decorated the floor of the INS office in Vienna and looked down at the street below. Shiny new automobiles zoomed past crowded streetcars that stopped frequently to let their riders off. People shopped for the holidays or met friends at one of the avenue cafés that still bristled with conversation and coffee despite the fact the weather made sitting outdoors out of the question.

As she watched the pedestrians bundled up in brightly colored coats navigate the sidewalks next to the organized and efficient vehicles, she thought about how far she had traveled in the last month. From east to west, revolution to stability, she had experienced a spectrum of emotions that reverberated inside her louder than the sounds now buzzing in INS's newsroom behind her.

A tap on her shoulder interrupted her reverie. She turned to see a young reporter holding an article he wanted her to review before he sent it to New York. Katharine took his paper and went back to her desk, reading as she walked. When the reporter left a few minutes later holding her edits, Katharine thought how strange it still felt, this new role. But this was her bureau now. Kingsbury-Smith had promoted her to run the entire office.

Turning back to her desk, she realized there was no more putting off the almost two-foot-high tower of correspondence that sat in her inbox as if waiting for one more addition that would topple it all over. She hadn't touched it over the last six weeks while she'd been in and out of Hungary. She sighed and tuned out the sounds of the newsroom still humming behind her with its ringing phones, clattering typewriter keys, and murmurs of conversation as she took her silver letter opener from her desk drawer and slit open the first few envelopes.

After reading this first batch of letters, she stopped.

On the desk before her lay a letter from Frederick Praeger, the publisher for *The New Class*. Dated December 4, 1956, it read, "This is to let you know the manuscript arrived today. Under the circumstances, I suppose we cannot expect the second half of the manuscript." Katharine was concerned. She had posted the second half of the manuscript on November 20. *Surely he should have received it by now*. Her eyes flitted between the open letter and the remaining unopened stack of correspondence.

She placed the letter from Praeger to the side. She pulled the next letter from the pile, hoping it held a more updated note from Praeger confirming receipt of the second half of the manuscript. Instead, she was met with another challenge concerning Milovan's books. Felix Morrow, the publisher for *Land Without Justice*, a man who Milovan had insisted be involved with one of his books because his political beliefs aligned with Milovan's, had written Katharine on October 31 detailing that, for various reasons, the manuscript Katharine had sent him "was not a book which I would publish and that in actual fact Harcourt, Brace would be a much better publisher for Milovan." Morrow shared that Harcourt, Brace was "very much interested in the manuscript." They had "gone to the trouble of having it read and reported on by a linguistically equipped person" who stated "the book was one of the most beautiful ever written in Serbo-Croatian." Morrow explained that Harcourt, Brace's agent was a man named Sol Stein, and Morrow expected Stein would reach out to Katharine "in view of the fact that you report that Djilases' mail is opened and/or kept from him."

True to Morrow's prediction, Stein had written Katharine. Stein informed her that he'd recently had lunch with the president and vice president of Harcourt, Brace, which Stein called "one of this country's largest and most responsible publishing firms." Stein went on to explain that the president of the firm, William Jovanovich, is "of Montenegrin origin himself and therefore extraordinarily sympathetic toward the proposal for publishing the Djilas book, however uncommercial the venture may turn out to be." He explained that Harcourt, Brace was prepared to draw up contracts but wanted to know answers to several questions about whether Felix Morrow was authorized to represent Milovan, how best to provide funds from advances and royalties for the book, and whether there was a more recent manuscript that dealt with Milovan's life after 1929. Stein assured Katharine that "Harcourt, Brace is prepared to publish the material already in its hands" but added that "there is of course greater interest in

Mr. Djilas' interpretations of the events in his life between 1929 and the present."

Katharine's head was spinning. *Why are so many men involved?*

Knowing she wouldn't receive an answer to her question, she kept on opening her mail. She learned that Milovan had been corresponding with Morrow and Praeger up until his arrest. Katharine hoped he had been able to find other people to pigeon his letters out of Belgrade so the secret police hadn't read his mail. She guessed Milovan had used alternative routes, as she did not believe the censors would have allowed correspondence on this topic to pass through.

Katharine sat at her desk staring at the letters, contemplating what to do. The last she knew of any of Milovan's intentions was to send Praeger the political book and Morrow the autobiography. Milovan had insisted Morrow be involved with his books. Katharine wished she could speak to Milovan directly. To know with certainty what he wanted. Or at least to ask Steffie. But both options were impossible: Milovan was in jail, and Katharine couldn't speak with Steffie about this on the phone, not even with the codes the two women had set up to get their messages across to one another. This topic went beyond their basic key. Katharine resolved to simply tell each man the original plan and be done with it. With that decision made, she put the letters aside to finish reading her other mail.

But the next letter she opened made her groan. It was from her editor, Kingsbury-Smith, who wrote, "A Swiss newspaper claims that Djilas, before he was arrested, smuggled to the United States a copy of his memoirs which are to be published under the title 'The

Country Without Justice.' [*sic*] I am wondering whether you might be able to find out for us whether this report is true, and if so, who possesses the rights to his memoirs."

This was a troubling development. Milovan's life could be at risk. Tito had remarked to many, including C. L. Sulzberger, the chief foreign correspondent for the *New York Times*, in 1954, when Milovan had been removed from his leadership posts, that "in other 'Eastern' countries Djilas wouldn't have lived 24 hours." But Katharine knew this was a truth that could easily become reality. In fact, just a month before, Sulzberger had written a piece for the *New York Times* asking the question, "Is this the moment of truth for that disillusioned revolutionary, Milovan Djilas?" Sulzberger had been referencing the bullfighting term known as "'the moment of truth': that instant when bull and swordsman face each other at the kill." Katharine shuddered now, fearing for her friend. After Milovan's letter to the *New York Times* sharing how he couldn't publish books in Yugoslavia, Tito would be incensed that Milovan's book, rumor or not, was smuggled out of the country.

Wanting to help Katharine closed her eyes and leaned back in her chair, rubbing her temples and contemplating what to do. The leak to the Swiss paper confirmed her suspicions that Praeger was unscrupulous. Katharine could not quite explain it, but something inside of her knew Praeger was somehow behind the leak. To Katharine's knowledge only Steffie, Praeger, and she knew about her role in bringing the book out of the country. Joan Clark and Ed knew she had brought out papers, but they didn't know what they contained. She also knew that none of them would have said anything to anyone let alone a Swiss reporter. And Katharine knew she had not said anything, which left Praeger. *Does he realize the damage leaking something like this might have on Milovan?* she thought. *Damn Praeger. Damn. Damn. Damn.*

She would have to explain everything to Kingsbury-Smith. She rolled a piece of paper into her typewriter and started at the beginning, giving her boss a summary of the book and a proposal that they write a series of articles about *The New Class*. When it was done, she set it aside to send.

Next Katharine turned her attention to the missing second half of *The New Class* for Praeger. There had been no additional letter telling her he received the second half of the manuscript which she had posted to him. Letting her mind wander through the rolodex of people she knew who might be able to help, she remembered the lovely Austrian vice minister of communications she had met at a party several months before. He'd been a gregarious man who had offered to help her in any way he could while she was a resident in Vienna. Katharine decided now was a good time to take him up on his offer. She walked over to the telephone and picked up the receiver.

After leaving a detailed message with the minister's assistant, Katharine set the phone's receiver down and turned her attention to the final drama with Stein and Morrow. She wasn't entirely sure how to handle the situation, as she wasn't quite sure she fully understood it, so she put their letters in a pile marked "Milovan" before she turned to her work for INS.

Katharine had written several articles while in Hungary, but she had more she wanted to write. But back in Vienna with its organized streets, bustling cafés, and working communication technology, everything she had seen and experienced just days before in Budapest felt very surreal. She closed her eyes and thought back on the last two weeks.

How can I begin to convey it all? The atmosphere. The devastation. The death.

When she and Ed had returned to Hungary after the Soviet takeover, Budapest had looked like one of the decaying corpses on the streets. They had headed again to the Hotel Duna under a faint fog that rolled in with the sunset. But the haze merely softened the newly created jagged edges of the city's baroque structures, their former curves lost and marked forever by shells and mortars. The insides of the buildings seemed to be on the outside, windowpanes were shattered, and entire walls had tumbled into the city's narrow, winding streets as well as the grand avenues. Shells of Soviet tanks burned out by Molotov cocktails littered the street. Overturned streetcars fortified by piles of rubble from nearby buildings or stones pulled up from the street served as miniature garrisons. Katharine knew from reports and pictures that these fortified streetcars had served as impromptu barricades for the freedom fighters.

For the second time in less than a month, the appearance of Budapest reminded Katharine of her first impressions of Berlin after the war. But the ruin of Budapest appeared even bleaker on her second visit. In October there had been a feeling of victory and hope. But now the city's spirit itself appeared to have been rolled over and crushed by the large green Soviet tanks that commanded street corners.

As Katharine thought back on the daily existence that had

been her life for the past two weeks, she decided to write about that, hoping her own perspective could bring to life the reality of the city. "There was the everlasting worry of a stray bullet in Budapest," she began. "You never knew where the gun was or from what direction the shot would come. It was no good going into buildings trying to see out windows. Police watched windows as carefully as street corners and you would be ordered away."

"But for the correspondent in Budapest, the real problem was transportation and communications," she added. Katharine tried to describe the situation for readers in the U.S. by sharing that the environment in Budapest was "a little like working Chicago without a map or telephone and against a decidedly unfriendly city hall."

Even the atmosphere at the Hotel Duna had been affected. Katharine spent hours on the fourth floor of the hotel each night "coaxing the telephone operators to try once again to reach London, Vienna or Prague." These calls were "so heavily monitored that it interfered with service," which often meant she missed dinner in the dining room. A new curfew prevented anyone from being on the streets between 9 p.m. and 6 a.m., which also meant that no dining room, even in a hotel, could be open during that time. "I got very tired of eating dehydrated soup prepared over canned heat," she wrote. Katharine acknowledged, though, that not once was the hotel without hot water, electricity, or heat. And it was a government policy to make sure there was always enough food at places where foreigners dined. Yet, "always, always there were the Hungarians," she noted. "What they thought and said and the way they lived, fought and died. So each day we reached a point of emotional exhaustion. How many times can the heart be broken? How can any reporter convey what that means? That was our real problem."

As she read back over what she had written, she felt a sense of satisfaction. Despite the devastation, she had seen so many small examples of resilience. She remembered a woman "pushing a baby carriage which groaned under the weight of a small coal range. The woman said that with a stove and a baby carriage anyone can make a new home." At the same time, Katharine had winced whenever she had heard a gunshot, reminding herself while running for cover from gunfire that "the right side's the one to turn to—your heart's on the left," to ensure she didn't suffer a fatal wound by making the wrong decision on which way to turn her body.

Katharine hoped all the details and the ironies would help readers back in the United States make some semblance of understanding. Sitting back, Katharine was both exhausted and energized, hoping that she had been able to explain the unexplainable. In that moment, she realized two things: that everything Milovan had talked with her about was manifesting itself over and over again in several countries behind the Iron Curtain, and that all of the focus her editors had wanted from her early in her career—a woman sharing human stories—was now to her benefit, allowing her to make her point by becoming part of the story instead of just an observer. She still shuddered thinking about when she had crouched behind a tank and the turret swung around to point at her. She hadn't dared move, unsure of what could be seen and not wanting to die.

Quickly all of her thoughts and emotions were replaced by

an abject sadness as she thought about the cold prison cell that Milovan was again calling home.

————

Several weeks later on the day after Christmas, Katharine picked up the telephone ringing in the hallway of her apartment and was surprised to hear the voice of the vice minister of communications himself wishing her a happy holiday. He had located her missing package addressed to Praeger, and it was on its way to her now. It had been in Austria the entire time, in a warehouse outside of Vienna.

Katharine was full of relief and excitement. She thanked him and then paced in front of their apartment door until the courier arrived an hour later to deliver the package directly to her. Katharine tore open the brown paper wrapping that bore her handwriting. She then rewrapped the second part of the manuscript and addressed it again to Praeger to take to the post office to mail. Before she left she drafted a cable to Praeger to let him know the balance of the book had been found and was now on its way to him.

Katharine had realized on her walk that she had never replied to Morrow or Stein. Consumed by this fact when she returned to the office, she went directly to her typewriter, rolled a new piece of paper into it, and started writing. She decided to write Morrow first. He had been her initial contact, and she knew Milovan wished for his involvement. The twisted web of people now involved with *Land Without Justice* overwhelmed her, and she wanted Morrow's reply back to her note before she sent anything back to Stein.

December 26, 1956

Dear Mr. Morrow,

I have had a letter from Sol Stein asking if you are authorized to represent Milovan Djilas in America in business or literary matters.

Since Milovan is now in prison and we can get no authorizations from him for anything I want to give you the history of his manuscripts and let you figure out what to do.

When Milovan wrote a series of articles for International News Service he did so at my suggestion and with my assistance on translating and rewriting. As a result of those articles he received a letter from you and one also from Frederick Praeger. Because I had helped the first time he asked my advice about your two firms. I, knowing nothing about publishing houses, asked friends in New York if you were reputable firms and on being assured that you were, I told Milovan both were ok and to make his own decision which to use. His decision was to send one type of book for you and another totally different to Praeger. The only other connection I have had with any of this is to bring the manuscripts out of the country and mail them according to instructions.

I have been told by both you and Praeger that the manuscripts have arrived. My understanding is that each of you is authorized to handle whichever manuscript you received. I cannot, however, make a flat statement that you or anyone else can handle all of Djilas' writings in America because that would be unjust to the other publisher. I do not however want to hurt the chances of publication of either manuscript.

Is it legal that we simply state that you can handle the publication of the manuscript in your possession? If so, please use this letter as such an authorization. I can swear on stacks of Bibles that you are the person he wanted to handle that particular manuscript.

I personally would be happier if you could be named as the person to handle everything about his writings—all of them—first because I feel certain it is better to have one person do it and secondly because Milovan knew your name and was anxious to have contact with you.

But I would hate to prevent publication of Praeger's or your manuscripts by having a rat race develop about rights.

At the risk of stepping on toes and butting in where I have no rights I venture to suggest that you might talk it over with Praeger himself. He might be interested in turning over his manuscript to you also for a fee.

The only thing I want out of all this is to make certain Milovan's writings are published. I not only believe that what he has to say is important. I also have a personal interest in knowing that he finds a market and that the future of his family is assured.

However this is clarified I also believe I can be of help in publicising the books. I am doing a series of articles about Djilas and his place in international politics for International News Service. They are based on the knowledge I have of his life, his family and his history and beliefs. I hope they will quicken the general public's interest in his writings.

Please let me know your thoughts on all this and what you
want me to do. I hope to see Mrs. Djilas in Belgrade soon and it
would be wonderful to have some news for her.

Most sincerely,
Katharine Clark

P.S. Sorry for all this delay but I came out of Budapest Dec.
14th and have been swamped catching up with the office here.

With the letter finished and put into an envelope, Katharine
believed that now her work with both manuscripts surely had to
be almost done. But she was wrong.

Before the end of the year, the mail brought her more information and, with it, more complications. She received a note from
Praeger that both incensed and further confused her:

December 31, 1956

Dear Mrs. Clark:

I am very grateful for your letter of December 26. The last page
on my manuscript is page 90, and the last sentence on the page
is cut off in the middle, so I would assume that the second part
which you have is the second half of the manuscript which we are
missing.

I am very worried about the situation with Felix Morrow at
University Books. Please treat this information confidentially.

University Books was a brand new firm. Their first year's program was not interesting. They did not get off the ground, and so far as I know all titles, or practically all titles have by now been partly remaindered or sold.

Mr. Morrow is a book salesman, and he is now concentrating on that only, and as a matter of fact he is representing us in the Middle East.

I have a suspicion, because I have heard rumors, that the manuscript that was sent to him has already been shown to various other people. I consider it absolutely essential in the interest of our manuscript which is extremely important and might become one of the great political books of our years, that the other manuscript is withdrawn from Mr. Morrow, withdrawn from circulation and simply kept at a safe place until either Mrs. Djilas or Milovan decide what should be done in consultation with me.

I believe you can take matters in your own hands and write to Mr. Morrow not to do anything at all, but hold the manuscript until he gets further instructions, or better yet, gives it to me, because I will put it into a bank safe for the next few weeks. I would suggest that you cable, because Felix Morrow is starting on his spring trip on January 6, and I would suggest you obtain an authorization from Mrs. Djilas to have the manuscript given to me until she makes a decision on the next steps.

We do not need a contract, because it is self-understood among decent people fighting for the same things, that the financial interests of Djilas will be protected, and I am not particularly worried about authorizations since your letter could serve as the expression of his intent to have us publish the book. Still, if we could get something in writing from his wife, it would be better. I am in any case drawing up a letter for our Contract File, and I am sending two copies to you, so that we have something reasonably official. After all, it is also possible that something happens to me.

I expect to be in Lenzerheide on January 12th, and I will phone you. I think it best that you send me the manuscript to New York. We will have the chance to look at it before I leave.

The contract draft which I am enclosing with this letter has better conditions than those usually applicable. But this is as it should be. I think that for the moment we will have to be careful about money, and I would suggest that you put this contract form either in a bank safe, or destroy it. Under no circumstances should you take it to Belgrade. I do not know the Yugoslav law, and I believe that under no circumstances should we show officially any opening that dollar income is actually accumulating. But if there is an opportunity, I can also send you money, and you will see whether there aren't some ways to pass it on to them. An open deposit in his or her name in New York is dangerous, but there are other ways, and I will discuss them with you on the 'phone.

All the best for the new year,

Very sincerely yours,
Frederick A. Praeger

Katharine was frustrated. Again she wished she could talk to Milovan—to let him decide what to do, to laugh with him about the proper mess they had created for themselves by having so many people involved with his affairs. The only thing she wanted out of all this was to make certain Milovan's writings were published. She had meant what she had written to Morrow—what Milovan had to say was important.

Katharine decided she was just going to ignore Praeger for now. More importantly, she decided it was time to visit Steffie.

SIXTEEN
BELGRADE

February 1956

Toward the end of February Katharine boarded a plane to Belgrade with a tourist visa she'd acquired that same day at the Vienna airport.

Several weeks before, Milovan had been tried and given a three-year prison sentence rumored to be a result of the two articles he'd written about the Hungarian Revolution criticizing the Yugoslav government's role. Following newspaper reports of Milovan's trial and sentence that ran in Western publications, forty-two prominent political and cultural persons from around the world urged Tito to free Milovan. Their message called his imprisonment "a grave violation of the principles of intellectual freedom." It was signed by global literary figures, politicians, and activists, including Cass Canfield, Leo Cherne, Senator Joseph S. Clark Jr., Senator Paul H. Douglas, Harry D. Gideonse, Sidney Hook, Senator Hubert H. Humphrey, Elia Kazan, Alfred A. Knopf, S. M. Levitas, Archibald MacLeish, Lewis Mumford, Senator Richard L. Neuberger, Reinhold Niebuhr, Dr. J. Robert

Oppenheimer, Walter P. Reuther, Dr. George N. Shuster, Senator Margaret Chase Smith, Norman Thomas, Diana Trilling, Bertram D. Wolfe, Norman Angell, T. S. Elliot, Malcolm Muggeridge, Raymond Aron, Albert Camus, Andre Philip, Max Brauer, Karl Jaspers, Suddhin Datta, Asoka Mehta, M. R. Masana, Jayaprakash Narayan, B. R. Shenoy, Moshe Sharett, Giancarlo Matteotti, Ignazio Silone, Taiko Hirabayashi, Taku Komai, Takeo Naoi, Kenzo Takayanagi, and Pablo Casalas. Katharine knew Steffie wouldn't be aware of the letter, so she had packed the news article for her to read.

In Belgrade Katharine made her way to the hotel she and Ed frequented when they visited the city. As she had promised, she called Ed to let him know she had arrived safely. Then she buttoned up her coat and walked the few blocks from the hotel to the Djilases' flat.

As Katharine approached the familiar building, she noted the absence of the black car outside it. A quick glance across the street proved there was no cameraman on the balcony either. But Katharine guessed that Steffie was still being monitored.

Katharine put these thoughts aside as she entered the building. When Steffie opened the apartment door, Katharine ducked inside, and the two women embraced. Reluctantly breaking the hug, Katharine leaned back and saw tears in Steffie's eyes along with a pallor of gray that hadn't been there the last time. Katharine hoped her friend was not ill.

Inside the flat, Katharine took in the familiarity of it with a newness akin to that of a sailor returning home after having been lost at sea. There was Aleksa sitting and eating at the table with his grandmother, a smile spreading across his face at her when she entered. His grin grew when Katharine produced a toy from Ed. She took a mental picture of the delight on the little boy's face to share with Ed later. Although Katharine tried not to glance at the seat where Milovan usually sat, when Steffie implored her to sit and eat, it was the only option for her to take. She sat down heavily and took the soup that Steffie offered.

When they were done eating, Steffie suggested that she and Katharine should go for a walk. Outside, Katharine turned to Steffie and finally allowed herself to talk freely. She explained the complications with both publishers and asked Steffie to write two letters addressed to Katharine authorizing her to act on Milovan's behalf so she could use them in her dealings with Praeger and Morrow to get the books published.

Steffie agreed. She explained to Katharine that Milovan knew *The New Class* had made it to the West. Following Katharine's departure with the manuscript Steffie had visited Milovan in prison and had "crossed her forefingers and then gave a flip of her hand" to let him know of the development. Milovan had been pleased. Several weeks later, during a break in his most recent trial, the two of them had a chance to speak to one another freely in whispers. The topic of *The New Class* came up. Jennie Lee, Aneurin Bevan's wife, had traveled to Belgrade after Milovan's arrest. When Steffie told her about the book, Lee had suggested halting publication. When she shared this sentiment with Milovan, he insisted, "This is for me to decide. The book must be published, come what may." Steffie asked Katharine to help her execute Milovan's wish. Katharine shook her head, amazed at how her friends constantly rose to the challenges put in their way. Katharine shared Jennie Lee's concern about *The New Class* but also wanted to do as Milovan wished, and she was glad to know exactly what that was.

The women returned to the Djilases' apartment. As Steffie made tea to warm them from the cold, Katharine pulled a piece of paper from her bag and started writing out in English what Steffie should copy. While Katharine worked, the women talked about their sons. They continued this subterfuge while Steffie copied the notes in her own handwriting and signed them.

When Steffie was done she handed the letters to Katharine and asked her if she wanted another cup of tea. Katharine was in the midst of saying yes but only got half the word out. As she scanned Steffie's version of the letter to Praeger to make sure it had everything she needed, a line of text caught her eye. Steffie had written, "This is to authorize you to tell Mr. Praeger that he may publish the book written by my husband, Milovan Djilas, which book has been delivered to him, subject to such corrections and for deletions as you personally make in accordance with my verbal instructions and requests. This further instructs and permits you to inform Mr. Praeger that you Katharine Clark must personally be satisfied that such corrections and deletions as I requested have been made before publication." She had added the last sentence on her own. When Katharine looked up, shocked, Steffie smiled, delight shining in her eyes.

When Steffie nodded at the second letter to Morrow, Katharine picked it up and read, "This is to give you permission to withdraw the autobiography written by my husband, Milovan Djilas, from University Books Inc. if University Books Inc. is not publishing it and transfer it to any publisher who will publish it. This also is to not only give permission for such action but to request you to withdraw it and have it published by [a] firm of your decision and choice." Again Steffie had added this last line.

Katharine couldn't have expressed her emotions with words even if she'd been able to speak freely without spies listening in. Steffie had empowered Katharine not to only help with Milovan's book and to deliver on his wishes but to make more executive decisions about them, permitting her to ensure that the books were in the best form and hands when they were published. The task weighed heavy on her.

Soon after, Katharine rose to go. At the door she paused and looked back at her friend, hoping it wouldn't be the last time.

With the letters buried deep in her bag, Katharine exited the building. She scanned the street and felt an eerie sensation of déjà vu. Progress was seemingly everywhere, but she could not shake the feeling that something bad was just around the corner.

PART III
JUSTICE

SEVENTEEN

VIENNA

April–August 1957

The rusty wheels of the mail cart interrupted Katharine's train of thought. It was mid-morning on April 8, and she was at her desk at INS brainstorming pitches. Since the beginning of the year, she'd only written continuations of stories from the prior year—the fate of Americans imprisoned by the new Hungarian regime and the effect the deportation of 4 million Poles displaced by war from the Soviet Union back to Poland would have on Poland's economy. She had also covered rumors of stashed atomic weapons in western Hungary as well as new protests being planned in Hungary. Four months into 1957, Katharine was ready to find new threads. But as she looked down at the blank paper before her, she welcomed the interruption of the mail placed with a thud in her inbox.

A thick air packet postmarked from New York caught Katharine's eye. She was expecting news from Kingsbury-Smith, so she grabbed it and ripped it open. But instead of a note with her requested research, she found a manuscript. There was no note. *Odd.* Looking through the other letters, she found an envelope from Praeger's publishing house. Inside, his secretary, Jean Wilcox, provided a terse update with the subject line *The New Class*:

April 8, 1957

Dear Mrs. Clark,

I am sending you today by air packet an unedited copy of the above manuscript. We have just received the first clean typescript of the completed manuscript and wanted you to have a copy without delay. In accordance with the arrangements made by you and Mr. Praeger, we understand that you will read the manuscript carefully and advise us whether there are any passages which should be deleted in your judgement as being potentially dangerous to the well being of the author. We shall be looking forward to your reply and meanwhile shall proceed with the job of final editing. When you have finished with the manuscript will you kindly send this copy to Mr. Trevor Cracker at Thames & Hudson Ltd 80 Bloomsbury Street London WC1.

Thank you,
Jean Wilcox

Turning back to the manuscript, she thought excitedly: *This must be the English translation of* The New Class! Katharine thought excitedly. Although Katharine had a general sense of the book's contents, she had not yet read it because Milovan had written it all in Serbian. Now she looked at it with giddy anticipation. During her February visit to Belgrade, Steffie had laid down some ground rules for the publication of the book in order to protect Milovan as much as possible. She had asked Katharine to look out for certain words or details that might further inflame the Communists in Yugoslavia. Katharine stared at the manuscript wondering what it held.

She had work to do before her upcoming travel, but nothing seemed more important than *The New Class*. She grabbed a pen and sat back in her chair. Opening the first page, she quickly lost herself in the book. The translation was smooth and cogent. The sentences were short. *It's far more reader friendly than the translated articles* Life *rejected two years ago,* Katharine thought.

Page after page, Katharine recognized her friend's journey. In the book she saw a deeper treatment from his articles for INS. "The Communist revolution, conducted in the aim of doing away with classes, has resulted in the most complete authority of any single new class. Everything else is sham and an illusion," Milovan wrote early on in the book. This was Milovan's central argument on the paradox of Communism: that instead of doing away with class, Communism created a new one. But Milovan didn't argue that the concept of the new class explained everything. "The fact that there is a new ownership class in Communist countries does not explain everything, but it is the most important key to understanding the changes which are periodically taking place in these countries, especially in the U.S.S.R." Those in power were wielding it and doing everything possible to hold on to it.

As a result, Milovan wrote, "Persecution of democratic and socialist thought which is at variance with that of the ruling oligarchy is fiercer and more complete than persecution of the most reactionary followers of the former regime." The irony, Katharine noted, was that Milovan was writing about the threat that he himself presented to Yugoslavia and to Communism. But when she came to the end of this chapter, she realized his previous assertion had only foreshadowed a stronger point. Milovan predicted, "History will pardon Communists for much, establishing that they were forced into many brutal acts because of circumstances and the need to defend their existence. But the stifling of every divergent thought, the exclusive monopoly over thinking for the purpose of defending their personal interests, will nail the Communists to a cross of shame in history."

After several hours, Katharine held just one last piece of paper in her hand. She reread the final sentences of the book several times, letting them sink in: "In any case, the world will change and will go on—toward greater unity, progress, and freedom. The power of reality and the power of life have always been stronger than any kind of brutal force and more real than any theory."

He was still optimistic. The world will progress. She knew how deeply Milovan believed that. It was why he had said and done everything that he had. But she wished it weren't so taxing on him or his family.

Katharine sat in her desk chair, the INS office awash in the pre-sunset afternoon light, wishing not for the first time that there was more she could do for her friends. Katharine tried to call Steffie twice a month, at least once right before her monthly visit to Milovan to signal to the UDBA who monitored the Djilases calls that someone in the West was still tracking them and a second time as Katharine's work travel permitted. She did not want to push the censors too much, but Katharine resolved to try Steffie later that night. If she got through, she would use their code to share that publication of *The New Class* was progressing. Steffie could then signal the development to Milovan with a hand signal or other code when she visited him in prison just as she had been able to tell him that the book had made it out of the country.

As Katharine's thoughts turned to Milovan himself, she wondered what he was doing at that very moment in Sremska Mitrovica. It was the same jail where he had served time in the 1930s, and it still lacked heat in any of the cells. Katharine prayed the long johns and gloves she'd arranged to be sent shortly after her February visit had made it to him. She and Steffie had also talked loudly in the apartment about Milovan's need for writing instruments and supplies—and she hoped the government had finally permitted him to have such items given she as a member of the Western press had voiced concern. She knew that carried weight.

Katharine closed her eyes, lost in thought for a moment, reflecting on the journey of Milovan and the books. A month later she would put them down on paper for Ed, giving him background for a story that his editors were asking of him due to the leaks: "Again and again I go back to the fact that for me he has proven man is capable of pure thought. Even in darkness of his mental and moral surroundings—all alone—he has searched for truth and shed at least the negation of falsehoods. And when I think of how hopeless it is for him I find myself thinking of courage in the abstract the way you know beauty in the abstract by remembering a tulip."

Katharine was in and out of Vienna looking for stories for the next several weeks. Yet everywhere she went, she saw proof of *The New Class*'s assertions. She began to share this evidence in her own stories. In mid-May the lead-in to one of her most socially provocative articles about Communist life began: "The social, economic and political misery of life behind the iron curtain has cultivated a moral climate in which prostitution has flourished into one of Communism's biggest problems."

In addition to statistics about the rise in divorce rates and venereal diseases, Katharine quoted someone who shared how high-placed Russian officials frequented "a health resort...that comes equipped with several brothels." *The new class's benefits truly have no bounds*, Katharine had thought as she interviewed this official.

She ended the article with a quote from Salomon Lastik, a writer in Poland, who summarized the situation perfectly: "In an atmosphere of falsehood, cynicism and actions differing from words," he said, "moral crookedness was bound to arise which against a background of penury and misery is speedily maturing to the widespread symptoms of thievery, hooliganism, and prostitution." It reminded her of something Milovan might say on the topic.

——————

On the fourth of June, she returned to Vienna from a two-week trip hoping to find a detailed update on *The New Class*'s publication in her pile of unopened mail. She walked to her desk at

INS and picked up the letters, scanning through them, searching greedily for anything from New York. Seeing three envelopes postmarked from there, she pulled them out.

The first was a letter from Felix A. Morrow with progress about Milovan's other book, *Land Without Justice*:

May 25, 1957

Dear Miss Clark,

At long last things have crystallized to the point where I can write concerning the Djilas autobiography. It is already in the hands of a translator and Harcourt, Brace will publish it about January 1958. I am signing a contract with them, I acting on Djilas' behalf; rather than describe the contract, I shall send you a copy as soon as the last details are ironed out between their attorney and mine. As you know, I do not have Djilas' express authorization to sign such a contract; I am therefore neither his agent or his attorney-in-fact. And, frankly, the form in which you cast your letter of December 26, weaving in the details about the Praeger ms., made it impossible to use even as collateral material. I should appreciate your now sending me a letter dealing only with how the autobiography came into my possession and your testimony concerning Djilas' desire that I handle it, his knowledge of my name, etc. etc. Your letter will not satisfy Harcourt, Brace which, short of getting Djilas to sign the contract or a letter from Djilas authorizing me to do so, would hold them free from harm (ie foot the bill) if Djilas or his heirs object later on. I am willing to give them such an affidavit but my attorney won't let me sign it unless and until I have <u>your</u> letter in hand backing me up. Please send your letter to the above address.

Since I have promised Harcourt the affidavit will be forthcoming, nothing has been stopped. Methuen has already bought for England—at terms very favorable for Djilas, again, I'll send you a copy rather than a description—and I think the big continental countries will follow suit very soon. LIFE [*sic*] will probably do a chunk or two on the eve of publication.

Which brings me to the money. Within a few months there will be money from advances which I shall arrange to deposit here in a trust pending possibilities of getting the money to Djilas and his wife. No doubt Tito is not Stalin, but I should imagine that certainly not the whole of the money should be shipped to Mrs. Djilas in Belgrade. Can you ascertain her wishes? Please also inform her that I have instructed my attorney to make part of the proceeding the fact that I shall transmit all funds without any deductions for myself. Were Djilas free I should certainly not hesitate to be reimbursed for my work but in the circumstances I consider it a matter of honor to get his work published. In the negotiations with Harcourt, I left them with enough elbow room in the way of their percentages on subsidiary rights and sale of rights abroad to assure their interest and activity—as a matter of fact. I think this will end up by being what we call a "big" book—but preserving the lion's share to Djilas and his family.

Sincerely,

Felix Morrow

PS—The Praeger book will be published in August. I
have not even asked Praeger the terms under which he is
publishing—I feel it is none of my business since he came
by the ms. without my having anything to do with it.

Katharine smiled. She knew how important the autobiography was to Milovan, and she was pleased with the update. *How
generous of Morrow to waive his fee.* She knew very little about publishing, but she guessed from the amount of work she was already
spending on Milovan's books that Morrow was forgoing a substan-
tial amount of money considering how much time he had spent on
Land Without Justice.

But what most struck her was the postscript. *Why is Morrow
once again telling me more about* The New Class *than Praeger himself?*

Katharine put this thought aside as she opened the next envelope. Inside was a note from Praeger's secretary, Jean Wilcox. It read:

May 28, 1957

Dear Mrs. Clark,

On April 8 we sent you by air packet an unedited copy of the
above manuscript requesting you to read it and advise us whether
there were any passages that in your estimation might jeopardize
the author's well-being.

Since we have received no reply, and because we are anxious
to hear from you before publishing the book, we are writing again.
I trust that the manuscript did reach you, and that you found

nothing in it of an objectionable nature. May we hear from you
by return mail?

As we requested in our previous letter, we shall appreciate
your forwarding your copy to Mr. Trevor Cracker at Thames &
Hudson Ltd, 30 Bloomsbury Street, London WC 1 when you have
finished reading it.

Sincerely yours,

Jean Wilcox

Katharine felt a pit form in her stomach. *Didn't I send Miss Wilcox
a reply after I read the book?* She turned to her files, looking for her
note. But after half an hour with nothing to show for her search, she
realized she had never responded to the earlier letter. She would
never forgive herself if she delayed the book's publication. Katharine
started riffling through her desk searching for the manuscript. She
found it at the bottom of a pile of other papers. She put those aside
and reviewed her notes, seeing there were only two edits to make
to the translation. Katharine turned immediately toward the task of
communicating this back to Miss Wilcox. She rolled a new paper
into the typewriter and quickly punched out her response:

June 5, 1957

Dear Miss Wilcox,

I have finished the book. There is nothing at all which would
harm Djilas except the book itself and we can't do anything about

that. I mean that I can find no passage which I think should be removed except on page 233 last paragraph, fifth line from bottom of page where he says 'party leaders—shamefacedly and stealthily, it is true—changed.' I think the words shamefacedly and stealthily might be deleted only as a matter of taste but it is not really important. I mention it only because it is the type of nastiness the Yugoslav regime will really hate.

Anyhow, the book itself is going to make them so mad it is splitting hairs to worry over the words.

Please tell Mr. Praeger I think the book wonderful, and despite the fact that a Western audience will read it I find it exciting. I believe even Westerners will also be excited after they get past the first section on revolution.

I am preparing three articles on Djilas and what he has to say in this book which my New York office will consult with Mr. Praeger about before publication. They will help sales and I am sure Mr. Praeger understands that is what I want to do.

I think many westerners will say it is all very well for Djilas to reach the conclusions he does but why not give some answer, some suggestion etc as to what to do about communism. I think it only fair to point out in an article that that would be asking too much of him. To have the ability to think logically and with a sense of moral right while living and being a communist (and never anything else) is as much as the world can ask of the man. His courage in expressing it is even more than we should ask. Therefore I want to write one article pointing out this situation so there will be no negative reaction to the book.

I will be in Poland a short time and will contact you as soon as I get back. Then I will go down to Belgrade to see Mrs. Djilas again and if there are any questions from you all I can get the answers then.

Sincerely yours,
Katharine Clark

Katharine placed the letter in an envelope, addressed it, and put it on her desk. Ever since she'd first learned of *The New Class* in the summer of 1956, she had committed to helping Milovan with it in any way possible. Given her profession, she naturally assumed part of this meant writing articles about Milovan and his ideas for INS. Katharine had already drafted three such articles.

Katharine was proud of the entire series, but she felt the last article was the most important. As she had written to Miss Wilcox, Katharine wanted to prevent negative reactions to *The New Class* because the book didn't answer the question about what the West should do about Communism. "Of course the answer to that is that Djilas doesn't know either," Katharine wrote in her article. "Nor is it possible for the West to expect the man to know. He is a product of Communism. His horizons have been limited by his background. It is too much for the world to ask him to solve the problem. The world should instead marvel that he has been able, despite his surroundings, to see truth." He had quite literally, Katharine believed, thought his way out of Communism.

Katharine traveled back to Poland, where a week turned into a month. In addition to commemorating the "Bread and Freedom" riots which occurred the year before in Poznan, she came across several more stories to highlight the different living conditions between East and West. For the first time the Americans had an exhibit at the international trade show in Poznan. The display was a fully furnished, three-bedroom model home with a living room, dining alcove, kitchen with a washing machine and toaster, and a den with a television set. Katharine observed hundreds of thousands of Poles pass through the exhibit, making comments like "Wouldn't it be paradise to live like this" and "All we would have to do is move in."

One husband answered his wife's entreaties with the pragmatism of someone who has lived under Communist rule for the better part of a decade: "Yes, but the housing office would send two other families to join us." Katharine understood this comment intimately. During this visit, she'd elected to stay with a Polish family who shared a three-room house with two other families. The home had a closet-size room off one bedroom for its kitchen, a bathroom with no basin and a toilet that didn't flush, and a courtyard "filled with bricks and the filth of the last war" where the children played. Katharine slept on a couch in the living room, immersing herself so she could accurately convey how a typical Polish family lived to readers in the U.S.

Katharine had returned to Vienna appreciating her bed and the peace and quiet of the Clarks' Vienna apartment. But now, on the second of July, Katharine sat at her desk at INS in Vienna fuming. Before her lay two letters from Praeger, posted while she'd been in Poland.

In the first note dated June 7, Praeger wrote to her:

It is still a bit too early to decide on publicity plans and to coordinate this with the story you wanted to write. We have a chance for a very big play by one of the big magazines, but because of that we have to hold our horses for the if and when and the eventual fixing of release dates and deadlines. Only then can we fix our publication date, which will be preceded by quite a bit of publicity. However, I would like to time this so that you, if you want to, will get a chance to file a story in plenty of time before publication date of the book (but not before the magazine story breaks).

To the bottom of this letter Praeger added in his own handwriting, "It has happened—*Life* will do a Crankshaw article with excerpts from Djilas' book."

In the second letter, sent nine days later, Praeger wrote:

June 16, 1957

Dear Mrs. Clark,

First, are you Ed Clark's wife?

The manuscript has been vastly improved and the improved version has been checked against the original for last corrections. We ought to have page proofs on June 20th.

LIFE [sic] has the world pre-publication rights and will bring long excerpts together with the analysis by Edward Crankshaw.

Unfortunately, I have no definite publication date yet. Probably between August 5th and 25th. I would be very happy if your articles could be timed so that they would follow LIFE publication without a long interval. They should, of course, not be published before the story breaks in LIFE. We would then like to follow with a long article in the *New York Times* and actual publication of the book with book reviews, etc. etc. Probably I shall also give a chapter to the *New Leader*.

I would be grateful if I could have your articles at an early date so that I can tie our own publicity in with what you say.

I understand from a NEW YORK TIMES [*sic*] story that Mrs. Djilas is in a very difficult financial situation. Is there anything we can do about it? As far as I am concerned, you certainly can give her up to, let's say $15,000. If it is possible for you to give her some money, we should immediately reimburse you. Perhaps you know of another way how we can help her? Can one send her food? Would it be better to send food from here or from Vienna? Whatever it is, I'll be glad to do it.

Very sincerely yours,
Frederick A. Praeger

Hold your horses? Chance for a big play? Am I Ed Clark's wife? How naive I've been. Here was a man who had been given Milovan's manuscript by luck, telling Katharine what she could and could not write about and when. Over the years INS had respected her relationship with Milovan, allowing her to choose when and where to publish his articles. Kingsbury-Smith had never pressured her to use her connection to Milovan for INS's advantage. And now Praeger was telling her she couldn't run the articles she wanted to in order to help Milovan and INS. That *Life* was getting the scoop. On top of that, with all of his questions about money and gifts, his letter showed her how ignorant he was. She would have to help him. She would need to spell it all out for him, but recognizing she was in no state to reply, she set the letters aside and threw herself into her work. She had a backlog of articles to write on changes in the Kremlin's leadership, jazz, and various economic statistics in Poland.

Two weeks later, after her temper settled, Katharine responded to both letters from Praeger.

July 15, 1957

Dear Mr. Praeger,

I have just returned from a month in Poland which accounts for my silence on the Djilas book.

First, please do not at this time try to send any money to Mrs. Djilas. She does need it, but I feel certain money sent through the bank in a regular way would be seized.

If you want to help please arrange through CARE that packages be sent to her. You could deduct the cost of such packages from the earnings of the book. I have sent things through CARE before and they are very good. The CARE official in Belgrade should be instructed through the New York office that she be called into the Belgrade offices and allowed to select the type of package she needs. Sometimes she wants food and sometimes clothing. I have even managed through CARE to get toys sent in for Aleksa.

Second, yes, I am Ed Clark's wife. I am glad that LIFE is finally going to show interest in Djilas, but I do hope INS gets a break on this also. I have sent articles to Mr. Milton Kaplan of INS, 235 East 45th Street, New York, N.Y. and I would suggest you contact him if he has not already contacted you.

You will note in one article I mentioned the possibilities of what may happen to Milovan. I believe all advance publicity about the danger to him may help offset that danger.

I believe that you can help protect Milovan also if you will send as soon as possible (pre-publication) copies of the book to Nehru, Aneurin Bevan, Ollenhauer, Oskar Pollock and any other good liberals you can think of (do we include Nehru in that category?! anyhow he should have a copy.)

The gravest danger to Milovan is the mention of the fact that some of the manuscript got out of the country after his arrest. I do not say this to protect myself but because it would involve his wife and any pressures on her would be a double pressure for Milovan.

The wisest thing to say is that he went to prison before publication of the book simply because (due to events in East Europe) he wrote a summation of his book for *The New Leader* which precipitated his arrest.

I can assure you that the Yugoslavs are already in a tizzy of the book. And I believe it is going to be very serious indeed for Milovan. What worries me most is whether any of us will actually know what takes place. I am certain it will be hard for me to get a visa to go down there. That is another reason why I hope you can get CARE started quickly. If Mrs. Djilas failed to show up at the CARE office they would report it to someone and if she had any worries she would tell the young CARE man about it. He is an American.

After publication I think it would help if Radio Free Europe did something about the book but for God's sake with better discrimination and less bombast than they have done some things. BBC also should have a copy.

And please send me a copy. I'm sending on this typewritten one I have to Mr. Cracker.

One last comment—if the fur starts to fly, even if Djilas is executed don't feel too badly about it. That sounds callous and I am certain you will feel as terribly as I will (although my feelings will have the double dose of having done it to a dear friend) but remember that he <u>does</u> want it printed. If he survives he is young and has a hope of leading his people. If not he has at least struck a blow against the tyranny of men over men and that's what Djilas is—a revolutionary against tyranny in any form.

Best Regards,

Katharine Clark

When she was done, she reread both pages of copy for typos, adding in missing commas here and there. When she got to the part about smuggling out the manuscript, she stopped. In her career, Katharine had benefited from the little sneaks of information that well-placed informants she'd cultivated for months, sometimes years, fed to her. But the leaks about *The New Class* weren't to

break a story or to get the truth out; they were for the express purpose of creating hype to sell more books. She had tried to artfully
communicate that to Praeger without outright accusing him. She
knew the Yugoslavs were already incensed. Since December, when
Kingsbury-Smith had first brought the rumors about the manuscript being smuggled out of the country to her attention, the leaks
had grown, taking on new legs that the papers had been snuck out
of jail. But she was respecting Milovan's wishes to move forward
with publication. She prayed that it wouldn't result in his death.
She resolved to do anything she could to raise publicity about him
to ensure that didn't happen.

She put the letter in an envelope and turned her attention to
her other correspondence. She still owed Morrow a response to
his letter from May. In addition to a more formal letter of authorization he requested for his lawyer, she wrote him a personal
note:

July 15, 1957

Dear Mr. Morrow,

I am sorry for the delay in writing you about the Djilas book but
I have just returned from a long tour in Poland.

I am enclosing a letter such as you, in your May 25th letter,
say you need for your attorney.

There is one hitch however. Mrs. Djilas has expressly asked
me to read the translation of the books he sent to America and
advise the publishers if there is any comment or "personalities"

which could cause Djilas further trouble and which are not essential to the basic belief or narrative of the books.

I am not mentioning this in the other letter but leaving it up to you to get at least rough translations to me so that I can check it. I can promise you that if there is anything to strike out it would be exceedingly minor. But neither Mrs. Djilas nor myself want Milovan to call communist individuals ugly names. I don't mean such expressions as "dictator" but as "fat slob."

I feel certain you understand Yugolavs well enough by now to know that indulging in remarks like that would cause far more trouble than ideological differences. When Djilas first started asking for greater liberalism in Yugoslavia he wrote articles which astounded us but he didn't get into any trouble until he called the wives of the regime snobs. In your interest also it is only something like that which could cause the Djilases to deny anything printed—because they know how serious it is.

The basic trouble is that neither Mrs. Djilas nor myself are certain about details in the book you have. She has a vague impression that there may be some derogatory remark in that book about Gomulka. And Gomulka is not a figure anyone wants hurt today.

Of course you realize also that when Praeger's book is out Djilas may be in such trouble that it won't matter if he calls Tito an epileptic. The present mood in Yugoslavia is very tense. They technically welcome the upsets in the Kremlin but their own part is so static, the Poles have moved so much further ahead, and there is still such muttering in the party rank and file over Hungary that party control has become almost entirely police control.

Ideologically they are static and about ready to pop at the seams.
With the Praeger book out and undoubtedly with the Kremlin
attack on them for permitting the book to get out a real witch
hunt may begin.

Sincerely yours,
Katharine Clark

Incidentally, my husband is Ed Clark of *Time Life* so we are
delighted to know *Life* has shown interest in the book you have.

Katharine realized as she wrote the postscript to Morrow the
irony between her attitude to being Ed's wife with Praeger versus
with Morrow. But she didn't let the detail tax her for long. To her
it was simple. Morrow was moral and principled. Praeger, she felt,
was not. So while Praeger irritated her, she was willing to help
Morrow however possible.

Next she wrote out an update to Kingsbury-Smith. She'd been
so busy that she hadn't yet sent Kingsbury-Smith her articles to
support the release of *The New Class*. She sent him the three stories along with a note questioning whether they should carry her
byline.

July 15, 1957

Dear Joe,

Here are three articles on the Djilas book, The New Class. [*sic*]

I am sending copies also to Milton Kaplan who wrote me about the book.

I told Mr. Kaplan that I did not want my name used on these articles. However, Eddie says I should leave it up to you. He claims that there is nothing wrong in my writing about the book. Additionally the Yugoslavs have already expressed their displeasure at me so I guess we have nothing to hide.

Ed asked for a visa last week and was told that if he was my husband he would never have a visa. We are saying nothing about this yet because Ambassador Riddleberger is working on it. The Yugoslavs have not stated any reason why we can not have visas.

If they try to say I brought the manuscript out that will be denied by the embassy in Belgrade and technically (because of the aid agreement) they can not bar American correspondents for simply writing about the book.

Anyhow it's in your hands now. I know the articles are too long but thought they could be cut for the American papers and probably used in long form in European papers.

Best regards,
Katharine Clark

As Katharine finished the letter, the memory of the look of indignation on Ed's face when he'd come home from the Yugoslav embassy made her smile. The embassy clerk asked if Ed was Katharine's husband, even though he had plainly written out this information on the application form. When Ed confirmed he was, the clerk told him his visa was being denied. He added a message for Ed to share with Katharine—if she even flew over Yugoslavia, she'd be arrested. Katharine had laughed at the ridiculousness of the threat. But she knew the secret police were not oblivious to her relationship with the Djilases. She felt it best not to rub it in their faces by having her name on these articles, but she would leave the decision up to Kingsbury-Smith. She had finally told him that she was the one responsible for smuggling the book out of Yugoslavia. He was a seasoned newsman, and she was confident he would know the right thing to do.

Two weeks later Katharine stared down at the telex message she had just sent Ed. He was working out of *Time's* Bonn bureau that week and had told her that a rumor was circulating there that Milovan had been transferred from Sremska Mitrovica to Goli Otok, the bleak rocky island prison where Tito used to send his worst enemies. Fortunately, the intelligence had been unfounded. Steffie had confirmed this for her last night. *Thank god*, Katharine thought.

Katharine had been thrilled when the operator told her the call was being connected. Given the incident at the Yugoslav embassy with Ed's visa, she was unsure if she would be able to get through to Steffie. Although the monitors had been listening, Katharine had also been able to share some other updates. Steffie had asked her about the article in *Life*. Someone had told her about its existence, but they had not known what it said. When Katharine had told her that Edward Crankshaw, considered one of journalism's experts in Soviet affairs, was the author, she could hear the pleasure in her friend's voice. Katharine had known it would be pushing it for her to detail too much of the article on the phone. The Yugoslavs had to be enraged. Even Katharine thought Crankshaw had overdone it.

In his article, Crankshaw wrote, *The New Class* "was to be a supremely important book. It was to be political dynamite, blowing the theoretical justification for Communism to smithereens. It was to show irrefutably how and why Communism does not and cannot work." He'd claimed, "The New Class, [*sic*] is probably the most devastating anti-Communist document ever written." It was "one of the most tragic and yet inspiring documents of our time. It is more than a book, it is in itself a historical act which marks an epoch."

While Katharine didn't disagree with any of the sentiment Crankshaw conveyed, the pomp had Praeger written all over it.

Praeger, Katharine thought distastefully.

Life had used the verb "smuggled" all over the article, despite Katharine's having told Praeger not to use this positioning or wording. But there it was on the magazine's cover: "A Smuggled Book that will Rock Marxism." And it was in the subtitle of the story: "Smuggled book by Milovan Djilas, a Tito prisoner, shows that Marxist system not only has evil results but is evil by nature." In the third paragraph, Crankshaw wrote, "The first half of the manuscript had already been smuggled out of Yugoslavia. The second half was spirited out of the country by friends under the very noses of the police just before the final arrest." Although this gave the right timeline—the book was out of the country before Milovan was in jail—she knew Tito would be furious at the implication that the police had missed intercepting the manuscript on two separate occasions.

The only thing Katharine was grateful for was that Praeger upheld her wish to withhold mentioning her name.

When Praeger had traveled to Vienna the month before, Katharine had met him at the café at his hotel. Praeger was an athletic man, with a nose like a long-billed bird which he accented with thick, dark round glasses to give him the appearance of intelligence. For a while, everything went smoothly, but when the topic of smuggling arose, Katharine felt her emotions escalate to a boil. He claimed to have had no involvement in the leak. She looked at him in silence, concentrating her eyes on the thick black glasses he wore, focusing to try to temper her anger. She was curious if he really needed them or wore them to affect the air of an intellectual. Whatever the answer, Katharine knew a phony lay underneath his veneer.

After she hung up with Steffie she reflected that she seemed "absolutely jubilant that the books are on their way and does not seem to be worried for the future." Katharine did not share her enthusiasm.

Knowing fallout was inevitable, Katharine took some comfort in the fact that she had taken steps to be able to ensure she could track whether anything changed with Milovan's location. She wrote Felix Morrow, "At present I believe the pressure of world opinion will keep him alive. Later, however, when the noise has died down I am certain he will be in real danger. Very confidentially, I have talked to Aneurin Bevan about this and the two of us have our way now of knowing whether Milovan remains where [he] is or disappears." But even Katharine acknowledged the limitation of her plan, pointing out that "it is not much of a preventive action."

On August 12, 1957, *The New Class* hit bookstores as an instant best-seller, already on its second printing before publication.

In addition to *Life*, dozens of other outlets covered the book's launch. A front page *New York Times* article on July 26, 1957, referred to the book as a "devastating criticism of Communist rule." The *New Yorker* stated, "This is one of the most tough-minded examinations of Communist theory and practice ever undertaken, and its proud impersonality makes it a far more moving document than it would have been if it were merely one more chronicle of personal disenchantment." The *Christian Science Monitor* wrote, "This is a book one would like to quote from page after page. For rarely has the true nature of communism and Communist states been analyzed as incisively and unsparingly. And never before has this been done by an ex-Communist who had held a positioning anywhere near to that of Milovan Djilas." And the *Saturday Review* stated, "Every once in a while a book comes along which helps influence the course of human events. Adam Smith and Karl Marx produced such works. And it just possible that in The New Class [*sic*] Milovan Djilas has written a volume that may deeply affect the thought and deeds of men for years to come in a good many ways that 'anti-Communist manifesto' is an extraordinary exposition of a man's faith."

Outside of print publications, Radio Free Europe was beaming daily broadcasts that read the book out loud to Eastern Europe. American specialists on Eastern European affairs in Munich indicated that "the book is a fundamental document for the study of communism and a work without parallel in the post-war world."

Before she celebrated, though, Katharine had one important detail to check. When she received the edition she'd asked Kingsbury-Smith to buy for her in New York, the first thing she did was search for a mention of her name. She looked at the foreword, in the index, and on the front and back book jackets. Finding nothing, she breathed a sigh of relief. In this, at least, Praeger had kept his word.

As the month approached its fiery end, Katharine received a letter from Praeger:

August 29, 1957

Dear Mrs. Clark,

I feel I simply have to write to you even if it is only a short letter bringing you more or less up to date.

The New Class [*sic*] is a bombshell. We are now on press with a 5th printing, bringing this up to 50,000 copies. The Congress for Cultural Freedom will distribute another 15,000 copies, but this is not for general consumption. Many translation rights have been sold, and as you have probably noticed the book is being serialized all over the world.

INS made its own break. They simply published when they felt like it without asking our authorization.

I have a feeling that this has become one of the main political issues throughout the world and that the Russians and their satraps

will not succeed in ignoring it. Actually, I have done little else but
work myself with two secretaries on the exploitation of the book.

Some of the sensational publicity got a little out of hand. The
claim that the book was smuggled out of a Yugoslav prison was
investigated but we were not at fault.

We have sent copies to everybody we could think of including
the people you mentioned, some directly, some through influential
friends.

You probably know what RFE and RL* are doing.

I have sent CARE packages using the method you suggested.
Is there anything else I can do? The book is actually making a lot
of money for the author and I feel rather horrible about not being
able to at least get enough food to Mrs. Djilas.

This is really the only thing that bothers me. In publishing
terms this is a real success story, but I feel I don't deserve the
success, that it is a hero's tale and we can not even let him know
about it. On the whole, it looks as if we have fashioned the most
potent anti-Communist tool anybody could dream up. It is going
to worry the Communists from here on in.

Sincerely,
Frederick Praeger

Katharine let out a small squeal as she read about the book's
success. A fifth printing! Serialized all over the world! Milovan

---

* Radio Free Europe (RFE) and Radio Liberty (RL) broadcast and report news in countries
where a free press is banned or not wholly established. The organizations merged in 1976
and receive funding from the U.S. government.

would be so pleased. But her enthusiasm evaporated as she read about the investigation of the leak. She had underlined the "we" in "we were not at fault" as she read the note, and now her eyes focused on the claim. *No*, she thought. *Just you. And I hope Milovan will be able to weather your mistake.*

EIGHTEEN

VIENNA

October 1957

In the early evening of October 4, 1957, Katharine and Ed sat in their apartment in Vienna listening to the radio detail the Soviet Union's launch of Sputnik into a low elliptical Earth orbit. As Sputnik's beeps came over the wire, the Clarks' telephone rang in the hall. Ed went to answer it while Katharine marveled at the satellite's symbolism. The Soviets had done it. They'd beaten the U.S. into space and shown the world that they still mattered. She wondered what the reaction was back home.

But her thoughts about satellites vanished when Ed returned to the room wearing a somber expression. He told Katharine the phone call had been from Stojan Bralovic, their friend from Belgrade who worked for UPI. Stojan had phoned from Sremska Mitrovica, the village that shared the same name as the prison where Milovan was serving a three-year sentence.

Stojan had arrived at the village's grimy stone courthouse a little before 8 a.m. that day to cover Milovan's new trial, but he, Elie Abel of the *New York Times*, and Dino Frescobaldi of *Corriere della Serra* were refused entrance to the courtroom. The reason a security official told them was that their pre-trial writings showed an "incorrect attitude toward the Djilas affair." All three of the correspondents had covered rumors of an investigation into Milovan days before the Yugoslav government publicly confirmed this work. As Abel observed, "What seemed to nettle the Belgrade authorities was that some Western correspondents obviously had reliable sources of their own outside of the Government and saw it fit to publish the news without waiting a week for the official announcement." While the other newspapermen had fared better and were allowed to enter the courtroom while the prosecutor read his thirty-minute indictment, when the prosecutor finished, the judge ordered the Western media to leave. Milovan protested, saying, "If there is a secret trial, I will refuse to answer any questions at all either by the judge or the prosecutor."

Steffie was allowed to stay and told Stojan that Milovan had been true to his word. Over the course of five hours, Milovan refused to answer a single question from the prosecution in order to protest the secret nature of the trial. When given the opportunity to state his defense, Milovan simply replied, "I should like to state that I stand by my book in the way it was written from the first to the last letter."

Sentencing was set for the following day, and Stojan told Ed he would call them again with the details.

The next day, Katharine worked from home. She tried to keep herself busy, but her thoughts were focused on Milovan, and she kept waiting for the phone to ring. She was within an arm's distance of the phone when Stojan called the next night. He told Katharine the government had allowed all the reporters access to the court-room to hear the verdict. The judge explained that Milovan was guilty of authoring a book that undermined "the peoples authority, defensive power and economic power" and that with it, Milovan "consciously wanted" to undermine Communism as an idea. The judge went on to state that the day before, Milovan had confirmed that he wrote the book and that it matched his manuscript.

Milovan's prison sentence was extended by seven years and he was stripped of his war decorations, including the top honor as the People's Hero, which Tito had given him for his role in defending Yugoslavia during World War II. After the judge finished, Milovan said, "I protest that the press here has falsely published that I yes-terday replied to questions during the proceeding." But the presid-ing judge cut him short and two policemen ushered Milovan out of the courtroom before he could make any further comment. Steffie hurried after him, and Stojan had not been able to find her after to learn anything more.

Katharine listened to Stojan, the hairs on the back of her neck standing up in shock. She had been expecting a reckoning for Milovan since she had learned in early September that Tito had banned *The New Class* as well as "all foreign publications con-taining excerpts from it." Katharine had struggled with conflict-ing emotions throughout the publication of *The New Class* while Milovan was imprisoned: she had wanted to follow his wishes but felt she was risking so much for him. *Now he was getting seven addi-tional years!* she thought. That was an eternity, especially as he was already serving a three-year sentence. Somehow Katharine found her voice to thank Stojan for the information. He had risked calling the Clarks two days in a row to make sure they were informed. He knew they had no direct channel to the Djilases anymore and could not get a visa to visit.

Desperate to hear Steffie's voice, Katharine dialed the number of the Djilases' phone. But the operator said the same thing she'd been telling Katharine for the last several months: the call could not be connected. Katharine put the receiver down, realizing that Steffie probably wasn't even back in Belgrade from Sremska Mitrovica yet. She walked back into the living room, picked up a pen and paper, and started to make a list of every reporter she had ever known and every reporter who had ever met Milovan. If she couldn't reach Steffie, she would have to help another way. She wanted the world to know what had just happened. By the time Ed came home, she had a list of more than a hundred people to contact. Katharine could use her weapon—her pen—and convince others to do so as well.

———

Two days later Katharine learned she was not alone in her campaign. Twenty-seven Americans, including several of the senators who had signed the letter sent to Tito in January expressing concern with Milovan's sentence in the wake of his articles after the Hungarian Revolution, joined men of the church and labor leaders as well as Mrs. Franklin D. Roosevelt to state, "We see the release of Djilas as a measure of the strength of the Yugoslav Government, and his continued imprisonment as a measure of its weakness."

Excellent, but we need more, Katharine thought when she read it.

So when Katharine received a letter from Felix Morrow the

next day providing an update on the contract for *Land Without Justice*, she was more than open to his idea. Morrow wrote her, "I should like you to discuss with Mrs. Djilas or Djilas' friends, whether they would like to have monies, as they come in, utilized by any existing organization but earmarked to be used for Djilas' defense; or whether a new ad hoc committee should be formed to defend Djilas. I have in mind such previous examples as the Trotsky Defense Committee from which eventually came into being The Commission for Inquiry into The Moscow Trials headed by John Dewey."

Morrow went on to explain, "Although superficially one might think Djilas is getting a great deal of publicity, the grim fact of the matter is, it is primarily due to the unusual interest of The New York Times [*sic*] and that there is no guarantee that this will continue long beyond the present trial. I know from bitter experience in the past the only way to keep such a cause celebre alive is to have a specific committee with its own personnel. If you send such a mandate from Mrs. Djilas, I shall undertake the responsibility of seeing to it that a Committee is formed, has a habitation, and a name and a functionary or two, and, when funds become available, a working Secretary."

Katharine thought about how she could get a message to Steffie. At the present she saw no way to communicate with her. She couldn't obtain a visa or connect via telephone. But as Katharine prepared for a trip to Romania, Bulgaria, and Hungary, she hoped that something would come to her in her travels.

When she returned to Vienna after several weeks, she found more letters from Morrow as well as the first fifty pages of *Land Without Justice* translated from Serbian to English. She appreciated that Morrow was sending her the book in sections rather than waiting until the end—it reduced the burden on her by spreading the work out. Katharine read the book and the letters with interest, and then she sent Morrow a long note:

November 19, 1957

Dear Mr. Morrow,

I seem to begin every letter to you by explaining that I couldn't write sooner because I've been away. But it is true. I returned from a trip through Rumania [sic], Bulgaria and Hungary and then started off three days later for Prague.

To answer all the letters I've had from you during this period: the best suggestion on Djilas photos would be International News Pictures. I sent the few personal ones I had to INP London. They are pictures only of Djilas, his wife, son and mother. I have nothing else.

I do hope you can work out something with INS. They have been very kind about my connection with Djilas and never pressed for anything leaving me free to try and choose the best market for him. I honestly believe that the European outlet for INS (Opera Mundi) would make a first class outlet for the autobiography.

I agree with the translator. From what I've seen there is

certainly nothing Mrs. Djilas would object to in this book so far. But I do have the obligation to Mrs. Djilas to read it for her.

Now as to Djilas being forgotten—I quite agree. I hope some sort of club or organization can be formed but I don't see how we could release any of her funds or his funds for such a purpose without specific permission. And I have no way of getting to her at this time. I am persona non grata in Yugoslavia. I believe it will blow over but for the next few months I'm certain I'll get no visa.

There does seem, however, one thing you can do. As an agent you undoubtedly keep an account of his expenses etc. and a certain amount of advertising I feel certain is justified. Some authors spend money on parties and making speeches etc. Others have cocktail parties to get a book going. Djilas will have none of those costs so couldn't you substitute a certain amount of "reminding"?

And on that score I will gladly do anything I can to help. I am returning to the States at Christmas. I will be in San Francisco for three days—Dec 17 through 19th. Then I go on to Washington DC and will be there at least three weeks. If there is anyone you want me to see or anything I can do I will of course be happy to help. I understand the Christmas period is difficult since few people are in their offices but if you have any suggestions let me know.

Sincerely yours,
Katharine Clark

The reply Katharine received from Morrow six days later confirmed to her again that Morrow was different from Praeger. Morrow informed Katharine that INS's feature editor, Milton

Kaplan, had a copy of the book and was considering running an exclusive article. He assured Katharine he would give INS the first right of refusal for a story. Morrow also shared that he would move forward with forming a committee on Milovan's behalf: "The authorization that I wanted from Mrs. Djilas really had nothing to do with funds. It will be quite easy to raise funds here without using Djilas' own money. Had it been possible to get an authorization from Mrs. Djilas herself for such a defense committee, it would have had a certain value. But I shall go ahead with it anyways sometime around the first of the year as soon as I can possibly find the time for this kind of exhausting work."

Katharine recognized a kindred spirit, someone who was willing to go beyond the day-to-day responsibilities of his work to help. It was the extra work that was critical to ensuring Milovan's safety, and Katharine was happy to have someone to help her in this effort. She sat down to write Morrow back with her address in Washington, DC, so they could coordinate a meeting face-to-face. Katharine realized she was looking forward to meeting him in person.

NINETEEN
VIENNA

1958

Katharine returned to Vienna from the States earlier than anticipated with a restlessness that accompanies one whose plans change abruptly in the middle. She had cut her time in Washington short and did not meet Morrow as planned. Instead, Katharine met unwelcome news from him in a letter he sent to her in Vienna. "INS turned down the Djilas manuscript. Just between ourselves, I haven't had any bite on it yet," he wrote.

Katharine was not wholly surprised. Before she left Europe in December, she had received and read the remaining portion of *Land Without Justice*. Steffie had believed the book contained details about Milovan's political life including conversations with prominent Communist figures. Steffie had reaffirmed this position during their conversation in February the year before when she asked Katharine to read the books and ensure there was not anything too inflammatory in them. It was anticipation of these tidbits that had prompted Katharine to write Kingsbury-Smith an effusive pitch in August 1957 in praise of the book: "I am certain that this book will be much more interesting for the west," she began. "As I understand the book the first part is Djilas' own childhood but the second part is a very intimate account of his intimate contacts with high ranking communists. I think it may be rather juicy because Stephanie [*sic*] begged me to watch for and remove a statement that Djilas consider Tito rather fond of small boys as well as large ladies. She said she wasn't sure he wrote it as his personal opinion or as a rumor during war days but to please take it out!" Katharine suggested, having learned the hard way with *The New Class*, "you will want to sew this one up before *Life*." But nothing salacious about Djilas's interactions with high-ranking Communists had been in the translation. Perhaps she had misunderstood, but she understood why INS was passing. *At least I gave them the opportunity this time*, she thought. *The fact they chose to pass is their decision.*

Despite INS's rejection, Katharine felt she owed Morrow. So as she wrote stories about international spy rings in Vienna, a young housewife in Poland caught pedaling millions of dollars of nylon on the black market, and restlessness in Hungary, Katharine tried to help Morrow land publicity for *Land Without Justice*. But neither she nor Morrow had much luck.

Harcourt, Brace published *Land Without Justice* on April 24, 1958, to much less fanfare than *The New Class*. The book garnered just three reviews from the *New York Times*, the *Saturday Review*, and *SR Syndicate*. The *New York Times* gave the book page-one treatment in its book review, with American author and journalist Stoyan Christowe noting that Milovan often "writes of seemingly commonplace things, with a Tolstoyan-like simplicity and naturalness and a Dostoevskian preoccupation with good and evil." A *high compliment,* Katharine thought, and one she knew Milovan would treasure. But as she kept reading, it was the review's eloquent end that moved her the most: "[Djilas] says, 'bravery means to tell the truth,' and that one must never 'renounce one's deep convictions or the necessities of life.' These are not the boastful sayings of a vain man, they are the beliefs of one who gave up high privilege for the solitary cell of a prison." Milovan had sacrificed it all for the truth. And it was that sacrifice, Katharine knew, that was hard for any man to grasp.

Land Without Justice's launch brought Katharine one more note from Frederick Praeger. He wrote her:

April 24, 1957

Dear Mrs. Clark,

Long time no see and long time no hear. Have you heard anything important about our friend, Djilas, or his family? You probably heard that we had a TV dramatization of the Armstrong Circle Theater show. Actually you were in it too, but as a man, completely unrecognizable, with all the circumstances completely changed.

I am trying in all directions to get some help to Mrs. Djilas. Do you have any suggestions? The book has been extremely successful, both in the trade and in the Book-of-the-Month Club special edition. None of the many foreign editions were particularly startling successes with the exception of the German one. But other countries, too, reached respectable edition sizes, such as Japan, Brazil, England and Argentina.

Aren't you ever coming back to the States even for a short visit? If not, I hope I shall see you in early October in Vienna.

Cordial regards,

Yours,
Frederick Praeger

How ridiculous, she thought, while at the same time feeling relief that Praeger still respected her wish to keep her involvement quiet. *Let them think a man did it*. Katharine set the letter to the side, thinking nothing more of the man or the matter. As was true after the last note she'd received from Praeger, Katharine would not be replying.

Katharine would have also ignored the letter from the dubious attorney in Belgrade, but it was not sent to her directly. Morrow shared with Katharine that Harcourt, Brace received a letter requesting that royalty fees from *Land Without Justice* be transferred to an account at the National Bank of Yugoslavia. "What particularly puzzles Harcourt," Morrow wrote, "is that an identical letter was also sent to the English publisher, Methuen. Why is money being asked for this new book, which has actually not yet earned its royalties, when Praeger has over $100,000.00 of monies owing to Djilas for *The New Class*?"

Katharine advised Morrow to have Harcourt, Brace ignore it. She knew it was a scheme to steal Milovan's earnings. But Morrow wrote Katharine again two weeks later that Jeannette Hopkins and Bill Jovanovich from Harcourt, Brace wanted to speak with her. "At this moment, I suspect that they think you and I are very hardhearted not to take a chance and send the money," he wrote, adding, "Perhaps I exaggerate, but they are very unpolitical about this."

In the envelope Morrow enclosed the latest note from the Belgrade attorney to Harcourt, Brace. After reading it, Katharine knew the secret police were behind it. The contents were all false except for one reference to a letter Morrow had sent to Milovan in the fall of 1956. Katharine recognized it immediately as the same content she'd received from Morrow after sending him *Land Without Justice*—that Morrow didn't feel he was the right publisher for the book and planned to forward it to an appropriate publisher. Katharine knew that the secret police had read or maybe even confiscated Milovan's mail, holding on to it for a time such as this.

Katharine had no doubt in her assessment and knew what Milovan and Steffie's wishes were, so she again replied to Morrow not to send any money. She hoped Morrow could talk sense into the publisher, but she knew she had the benefit of actually having lived and traveled widely in Communist states. What was so obvious to her was not to most in the West.

————————

With both books published, the work she promised to do for Milovan was done. And after five years in Europe, she and Ed craved change. Ed accepted a job at *The New York Herald Tribune* in Seoul, Korea, and Katharine found work with NBC News. After a vacation in Moscow, they planned to spend time back in the United States with family—first in Washington, DC, and then San Francisco—and would ship most of their furniture and other belongings to store in the U.S. while they were in Asia.

As Katharine packed up to move, she also closed out open items regarding the Djilases. Knowing they would be separated from their possessions for an indefinite amount of time, she gathered all the remaining papers she had smuggled out for Milovan and put them in a large manila envelope addressed to Bill Jovanovich at Harcourt, Brace in New York.

Katharine already had ensured the Djilases' daily needs would be covered. On her last trip to Poland, she had convinced Paul Underwood, a reporter for the *New York Times* in Warsaw who was moving to Belgrade, and his wife, Mary, to look after the Djilases for her. With the weight of the *New York Times* behind him, Paul was in a unique position to help protect them by writing about injustices toward them in the Western press. Mary agreed to look after Steffie and to let Katharine know what they might need. Katharine also took comfort knowing she still had the CARE channel open as a way to send items to her friends.

On their last night in Vienna, Katharine picked up the phone to try to get through to Steffie. She was not surprised to hear the operator state that the connection could not be made. It had been that way now for a year. Yet Katharine persisted, calling every few weeks, always hoping the situation would change.

The next day, she and Ed left for Moscow. It was Katharine's first visit to the country that had spawned the system whose impact she had lived under and covered for the better part of a decade. Katharine wanted to experience it first-hand, not realizing she would soon be back in the region covering its shadow once again.

TWENTY

WARSAW, BERLIN, AND WASHINGTON, DC

1962–1968

In early February 1962, after an "insoluble dispute" between Ed and his editor at *The New York Herald Tribune*, Katharine and Ed landed at Warsaw-Okecie Airport in Poland, excited to return to work in a region with which they were intimately familiar.

Three years had passed, but very little appeared different at first. Warsaw was a beautiful city. The grand avenues were lined with square, modern buildings, their short, squat stature commanding attention and respect, begging the question of whether the architect's inspiration hailed from Paris or Moscow. Almost eighty percent of the city had been destroyed during World War II, which had led to a construction boom. But the sheer number of buildings that needed work meant that while the government had made progress, every few blocks a ghost building—utterly destroyed and uninhabitable—reminded one of the earlier devastation to the city.

Now, as they traveled in a hired car to their new apartment, Katharine felt like she had returned home in a way. Although she had enjoyed living in Asia, something about Europe had always tugged at her. She was grateful that James Bell was again the bureau chief of *Time's* Bonn bureau and had made their return possible when he offered Ed the post in Warsaw.

Two days later, while covering the private visit of Edward Kennedy to Poland, they'd been following the U.S. president's brother in their car, through a blizzard, when they'd hit a patch of ice and run straight into a truck. They'd been lucky to escape with only minor cuts and injuries. Katharine couldn't shake the feeling that the accident was a bad omen, a terrible start to their return to the region.

Their luck worsened a week later when she and Ed walked into the spartan lobby of the Polish foreign ministry to apply for their media identification papers at the press office. The credential was issued to all foreign newspeople and consisted of two parts: a top portion with a photograph and a brief personal description, and a bottom section carrying special instructions stating that anyone shown the paper provide assistance to its owner in the execution of their duties as a journalist. These papers, along with a passport, were required to be shown to every person upon whom a correspondent called, as well as at hotels.

Soon after filling out their applications, they had their papers. But while Katharine's papers were complete, Ed's papers contained only the top component. She knew this was about Milovan. The UDBA had gotten word to the Poles. There was no other explanation. But the reason she had full papers she realized was that the secret police couldn't believe a woman had outsmarted them. They blamed Ed fully. She would have laughed if she didn't feel so bad. Ed was being punished for something she had done to help Milovan. Although she was still working for NBC, she helped Ed gather information, relegating him to the role of her "overpaid driver."

Now that she was back in Europe, every several weeks Katharine tried to call the Djilases. In January 1961 Milovan had been granted a conditional release from prison, a fact she learned by a cable from Al Friendly, the managing editor of the *Washington Post*, who asked her to write an article about it. She had promptly provided the *Washington Post* a lengthy story on Milovan. But Katharine still could not get through to them by telephone. Nor could she get a visa to visit. She settled for knowing Milovan was reunited with his family. But this would not last.

Katharine learned of Milovan's re-arrest via a cable from Friendly too. On April 7, 1962, Friendly sent a radiogram informing Ed and her of Milovan's arrest and asking if they would provide color on the real reasons for it. Friendly added that he would also welcome any details of Milovan's recent writing, including rumors of an unpublished book entitled *Conversations with Stalin*.

Katharine's spirits fell as she read the message. *What are the Yugoslavs thinking?*

She looked up at Ed. He knew she took every opportunity available to keep the world aware of Milovan. Inspired after the last cable from Friendly, she had secured coverage in *Chosun Ilbo*, an outlet in Korea about Milovan's plight. Ed had told Katharine it was wasted effort, that the Koreans had no interest in Yugoslavia. Katharine had persisted anyhow.

In Communist Poland, things were more complicated. There was an unwritten rule that foreign newspaper journalists should report nothing from Poland except news about Poland. The country was never to be used as the center for collecting or transmitting information about other countries in Eastern Europe. Ed knew this intimately. In 1956, Henry Luce had had the idea of moving all of *Time's* Bonn bureau en masse to Warsaw, but the idea was killed when the rule was brought to Luce's attention. Now Friendly was asking Katharine and Ed to break it.

Ed and Katharine deliberated. *Should we ignore the cable?* On top of the political risk, the *Washington Post* was "notoriously cheap." In the end, despite all this, they took the risk in trusting Friendly, who had been Ed's classmate at Amherst, believing the coverage would help Milovan. There was one stipulation, they told Friendly—the article needed to carry Belgrade, not Warsaw, as its location of origin.

When Friendly agreed, they turned to how to gather the information. Neither one of them could travel to Yugoslavia, and Katharine still couldn't connect with Steffie by phone to collect any details.

After several days, Katharine phoned Stojan, who was still with UPI in Belgrade, to gather color for the story. Katharine learned the new book discussed Milovan's impressions and interactions with senior members of the Communist Party in the Soviet Union. She realized it sounded like the parts of *Land Without Justice* that she had been expecting to find and never did.

More than anything, what Katharine learned about Milovan's re-arrest left her with a poor opinion of Harcourt, Brace, the publisher of *Land Without Justice*. Bill Jovanovich had let it be known Milovan received a $3,000 advance for his new book, *Conversations with Stalin*. This not only gave the Yugoslav government advance notice of the book but also a concrete reason to punish Milovan. Bill then made it worse by offering not to publish the book at all in the hopes it would do Milovan good. The offer to rescind publication didn't matter; the damage had been done. Katharine knew public knowledge of the advance and the manuscript was enough to expedite Milovan's return to jail. *How had Bill been so ignorant?* she thought angrily. But then she remembered Morrow told her that, against her advice, Bill had ended up sending books and money to the attorney in Belgrade, running the scheme about royalties for *Land Without Justice*. Bill clearly was gullible and soft-hearted—two traits that would not get him far in a Communist country.

Katharine put these thoughts aside to write the story for Friendly. She detailed not only what Friendly had asked but also the way Milovan now lived. Given Ed's already tenuous situation in Poland, they agreed Ed would commit the "cardinal sin" and take the fall by filing the report to the *Washington Post*. When Ed submitted the article, it was datelined as "by telephone from Belgrade."

Katharine soon regretted their decision to work with the *Washington Post*. When Friendly sent the clipping of the story that ran in the paper, the dateline read Warsaw instead of Belgrade, and Katharine saw that Friendly had culled all the lines Katharine hoped would help Milovan. The piece only included new, unknown details about *Conversations with Stalin*. The book had

not yet been distributed to reviewers and bookstores, so this was a
real scoop for the *Washington Post*. The coverage provided no help
to Milovan and potentially risked his safety and it would likely
get Ed in trouble with the Polish government. Incensed, Katharine
raged around the apartment in Warsaw, unable to do much else.
The article reduced Ed's professional situation to the point of no
return overnight. In late May *Time* transferred Ed to Berlin, putting them in a city that straddled East and West.

———————

The move to Berlin delayed attempts by Bill to track Katharine
down. He had tried to find her with a June 4 letter addressed to
NBC in New York but eventually reached her in Berlin on July 27:
"I should be glad to give you all the information I have on Milovan
Djilas. His and Stefanie's regard for you is both respectful and
affectionate and both expressed desire...that we should meet. You
had no doubt read my abortive attempt to aid Milovan by offering
to withdraw Conversations with Stalin. [*sic*] Since that time the
book has, of course, been published and won for Milovan a world-
wide sympathy and interest."

But she soon saw his real purpose for writing was to inquire
about missing manuscripts. "I have in my possession three further books of Milovan's," he wrote. "I had from Milovan and more
lately from Steffie, instructions about the publication of the two-
volume autobiography whose manuscripts you have. Steffie was
to write you, asking that you turn over the manuscripts to me, so
that I could publish them as sequels to Land without Justice [*sic*]
when the time is right."

Katharine put the letter down and reflected on its contents. She had been so sure all of Milovan's papers had gone to Harcourt, Brace before they'd moved to Asia in 1959. *Do I have anything else?* She racked her memory. She knew there wasn't anything currently in their possession, and she could not imagine where else these papers might be.

Katharine fretted for over a week before responding to Bill. Although she was angry at him for his bungle of *Conversations with Stalin*, she knew he wasn't entirely to blame for Milovan's re-arrest. Earlier in the week she had read Paul Underwood's article in the *New York Times* relaying Tito's assertion that Yugoslavia had "gone too far" in giving freedom to writers. Tito had told a recent party meeting, "We shrugged our shoulders thinking nobody would be harmed if we allowed people to say and write what they wanted." Tito further qualified, "We certainly do not want to teach writers and tell them what they must write, but we will not allow anyone to write nonsense and caricature and distort our social life." Against a backdrop such as this, Katharine knew any little detail could be inflamed. And though Katharine felt Bill naive, she recognized that he was still able to travel to Yugoslavia while she was not. He could see Steffie and Aleksa, and Katharine craved another channel to reach them. The Underwoods were still in Belgrade, but Paul was busy, and Katharine tried not to contact them too frequently to preserve that line of communication.

So Katharine found herself before her typewriter on August 15 responding to Bill with a polite and lengthy—albeit slightly frosty—note:

August 15, 1962

Dear Mr. Jovanovich,

Your letter of July 27th enclosing a copy of your June 4th letter has just reached me. I had not received the June 4th letter nor the copy of Conversations with Stalin. [sic]

I had, of course, heard all about your trip to Belgrade and once even telephoned from Warsaw to Belgrade to talk to Brailovic of UPI about the situation. As you know I can not get a call through to Stephanie [sic] nor any letters to her.

As for the autobiography which you mention, I would of course turn over anything to you if I had it. It is difficult for me to remember all the details of the papers at that time but I don't believe I have a thing left of Milovan's. As you probably know, I do not read Serbian but I was under the impression that everything of Milovan's in Serbian, other than New Class, [sic] had been sent to you. Would you look through all the papers sent at that time and see if by chance there remain some unpublished notes?

It is true that all my possessions have been in storage in the States since we left Vienna in 1959 and that there might be among them some papers I have forgotten but I simply don't think so. Both my husband and I have tried to reconstruct all we did about the papers and neither of us believe I would have put away anything of Milovan's but would have taken it with me. I do know that in my files in storage are the originals of the articles he wrote for INS—those original articles which brought him to the attention of people like you and Mr. Praeger—but he dictated to me and they were written in English.

After Vienna we were in the Far East and went from there to Warsaw. I took nothing with me to Poland other than suitcases and now that we have moved to Berlin I still have only the few things we had in Warsaw. But while I would have bent over backwards not to take anything of Milovan's to Poland I would also have remembered that there were items which should not be taken there. And neither of us have any such recollection.

I will wait until I hear from you again and then see if my son can perhaps go through things in storage to look for anything written in Serbian. Both my husband and I are terribly upset to think we might have had something of Milovan's which had not been given you.

If you do get into Belgrade again please give them all our love and please do let me know how Aleksa and Stephanie [sic] are getting along. I tried sending CARE packages but she refused to accept them because my name was on them and I think she was quite right. Then I understood from Paul Underwood of the NY Times that some funds were reaching her and I was not quite so worried. The Yugoslavs have told me I can not even transit Yugoslavia and that I will never be given a visa again so I have faint hope of seeing them all. If by some miracle any or all of them get out I hope you know they could come to us for as long as they want. Berlin is not exactly the place for them but we do have a house in Washington and it is theirs if they get out.

We look forward to seeing you in the spring and hearing

from you firsthand how the family is. We have been especially concerned about Aleksa—his life was so abnormal for a small boy.

Most sincerely,
Katharine Clark

She received Jovanovich's reply nine days later, confirming the accuracy of her assessment of him as an ally: "The general feeling here (that is, among foreign correspondents and people in Washington who are concerned about Djilas) is that the more books of his that I can keep issuing, the more pressure will eventually be exerted upon the Yugoslavs to treat him humanely." This made finding any missing manuscript especially important, Katharine realized. She would write to Sandy to look through their storage unit as soon as he was able. Bill also told Katharine how Milovan described how she "spirited" documents out of the country. Recognizing Milovan would not have told this information to anyone who he did not believe would keep this secret, Katharine resolved to keep her mind open about Bill.

In early 1963, out of the blue, Yugoslavia recognized East Germany as a nation. In doing so, West Germany severed ties with Yugoslavia, acting under a precept laid down by Chancellor Konrad Adenauer that called for this action toward any country that recognized East Germany. Overnight Yugoslavia's interests in West Germany were assumed by Sweden.

Sensing that this was their opportunity to finally obtain visas to enter Yugoslavia, Ed and Katharine sent their passports and requests to the Swedish embassy in Bonn. A week later, their passports arrived with visas good for three months. Elated, Katharine and Ed both agreed to travel only when there was a reason for work—it took time and money to travel to Belgrade, and having a professional reason for a visit also provided a necessary cover.

Fortunately, they did not have to wait long. Ed's chance to visit came in May 1963. Dean Rusk, President John F. Kennedy's secretary of state, was stopping in Belgrade to visit with Tito on the last leg of a European trip. Although Katharine now worked for the *Washington Post*, she did not join, as she was working on a different story.

When Ed returned to Berlin, he told Katharine that Steffie seemed a bit piqued and very worried. She had only brightened when Ed told her of Katharine's constant attempt to reach her by phone and had replied that "she hoped she would keep trying."

On May 14, 1964, Katharine called Steffie later than her usual attempted times and was overjoyed to hear her friend's soft voice on the other end of the line for the first time in six years. But worry soon replaced joy when Steffie shared with Katharine that she had been very ill with kidney troubles. Although Katharine could hear the fright in her voice, she pushed Steffie for more details, and Steffie told Katharine the name of a drug she needed very "seriously" as well as information about her doctor.

Steffie was also able to tell Katharine a little about Milovan, sharing that he was "not so bad—like always." She remarked that the long underwear Bill had sent to Milovan in prison was "too good" and the officials had not allowed him to have it. Steffie also requested a copy of *Paradise Lost* in Russian for Milovan, which was "very important." As she hung up the receiver, Katharine wished, like she always did, that they could speak more freely and for longer, before turning her energy to executing Steffie's requests.

The next day hope rose and soared around Katharine, gliding like a bird whose wingspan had just come in, reveling in the movement fully for the first time. An agency report had come across INS's wires the night before that the travel of an American attorney, James B. Donovan, to the region had something to do with Milovan. Two years earlier, Donovan had successfully negotiated the exchange of two Americans captured and held by the Russians for Soviet spy Rudolf Abel and the release of American prisoners from Cuba after the failed Bay of Pigs invasion. Katharine put her work aside and called Bralovic, who confirmed that similar rumors were swirling in Belgrade.

With little to go on but the need for an outlet for her hope, Katharine wrote Bill on May 16, 1964: "If you are in contact with Donovan and there is any truth to the report I hope you will make certain Donovan arranges for the release out of the country of all three of them." She and Ed "would like to be wherever they go to sort of tide them over a bit at least emotionally." Letting her imagination carry itself to its extreme, Katharine even offered their home in Washington, DC, for the Djilases to live in if it was useful.

Bill's reply to her nine days later held little news, neither good nor bad. "Donovan is acting outside the channels of the people I am acquainted with who are working to help Milovan—if, indeed, Donovan is doing anything at all," he wrote. "I've tried to get information on this in Washington, but no one says anything."

He concluded with the pragmatism of someone who realizes there is little he can do in matters out of his control: "Until Donovan returns there isn't much chance of discovering whether there is truth in the rumors or not." Katharine realized she would have to adopt this approach as well.

But Katharine allowed herself to hope a little more when on June 3 the *New York Times* ran a story with the title "Donovan Hints Success in Europe on Prisoners." Donovan had returned from his trip the day before and told the press of "a visit to Yugoslavia on a 'private legal mission.'" Donovan shared that the U.S. State Department was aware of his trip and that the trip had been successful regarding Milovan's release.

But two weeks later, after Romania announced the release of all of its political prisoners and there was still no news from Yugoslavia, Katharine deflated. She finally resigned herself to the fact that the rumors had been unfounded or, worse, Donovan had been unsuccessful.

In the fall of 1964 Bill made contact with Stella Alexander, an officer of a Quaker organization, the Peace and International Relations Committee, who traveled frequently to Eastern Europe to help him care for the Djilases. The timing was fortuitous, as the Underwoods had recently been transferred out of Belgrade, and Stella had no problems securing a visa to Yugoslavia. To ensure they were all aligned, Bill convinced Katharine to visit New York while she was home in the U.S. over the holidays to meet him and Stella in person.

So it was that on a warm spring day in 1965, the three of them met in New York to discuss their common goal of assisting Steffie and Milovan. As Katharine walked into Bill's plush top-floor office, she was instantly put at ease. Bill had the eyes of a dreamer and the face of a shrewd businessman with a strong jaw, sharp nose, and a mane of black hair that rivaled Milovan's mop. His voice was both warm and authoritarian. Katharine liked him immediately. In Stella, Katharine found someone with whom she shared many similarities. Both women had spent their childhoods abroad and had married men whose careers required constantly changing postings that strained their relationships. Like Katharine had years ago, Stella had separated from her husband. Unlike Stella, Katharine had returned to her marriage. So when Katharine took in the round-faced, petite woman who stood smiling before her in Bill's office, she felt she was almost looking in a mirror of her soul. Katharine had never been very religious, but something about Stella's cherubic face and angelic smile drew her in. She wasn't surprised that she now served a religious mission.

The three of them discussed Milovan and Steffie, agreeing to write letters to one another to keep the others informed of any important conversations or developments.

When Katharine returned to Berlin in June, she placed a call to Steffie. Katharine had been abroad for several months and wanted to speak with her directly. The first time the operator told Katharine the call could not go through. But she insisted the operator keep trying. Over and over Katharine repeated her entreaty. Four hours later the line finally connected and she heard Steffie's voice, but it sounded different—softer and more strained.

When Katharine asked her what was wrong, Steffie shared that her health was still poor. "Some days I am on foot and some days in bed. Some days I go to work," she said. But she finished by telling Katharine "not to worry too much." When Katharine offered to visit her in Belgrade, Steffie asked her to wait to travel in case she needed someone to help her on a trip to see doctors outside of Yugoslavia. Bill had found experts in Switzerland and had been urging Steffie to consult them. Steffie turned the conversation to her upcoming visit to see Milovan in mid-July. She told Katharine that if she felt better, she might accompany Aleksa to the coast afterward.

As the two women said farewell, Katharine realized she needed to write to Stella in New York immediately. Stella had told Katharine she planned to visit Belgrade in mid-July, and Katharine didn't want her to worry if Steffie wasn't home when she visited.

Several weeks later, Stella took the chance and traveled to Yugoslavia. She had responded to Katharine's update that she would take the risk to visit Belgrade, writing, "I think it is important that someone should speak to her face to face and <u>freely</u>, and be able to judge better her real state of mind." Stella found Steffie in the city and visited her every day for over a week. But Stella was so concerned with what she saw that she wrote Katharine a handwritten update and risked mailing it from within the country. Stella wrote that Steffie "was more alone than ever." She also confirmed what Katharine already suspected regarding the gravity of Steffie's illness and that Steffie hoped that Katharine or Ed would soon be in Belgrade. Katharine immediately started making plans to visit her.

———

Katharine and Ed arrived in Belgrade on August 20, two days before Steffie's monthly visit to Milovan at Sremska Mitrovica, the prison he'd been in since 1956. Steffie had been hiring a car to drive her there since the onset of her kidney issues. When she asked the Clarks shortly after they arrived if they would drive her and Aleksa, they happily agreed.

A little before eight thirty on the morning of August 22, Katharine and Ed drove up in front of the Djilas flat on Ulica Palmotićeva in their Mercedes complete with Virginia license plates and a large USA sign in the back window. They had driven from Berlin to Belgrade in it. Though they were slightly early, Steffie and Aleksa were already waiting outside with the Djilases' Boxer named Jolly.

Steffie had been a bundle of nerves since they arrived. Katharine learned that the prison permitted the exchange of telegrams between Steffie and Milovan regarding health issues only, and Milovan had recently sent Steffie a message that he needed an operation. Steffie was barely coherent when she spoke to her. In the moments where she made sense, Katharine was able to understand Steffie was concerned for two reasons. First, she worried the news about Milovan's health might be true. But she was equally concerned that it was a provocation from the government to trick Ed or Katharine into writing something about it, which the government would then deny and use as an excuse to keep Ed and Katharine out of Yugoslavia. *What heavy options to have to consider*, Katharine thought.

On that morning, Katharine also saw how big Aleksa had gotten—he was now twelve years old. For the past two years, Ed had frequently traveled to Belgrade for work, and he always took Aleksa a toy—a pogo stick, a Harlem Globetrotter basketball, a bow and arrow—but those toys seemed so small now. Katharine's heart went out to the boy. She worried that Milovan's prison sentence had also meant one for his son. Despite Milovan's protests, Steffie refused to let Aleksa use his father's record player or desk or radio. And she would not permit social gatherings at their apartment, even for birthdays or Christmas. Katharine planned to say something to her later, after the prison visit. He was a wonderful boy, and she wanted to help make his life more normal.[*]

Just after ten in the morning, 44 miles northwest of Belgrade, Ed pulled off the autoput toward Sremska Mitrovica and turned left into the prison grounds. The large, yellow-brick buildings cut a sharp, imposing contrast against the clear blue sky above.

According to legend, under the Austro-Hungarian empire, Vienna offered to give the town of Sremska Mitrovica a new building to appease the rebellious residents. Instead of a new school or town hall, the inhabitants opted for a prison with the logic that the locals would not have to go so far to visit their relatives that way. When construction ended on the expansive structure in 1899, the prison's yellow bricks signaled its Hapsburgian sponsorship. Some twenty years later, at the end of World War I, Austria-Hungary would dissolve, but the prison remained.

After dropping Steffie and Aleksa off at the entrance, Ed drove

---

[*] Steffie did become less strict.

the Mercedes with all its U.S. markings just a few feet to a small area for visitors in front of the prison. Katharine noted, "Perhaps it is a measure of the new Yugoslavia that they now must provide parking spaces for the relatives of prisoners." Katharine watched as Steffie and Aleksa joined a small group waiting for entry to the prison. Steffie had told Katharine that she met Milovan in a white administrative building in the prison's center compound. Before Steffie was allowed in, bells rang and prisoners were cleared from the area to prevent the other prisoners from seeing Milovan. Steffie warned Ed and Katharine they might have to wait a long time. Although Aleksa and Steffie's actual visit with Milovan would only last for thirty minutes, the preparation work to clear the rooms and grounds could take over an hour. Later Katharine would learn that the prison also made every effort to avoid using the name Djilas. He went by Milovan only and she by Steffie. The lengths the government were taking were astounding.

In the back seat, Jolly's whines and barks signaled she wanted out. Katharine knew she was nervous because her two humans—Steffie and Aleksa—had left her. Seeing what looked like a park a couple hundred feet away, Katharine put Jolly on a leash and walked her over. Soon a troop of little boys had joined them, and when Jolly started panting heavily under the heat of the late-morning sun, Katharine asked one of the boys to knock on the door of a nearby home. It turned out she was in the living area of the prison's guards and officers, and the man who answered gave Katharine a bowl of water, only asking after the name of the dog.

Twenty minutes later, when Katharine returned to the car, she observed casually to Ed that the many boxcars in the train yard opposite the prison would be "helpful for a fugitive once he had made it out of the cell blocks and over the walls." Milovan's escape was never far from her mind, especially now. But Ed prudently told her to "forget that kind of thinking, particularly out loud." Considering where they were, his counsel made sense. Still Katharine shared her scheme with Bill, concluding, "I don't think we could do it without a helicopter." Steffie and Milovan had also discussed his potential escape during the time he'd been released in 1961 and 1962. Milovan had reached the same conclusion as Katharine. The only other alternative he thought might work was "the help of a good guard and fast car outside."

Less than an hour later, Steffie and Aleksa emerged from the prison wearing wide smiles. Steffie told Katharine and Ed about the visit as the foursome drove to a little fish restaurant on the bank of the Sava River, which skirted the town. Milovan had said his health was much improved, and he would not need an operation. Aleksa and Steffie had also told Milovan that Ed and Katharine were nearby without giving too much away. As Steffie and Aleksa had prearranged, Aleksa told his father that he had eaten caviar for the first time. When Djilas asked where, Aleksa replied, with "Ed and Katharine at the Majestic Hotel." With this Milovan knew Ed and Katharine were in Yugoslavia. Steffie then told Milovan that Jolly was with them. Milovan told her he didn't want Jolly to come in because the dog would become too excited and the time was so short, but Steffie told him Katharine was walking him and that Ed was her new driver. He was pleased, immediately understanding that Ed and Katharine weren't just in Yugoslavia but were outside the prison at that very moment. Djilas knew people called on Steffie in Belgrade, but the fact that Katharine and Ed were "outside his own door" meant Ed and Katharine were "friends like just before." Soon Milovan was escorted from the room. As he left he stepped behind a guard, raised his right arm, clenched it in a fist, and said, *"Zdravo."* Katharine and Ed smiled, understanding Milovan's directive to "keep up the good fight."

After a lunch of fried fish and rice with grilled vegetables, they had to drive past the prison to get on the autoput back to Belgrade. As the yellow bricks rolled by the window, Steffie remarked that she had almost forgotten where she was. After every visit she returned to her normal routine for several weeks before the excitement of being able to see Milovan began to build up again. As Ed pulled onto the autoput, Steffie fell asleep on Katharine's shoulder.

Katharine wrote Stella Alexander about the trip when she returned to Berlin, telling her, "I learned, through Yugoslav communists and even from one in the Foreign Office, that it is now accepted that Stefanie [sic] and I are friends and that we see each other as friends, not as journalist calling on a source. Even Yugoslav newsmen accept this now and I am very pleased about it. I think it means the telephone calls and visits will not be stopped." As she wrote this Katharine shook her head. She had considered Steffie and Milovan friends for over a decade now. *The Yugoslavs have finally caught up*, she thought.

In the spring of 1966, Katharine flew to Washington, DC, for the first time in several years. Her mother was ill and had taken a turn for the worse, so Katharine spent several weeks in the redbrick house on Tilden Street where her sister and youngest niece also lived. When her mother's health improved, Katharine prepared to return to Berlin. Before she left, she remembered she wanted to audit what items of Ed and hers were stored in her mother's attic.

As Katharine stood in the room that served partly as her nephew's bedroom and partly as a storage area, she surveyed the contents against the far wall—boxes, sports equipment, and a hodgepodge of furniture stood at attention for her review. Out of the corner of her eye she caught a glimpse of the camphor wood chest she'd purchased in Peking on her family's tour through Asia after her father's posting in the Philippines. Something pulled her to the chest. Katharine knelt down before it and lifted up the top to reveal a set of neatly folded curtains from their house in Belgrade. Beneath them, tucked among her old clothes, a brown paper package poked out from the corner.

"Eureka!" Milovan's missing papers. She had been searching for them since Bill's note to her in 1962. She had completely forgotten about this trunk. Relief flooded through her as she descended to phone Bill with the happy news.

In late May 1966, Katharine returned to Berlin and then flew with Ed's nephew Paul on a trip to Belgrade. She wanted to return the papers from the trunk in Washington to Steffie, and she knew the only safe way to deliver them was by hand. Paul was spending the spring semester of seventh grade with her and Ed in Berlin learning German. Using tourist visas granted by the Swedish authorities at the airport in Berlin, Katharine and Paul landed in Belgrade without incident. They stayed at their regular hotel where the owner and concierge knew her and Ed well. When they reached the room, Katharine phoned Ed to tell him there had been no trouble.

Later that evening, after eating supper and settling Paul into his hotel bed with a book, Katharine walked the few blocks to the Djilas flat with Milovan's papers in her bag. She and Steffie had a long talk catching up on each other's lives. Then, wanting to speak freely as it was a balmy night, Steffie accompanied Katharine back through a little park where they talked about things they did not want the secret police to hear. Just before they reached the hotel, Katharine bade Steffie farewell, and she stepped into the lobby, lightened by the fact she had delivered important papers back to their owner as well as by the time she'd been able to spend with a dear friend.

But when the concierge at the desk, an old man whom she had known for over twenty years, gave Katharine her room key, his hand was shaking. He told her that while she was out, the secret police had come to the hotel and gone to her room. With tears in his eyes, the man relayed the message the secret police had left for Katharine: she must leave Yugoslavia immediately.

Katharine ran to the room. Inside she found Paul wide awake and very excited. With a grin on his face, he told his aunt that the police had come to the room while she was out. They had told Paul that he and Katharine had to leave the country that very night. Paul recounted all of this as though it was a routine chapter in a story, assuming Katharine and Ed were constantly being thrown out of countries. Katharine dialed the duty officer at the embassy to inform the embassy what had happened before falling into bed for some fretful sleep. When they woke, Katharine hired a car to take them to the U.S. embassy, where she told the political officer that she was not going to leave Yugoslavia until her planned departure the following day.

And so it was. As scheduled, the next day an embassy officer drove Katharine and Paul to the airport and saw them off without trouble. When Ed greeted them at the airport in Berlin, she told him that she regarded her departure-as-planned as a victory. Ed observed it was somewhat pyrrhic, but Katharine disagreed, convinced she had left on her own terms.

For the next several months, Ed lobbied Katharine for a return to the United States. He viewed Katharine's ouster from Belgrade as a "watershed" moment. Combined with Jim Bell's recent departure from Bonn resulting in a new boss for Ed, her inability to visit Yugoslavia left them with no reason to remain in Europe.

At first Katharine resisted, but she slowly she came around. On New Year's Day 1967, with their house in Berlin packed up and everything sent ahead except what they needed for their voyage out of Antwerp, Katharine made her last and final call to Steffie from Berlin.

As she waited for the line to connect, Katharine took comfort knowing that Bill and Stella were in place to monitor the Djilases and, in fact, could do so better than she could. Steffie answered the other end of the line wildly excited. She told Katharine that

Milovan had been released from prison the day before and had returned home. When the prison had called Steffie with the news, she had fainted. Milovan was out seeing his daughter from his first wife, Mitra, but Steffie told Katharine when to call back and said she would go get him.

Katharine couldn't contain her excitement for her friends. They had been apart for so long, had endured so many hardships— but now Milovan had been amnestied, released only with the condition that he not publish for five years. Katharine paced the apartment in front of the phone whiling away the minutes until she was due to call back. When the line connected, this time it was Milovan who answered.

"Come at once to Belgrade," he said. "I must see you." A deep pang of regret struck her as she and Ed told Milovan it was impossible. They were leaving "for home for good"; they had no visas and could get none.

Katharine could hear the disappointment in his voice. She matched it in her own.

EPILOGUE
NEW YORK CITY AND WASHINGTON, DC

1967

A letter from Milovan and Steffie awaited Katharine when she arrived in Washington in March 1967. She opened it greedily before she even unpacked.

Feb 25, 1967

Dear Katharine,

A few days ago came your postcard to Alex and immediately after we received Stephanie's letter. Stephanie and I have decided that this time I shall write—for the first time and after so many years.

During all these years I have felt, and from Stephanie's and Alex's remarks on visits I have known that our friendship, which began in the days most critical to me and most difficult for my family, was to continue in the years of my imprisonment. After coming out of prison Stephanie impressed me with your unselfish friendship whose warmth filled me from your letter also.

There is not anything I can say for myself besides the things you already know. This second, five year imprisonment I have undergone through calmly and patiently and was able to continue it peacefully. I can only criticize myself for not writing more, but with age one works slower, yet—some say more mature. My health is good—only for the occasional headaches and hyperacidity. On the first day even I managed to adjust to the new conditions receiving great help from Stephanie and Alex. With them it is so nice, that it seems to be the first time I have felt the sweetness and the value of every-day life.

But life is not without troubles and problems.

My literature work begun at the prison, has already horrified me by its volume: if I was to have no other duty but this I would need a few years work to finish it. It seems I will have [to] carefully plan both my time and obligations which will not be easy, for I am not so alone as I was when we met: Stephanie and I failed to organize time and space belonging to us only and it looks as if we will not manage to. We have even been pressed by such meaningless things as a scanty and demode wardrobe.

Alex is growing and progressing. He has just arrived after ten days skiing at Kopaonik with his friends. He is above his age and often surprises us by his knowledge and observation. Through him we live our own eternity and feel the forming of a new world in which people will think and exist outside the national border and the border of ideas.

My gratefulness to you has no limits, just as your friendship towards me.

Yet between us something much stronger than gratefulness

and friendship has been created: our destinies have become identical. The lightest and the hardest moments of my being are unbreakably tied to you. Time and space are not able to weaken our relationship. What is more, it is being purified and made eternal by distance and years. My memory will always be guarding you and my hopes will be within you.

We are hoping that we shall meet, even if that is not to be soon. I understood Katharine very little over the telephone, so that we hoped you would come here after Washington. Now we are awaiting Sandy—as a part of you and so dear to us that it seems you are coming.

We hope you will find more peace and quiet at home. For you have too in a different way to us—had to part from the normal life conditions and sacrifice a lot for unpersonal ideals and duties. But that is how it should be with all who live not just for themselves and their time.

With all of our beings we would like to return to you something great and unforgettable. For when we note down so many of our friends—you with your unselfishness and loyalty occupy a special place.

We hope that these words, which we send from the heart and mind, will contribute to our love and devotion towards you both.

Again, we are waiting to hear news from you.

With Love,
Milovan and Stephanie

When she finished, Katharine wiped tears away from her eyes. Milovan had managed to capture through his beautiful writing how special their friendship was and the important ways they had touched each other's lives over the years.

Over the next several months, Katharine and Ed kept up correspondence with the Djilases as they settled into life in Washington. But their relationship naturally changed. The shift had more to do with the fact that Milovan was now out of prison than the geographic distance between the couples. However, increasingly, Bill Jovanovich provided the Clarks with more regular updates on their friends.

Then in October 1968, a day that Katharine had never thought would be possible, came to pass. Steffie and Milovan had been granted permission to travel to the United States.

Katharine and Ed were there to welcome them when they landed at John F. Kennedy Airport in New York from several weeks spent first in the United Kingdom. At first glance the Djilases looked the same, but older. Katharine, who had not seen Milovan in twelve years, looked past his gray hair to see his eyes, recognizing the same spirit she had seen at the courthouse on that January morning in 1955. The two couples hugged each other, pleased at the opportunity for a reunion.

Milovan's visit would be a mix of work and rest. He had traveled to the U.S. as part of a speaking tour, the centerpiece of which was a fellowship at Princeton University. Other institutions had invited Milovan to speak, but it was unclear how many trips he would be able to make. Katharine had already convinced Bill to forego a huge, public press conference. Instead Milovan would spend some time with both the editorial boards of the *New York Times* in Manhattan and the *Washington Post* and *Newsweek* in Washington, DC. Part of the trip would involve rest at Katharine and Ed's vacation cottage in West Virginia.

But Katharine and Milovan had work to do first. She had trodden in the footprints of her old habits, pitching her new editors at *Reader's Digest*—Kenneth Gilmore, the editor, and John Barron, the editor of the Washington bureau—about Milovan, as "the highest ranking communist to ever renounce and denounce communism and the only one who ever did it from behind the curtain." Trying to help the younger editors with the full context, she wrote, "I don't want to sound like your grandmother but I do hope you will understand that New Class [sic] was the greatest and most important single political action since world war two [sic]. Then and today Milovan is the greatest threat the Kremlin faces. There are new forms of Djilasism now but they all bear his name." They had agreed to print an article written by Milovan as well as to pay him $7,000 for it.

This time her work with Milovan was different. Katharine noted his improved English. The irony was not lost on her that during his first imprisonment as a young, aspiring revolutionary in the mid-1930s Milovan had studied Russian but that during his second sentence he had learned English.

Milovan began the article with a memory about a meeting with Winston Churchill in 1951. As Milovan rose to leave the room after a discussion with Churchill about Yugoslavia's yearnings for freedom, Churchill told Milovan, "You know, I think you and I are both on the same side of the barricade." "Today," Milovan wrote, "the Soviet invasion of Czechoslovakia makes these words of Churchill all the more poignant for me. For the brutal march into Prague betrays a sinister and fundamental change within the Kremlin which puts all men who cherish freedom—wherever they are—behind the same barricade."

In the article Milovan expanded on the meaning of this invasion by the Russians into Czechoslovakia and sounded a "somber warning" to the United States exposing "the fact that Soviet leaders are now adding military force to their 'Cold War' efforts to conquer the world." Milovan cited the "naked use of force" by the Red Army in their invasion of Czechoslovakia earlier in the year as proof. To combat this, Milovan offered that the West invest in military force such that "the margin of Western military superiority must be so clearly greater than even the Soviet bureaucracy can understand it. Otherwise they will risk adventures in increasingly wider areas, and the ideas of reformers within the Soviet empire will have no chance."

It was, Katharine thought, a fitting end to her work with Milovan. After she submitted the article to Gilmore and Baron, Ed and Katharine returned to Washington, DC, while the Djilases spent a few days with Bill and his wife, Martha, before continuing on to Princeton.

Several weeks later, in the early afternoon of November 21, 1968, a chauffeur-driven black sedan slowly pulled to a stop in front of the Clarks' home in Washington, DC. Watching from one of the windows that flanked the front door to the house, Katharine clapped her hands together before she flung the front door open and ran outside to greet her friends. Milovan and Steffie would be traveling with Katharine and Ed to their cottage outside Washington in West Virginia for a much-needed vacation.

But before that, Ed took Milovan to two official events. The first one was a luncheon with Katharine Graham, publisher of the *Washington Post,* and her editors from the *Washington Post* and *Newsweek.* Ed and Milovan were met at the door of Mrs. Graham's office by Al Friendly, still managing editor of the *Washington Post,* who stopped Ed at the door, telling him the session would just be between Milovan and the editorial boards from the two publications. Taken aback, Ed cheekily asked to be alerted when Milovan's driver should pick him up. Later, after Milovan left Washington, the *Washington Post* published a series of three articles under his name. Ed realized that was why Friendly hadn't wanted him in the room. Ed would have stopped them from tape-recording Milovan's off-the-record comments, which now had been turned into very on-the-record pieces.

Ed also escorted Milovan to a foreign policy group in Washington whose members were interested in discussing Eastern Europe problems with him. There, Milovan was not tape-recorded, and Ed was welcome. Despite the courtesy, Ed had quite a shock. After seating himself in a chair at the rear of the room, Ed saw that Milovan was seated at a dais next to Allen Dulles, the retired leader of the Central Intelligence Agency. Ed apologized to Milovan after the meeting for putting him in that predicament, knowing the UDBA would not want Milovan to be anywhere near a former leader of the CIA. But Milovan told Ed he had immediately figured out who Dulles was from photos he had seen. Besides, Milovan noted, Dulles had slept most of the meeting. He assured Ed that if the UDBA ever learned of the meeting, they would be as amused as Milovan had been.

With Milovan's professional obligations complete, the foursome, along with the Clarks' two basset hounds, drove to the country. As Washington's suburbs faded from view, with Sam, one of the dogs, barking his head off whenever Milovan and Steffie spoke in Serbo-Croat, the couples traveled back over time and distance, falling into the steady rhythm of their friendship, picking up as if no time had been lost.

With nothing but a river current as backdrop, Steffie and Katharine cooked and laughed while Ed walked the dogs and read and Milovan, unable to fully rest, redid his translation of *Paradise Lost*. His original translation, laboriously penned month after month on toilet paper in Sremska Mitrovica before Steffie mailed it to New York, had been ruined beyond repair. Unbeknownst to anyone, one of Bill Jovanovich's staff, whose "command of Serbian far exceeded his judgement," had retranslated the entire epic poem into modern Serbian and destroyed the toilet paper toils from Milovan's effort to translate the poem into the seventeenth-century Serbian of John Milton's time.

Several days later, it was with a heavy heart that Katharine hugged her friends goodbye and waved as they drove off toward the airport. Milovan was due to receive the 1969 Freedom Award from Freedom House in New York, an organization dedicated to strengthening free institutions around the world. The award is "dedicated to men who loved human liberty," and its previous recipients included Dwight D. Eisenhower, Winston Churchill, the Hungarian Freedom Fighters, and Martin Luther King. Freedom House noted in their announcement of the 1969 award that they selected Milovan in "recognition and encouragement to the millions of fighters in eastern Europe who are proving that freedom cannot be extinguished."

Katharine had helped Milovan with his acceptance speech and read eagerly the coverage of the ceremony in the newspapers the next day. Milovan had detailed that his struggle for freedom began with an urge "to seek a way out of the closed circle in which national and social communities still live in Eastern Europe." He then stressed, "All of eastern Europe is filled with the urge for freedom—for new forms of life...The movement to freedom in those countries today is inevitable and vital. And if the recent renaissance of Czechoslovakia is any example of these tendencies and possibilities, the invasion of that country demonstrates the barriers which east European people still encounter. And my country, Yugoslavia, though it has not yet reached the necessary and desirable degree of freedom, is an example not only of national courage but also those democratic processes which reactionary bureaucratic forces are no longer able to halt."

But even Katharine had not anticipated the protestors at the Hotel Roosevelt who carried banners protesting Djilas. The demonstrators were New York Serbs who had been driven out of Yugoslavia during the period immediately following World War II when the Partisans, of whom Milovan was one, and Chetniks, whom these New York Serbs were a part of, had clashed for control of Yugoslavia in what many might call a civil war. The picketers knew the Milovan of old—the one who worshipped Tito and Stalin. They did not know the new Milovan—the repentant one who had taken on Stalin, Tito, and communism itself with his pen. The man who now had a bronze plaque from Freedom House that read: "heroic leader and rebel—his reason and conscience turned him against tyranny."

It was a complexity that Katharine knew well. She had encountered it many times over the years, most notably with Jim Bell when she had tried to convince him to do a cover story on Milovan for *Time* and been met with a deep-seated grudge against Milovan for comments he had made as a revolutionary against C. L. Sulzberger of the *New York Times*. Katharine herself had felt the same about Milovan until that moment at the trial so many years before. But as she worked with him, she had seen him change and transform. Milovan himself acknowledged, "Man is not simple, even when he is one piece. That piece has many corners and sides." Katharine agreed and believed American journalist John Chamberlain summarized the sentiment best in his review of the Freedom House award ceremony and Milovan: "I honor the man for changing his mind about Communism."

When the wheels on the Djilases' plane lifted for takeoff from New York en route back to Belgrade, it was not the last time the two couples saw each other. Over the next two decades the Clarks and the Djilases maintained a relationship via correspondence and occasional visits. But the world in which they had become friends was changing.

The thaw of the Cold War was just beginning in the mid-1980s, but Katharine would not live to see the end of it. On a frosty February morning in 1986, she did not open her eyes. But ever the planner, shortly after her cancer diagnosis, Katharine had dictated her obituary to Ed. Under the headline "Katharine Clark, Prize-Winning Journalist, Dies," four paragraphs in, she had directed Ed to write, "Beginning in 1948, she and her husband Edgar began filing stories from central and eastern Europe. During the 1950s, she worked for the old International News Service in Belgrade and Vienna. Among the stories she covered was the historic break between Yugoslavia's leader, Marshal Josep [sic] Broz Tito, and his chief lieutenant, Milovan Djilas. Mrs. Clark smuggled manuscripts of some of Djilas' writings out of Yugoslavia. These manuscripts included portions of what were published as 'The New Class'[sic]...'"

In the end, with her death, Katharine finally publicized the role she had played in smuggling Milovan's papers out of the country. But even in this, she held back, omitting any detail of that friendship, having decided years ago not to write about the Djilases for professional gain.

More than half a century later, the story deserved to be told.

ACKNOWLEDGMENTS

Writing this book has been the adventure of a lifetime, and one that I feel lucky to have had the chance to experience.

As I wound through the twists and quirks of the past as well as the writing process itself, I discovered both wonder and challenge. While I obtained the bones of the story from newspaper articles, books, and documents preserved by my great-aunt and donated to Georgetown University by my great-uncle, there was still so much to bring to life. Living memory served as the solution to many of the mysteries presented by the primary documents' contradictions or omissions.

I am grateful for the time and information my mother and uncle provided to me about Katharine. Each spent time with her in various settings—my mother in Washington, DC, and my uncle in both Philadelphia and Berlin. Their firsthand accounts of Katharine and her work gave color and clarity to a complicated woman.

The kindness of Rebekah White at *Harvard University Press* for connecting me to Aleksa Djilas will forever be something I aspire to pay forward. Corresponding with Aleksa was by far the most extraordinary development to arise from my pursuit of this story. I owe him a debt of gratitude for the many emails we exchanged about various discrepancies and missing details that he painstakingly helped me answer based on his own memory and expertise and by providing me various articles, videos, and photographs.

Since that first moment in Georgetown's library when I saw the plaque for Ed and Katharine's special collection, my parents have encouraged me on my journey in the way they have done all my life. I appreciate the fact my mother read *every* single draft I wrote as well as the unvarnished feedback both my parents and my sister provided to me along the way. Thank you three for always believing in me.

Numerous friends also read versions of my book—giving me their time and thoughts. Each of you know who you are, and I cannot thank you enough for helping me see my writing through fresh eyes by sharing your candid feedback with me.

To my agent, Elaine Spencer, thank you for taking a chance on this unique story and for all your advice along the way.

To my editor, Erin McClary, who not only believed in this story but also helped me shape it, reading it over and over, and over once again—thank you. The manuscript has benefited significantly from your attention to detail and storycraft. My thanks also extend to the entire, wonderful team at Sourcebooks for helping to bring this book into the world: Sarah Otterness, Jillian Rahn, Stephanie Rocha, Brittany Vibbert, Bret Kehoe, Liz Kelsch, Deve McLemore, and Tina Wilson.

A large part of what prompted me to start writing this book was my own entry to motherhood. I am thankful that my children allowed me to carve out time to pursue my dream and always had just the right words of encouragement and doses of reality to help me whenever I needed them. My final thanks is to my wonderful husband: thank you for your unwavering support and love. I couldn't have done this without you!

This book would not exist without Katharine Clark or Milovan Djilas, two extraordinary people who were each remarkable in their own way. I am indebted to Katharine's foresight to keep many important papers from this period of history (and for Ed's initiative to donate them to Georgetown) as well as to Milovan's dedication to document history in the many books he wrote during his lifetime. Katharine's belief in and determination to help Milovan inspired me. Partway through writing this book I found a letter Katharine sent to me in April 1984 when I was a little girl. At the end of it, as she was wondering about my future, she wrote, "You have the biggest job—Katharines always do!" I hope I have lived up to her expectations.

READING GROUP GUIDE

1. How did Katharine being a woman impact her career in a male-dominated profession like journalism? How did she overcome those obstacles? In what ways was her gender beneficial in this line of work?

2. How did Katherine's upbringing—as the daughter of an Army general—influence her career and aspirations later in life?

3. Katharine was ahead of her time in many ways when it came to how she approached her career and motherhood. Did it surprise you that a woman during the 1950s would make those choices?

4. Initially, Milovan had asked to work with Ed to publish his articles. Why do you think Ed failed to do anything with Milovan's writing, and why do you think Katharine was so successful?

5. Katharine only disclosed that she was working with Milovan to a few trusted colleagues, and much later in her obituary. Why do you think Katharine was hesitant to disclose her involvement in smuggling Milovan's papers out to the West?

6. There are endless stories throughout history of men getting credit for the important work that women did, and Ed getting credit for the legwork and stories that Katharine uncovered is no different. Can you think of other instances where this has happened, both throughout history and in modern times?

7. Why do you think Katharine initially chose to keep her plan to help Milovan a secret from Ed?

8. Discuss why you think Katharine was so driven to work with Milovan and to help him expose his writing to a broad audience.

9. Milovan had once been one of the top leaders within the Communist party in Yugoslavia and a liaison with Stalin. What do you think contributed to Milovan's disillusionment of Communism and his eventual renouncement of the Communist party?

10. Steffie played a quiet yet influential role throughout the story. Discuss in what ways you see this and why she was instrumental in helping to get Milovan's work published.

11. At one point in the book, Khrushchev called journalists "dangerous people." Discuss why journalists were often perceived as the "enemy" by government leaders. Do you think there is evidence of that happening today, either in the United States or abroad?

12. Communist governments behind the Iron Curtain were desperate to keep the truth about what was happening in their countries a secret. Why do you think they felt the need to distort the truth and suppress freedom of speech and discussion? In what ways is this still happening today?

13. The author, Katharine Gregorio, unearthed much of her great-aunt's story by reading journals and correspondence, but also by listening to stories passed down through the generations. What's something interesting you've learned about your family through lore?

14. How is Katharine's story relevant to what's happening in journalism and the media today?

15. What surprised you most about the book?

CONVERSATION WITH THE AUTHOR

Katharine Clark is your great-aunt. How did you first come across this story? What was the impetus for writing about her?

My mother is a wonderful storyteller, and I grew up hearing all sorts of family stories. In particular, because Katharine and I share the same name, I always paid attention to the stories about her. I knew that she had been a reporter abroad, a reluctant mother, and the first woman American reporter to enter Berlin and Warsaw. She also had covered the Hungarian revolution with her stories featured on the front page of the *Washington Post* and had been a regular on *Meet the Press* (which I don't cover in the book).

There also was always this story about how she smuggled papers out in her brassiere, but my mother was fuzzy on the details and I really did not pay attention to this thread until I saw the plaque for the special collection at Georgetown University. The existence of the special collection made me curious, and over time as I unraveled more and more details, I just could not stop thinking about the story and how to tell it. After my second child arrived, during many sleepless nights, I started crafting a narrative in my head and then eventually put pen to paper.

Do you share any personality traits with Katharine?

While Katharine and I are very different, the one trait we likely share is determination. As we see in *The Double Life of Katharine Clark*, the act of writing a book can often be the easy part on the path to publication. To find an agent, get it published, and market it is challenging. Nothing happens quickly, so a consistent and persistent mindset to overcome challenges and detours that arise on the journey is critical.

What was the most surprising thing you learned about your great-aunt while researching and writing this book?

My great-aunt was a character in the fullest sense. However, the most surprising thing I learned about her is something I don't even cover in my book. She was friends with two interesting women: Martha Gelhorn, another female correspondent who was married to Ernest Hemingway for a period of time, and Svetlana Alliluyeva, Joseph Stalin's daughter. I can only imagine the conversations she had with each of them!

When writing historical narrative nonfiction, it can be difficult to fill in the gaps of a story. How did you go about making a cohesive narrative based on what you discovered? What was your research process like?

The *narrative* in historical narrative nonfiction is the key. While there are different approaches, I made the decision to be a purist and to only use quotes that I could cite from sources, which meant any dialogue I used had to have been documented by someone, somewhere. This led me to one of my favorite parts of writing about history—the research!

I was incredibly fortunate to have a vast foundation of primary documents to work with. In addition to numerous letters and reports that Katharine saved, I had both her and Ed's articles as well as Milovan's detailed accounts of his life which he documented in his numerous books.

From this I outlined a chronological sequence of events and then determined what the best story arc would be—this helped me identify areas where I needed to research or understand further. I was fortunate to be able to access first-hand accounts from Katharine's and Milovan's contemporaries and from my mother, uncle, and Milovan's son Aleksa Djilas.

When writing about history, it is easy to get lost in the detail of the facts, but I always was pushing myself to bubble up to the "so what" and tying it back to the story—to show versus tell. Ultimately I tried to write a book that I would want to read.

What do you think your great-aunt would think about you writing a book about this incredible chapter of her life?

She would love it! She didn't write deeply about the Djilases in her lifetime because she wanted to protect them, but her friendship with the Djilases transformed her. She did what she did because she wholly believed in Milovan and what he had to say. She would think my writing this book was another way for her to help tell his story and share his ideas with a new generation.

What was your writing routine while crafting this story? How did you keep all of your research and drafts organized?

Given I wrote this book while working full time and raising two children, my writing routine was to wake up early every morning and write for one to two hours. I also was able to work in the evenings after the workday and bedtimes.

I fortuitously took photos of every single document Katharine and Ed donated to Georgetown, and along with their newspaper articles and Milovan's books, I had a digital and physical archive I could consult whenever I needed. I also used Google docs to track and name my various drafts which allowed me to access my writing while commuting or waiting for an appointment to review and comment.

Do you tend to read more fiction or nonfiction? What books have you read recently that you've loved?

I read everything, and sometimes more than once. I love books that teach me things, transport me to different worlds or times, and challenge the way that I see the world. Given all the references to Fyodor Dostoyevsky by Stalin to Milovan, I recently decided to reread *Crime and Punishment* and *The Brothers Karamazov*, which then prompted me to reread Leo Tolstoy's *Anna Karenina*, Mikhail Bulgakov's *The Master and Margherita*, and Nikolai Gogol's *The Nose* and *The Overcoat*.

NOTES

AUTHOR'S NOTE

"From Stettin": Winston Churchill, *The Sinew of Peace*, delivered at Westminster College, Fulton, Missouri, March 5, 1946. https://winstonchurchill.org/resources /speeches/1946–1963-elder-statesman/the-sinews-of-peace.

ONE

"youthful enthusiasm": letter from Sanderford Jarman to Smith College president William Nielson in January 1933, in The Office of President William Allan Neilson files, Smith College Archives, CA-MS-00013, Smith College Special Collections, Northampton, Massachusetts.

"The foreign newspaper men": Jack Raymond, "Djilas and Dedijer Found Guilty; Yugoslav Court Suspends Terms," *New York Times*, January 25, 1955, 7.

"undermine the": Ibid, 1.

"Purged Yugoslav Asks Two Parties, More Democracy": Jack Raymond, "Purged Yugoslav Asks Two Parties, More Democracy: Djilas, Former Vice President Expelled by Reds, Calls for New Socialist Grouping," *New York Times*, December 25, 1954, 1.

"Traitor! Bandit!": "Yugoslavia: Surprise Ending," *Time*, February 7, 1955, 20.

"I am giving": Jack Raymond, "Purged Yugoslav Asks Two Parties, More Democracy: Djilas, Former

Vice President Expelled by Reds, Calls for New Socialist Grouping," *New York Times*, December 25, 1954, 1.

"the very" : "Yugoslavia: Heresy in Titoland," *Time*, January 10, 1955, 21.

"Every honest": Jack Raymond, "Court Opens Case of 2 Tito Ex-Aides: Djilas and Dedijer Accused of Moves to Hurt Yugoslav 'Vital' Interests Abroad," *New York Times*, December 31, 1954, 3.

"Sretno": Edgar E. Clark Collection, Box 2, Folder 6, "Ed's Report to Time on January 1955 Djilas-Dedijer Trial," January 26, 1955, Georgetown University Library, Booth Family Center for Special Collections.

"Kush": "Yugoslavia: Surprise Ending," *Time*, February 7, 1955, 20.

"Mr. Dedijer, did you": Edgar E. Clark Collection, Box 2, Folder 7, "Katharine's notes on January 1955 Djilas-Dedijer Trial," January 26, 1955, Georgetown University Library, Booth Family Center for Special Collections.

"No, I did not": Ibid.

"Mr. Djilas": Edgar E. Clark Collection, Box 4, Folder 1, "Associations with Milovan Djilas," December 1976, Georgetown University Library, Booth Family Center for Special Collections.

"Vera": Edgar E. Clark Collection, Box 2, Folder 7, "Katharine's notes on January 1955 Djilas-Dedijer Trial," January 26, 1955, Georgetown University Library, Booth Family Center for Special Collections.

"Good morning": Ibid.

"No ticket, no entry": Edgar E. Clark Collection, Box 2, Folder 6, "Ed's Report to Time on January 1955 Djilas-Dedijer Trial," January 26, 1955, Georgetown University Library, Booth Family Center for Special Collections.

"No tickets, no entry": Edgar E. Clark Collection, Box 2, Folder 7, "Katharine's notes on January 1955 Djilas-Dedijer Trial," January 26, 1955, Georgetown University Library, Booth Family Center for Special Collections.

"We hate you": Edgar E. Clark Collection, Box 2, Folder 6, "Ed's Report to Time on January 1955 Djilas-Dedijer Trial," January 26, 1955, Georgetown University Library, Booth Family Center for Special Collections.

"I have nothing": Jack Raymond, "Djilas and Dedijer Found Guilty; Yugoslav Court Suspends Terms,"
    New York Times, January 25, 1955, 7.

"Nista": Edgar E. Clark Collection, Box 2, Folder 7, "Katharine's notes on January 1955 Djilas-Dedijer
    Trial," January 26, 1955, Georgetown University Library, Booth Family Center for Special
    Collections.

"Is this trial secret": Jack Raymond, "Djilas and Dedijer Found Guilty; Yugoslav Court Suspends Terms,"
    New York Times, January 25, 1955, 7.

"No it is public": Ibid.

"Detriment": Edgar E. Clark Collection, Box 2, Folder 6, "Ed's Report to Time on January 1955 Djilas-
    Dedijer Trial," January 26, 1955, Georgetown University Library, Booth Family Center for Special
    Collections.

"Titoland": Ibid.

"All the cats": Ibid.

TWO

"western circles": Ibid.

"even Communists in Belgrade": "Yugoslavia: Surprise Ending," *Time*, February 7, 1955, 20.

"West to think": Ibid.

"Djilas is": Edgar E. Clark Collection, Box 2, Folder 9, "Note about Foreign Press Dinner with Tito
    February 25, 1954," December 1976, Georgetown University Library, Booth Family Center for
    Special Collections.

"advance history lessons": LeRoy Haden, "This Is Radio," *Philadelphia Inquirer*, September 29, 1942, 26.

"to the microphone": "Today's News for Children," *Billboard*, October 24, 1942, 8.

"kiddie": LeRoy Haden, "This Is Radio," *The Philadelphia Inquirer*, September 29, 1942, 26.

"Less work for mother": *The Children's Hour* song, http://www.broadcastpioneers.com/childrens.html.

"neither the quality": LeRoy Haden, "This Is Radio," *Philadelphia Inquirer*, April 30, 1943, 12.

"constant crusading": *Variety*, February 1945, 16. https://archive.org/stream/variety157-1945-02/
    variety157-1945-02_djvu.txt.

"unbiased, liberal": Ibid.

"There is a saying": Edgar E. Clark Collection, Box 4, Folder 1, "Associations with Milovan Djilas," December 1976, Georgetown University Library, Booth Family Center for Special Collections.

FOUR

"repeats statements": Letters to the Editors, *Time*, February 14, 1955, 6.

"TIME Correspondent": Ibid.

"I will": "Khrushchev's Secret Speech, 'On the Cult of Personality and Its Consequences,' Delivered at the Twentieth Party Congress of the Communist Party of the Soviet Union," February 25, 1956, History and Public Policy Program Digital Archive, From the Congressional Record: Proceedings and Debates of the 84th Congress, 2nd Session (May 22, 1956-June 11, 1956), C11, Part 7 (June 4, 1956), pp. 9389–9403. http://digitalarchive.wilsoncenter.org/document/115995.

"Dear Comrade Tito": "Yugoslavia: Come Back, Little Tito," *Time*, June 6, 1955, 28.

"splendidly adorned": Ibid.

"sat in his Rolls-Royce": Ibid.

"traitor": Ibid.

"unrepentant": Ibid.

"there, half": Ibid.

"Khrushchev happily": Ibid.

"Wistful": Ibid.

"dark and sour": Ibid.

"alongside his taller": Ibid.

"Tito stood still": "Yugoslavia: Come Back, Little Tito," *Time*, June 6, 1955, 28.

"It was the face": Publisher's Letter, *Time*, June 6, 1955, 19.

"Ti-to": Ibid.

"Some time ago": "Yugoslavia: The Rover Boys in Belgrade," *Time*, June 13, 1955.

"A dancer": Ibid.

"Well, Khrushchev never": Ibid.

"How about you?": Frank Kelley, "Visit Russia at Any Time, Khrushchev Tells Newsman," *Boston Globe*,
June 3, 1955, 5.

"I am satisfied": Ibid.

"Journalists": "Yugoslavia: The Rover Boys in Belgrade," *Time*, June 13, 1955.

"Oh. They": Ibid.

"The trouble is": Frank Kelley, "Visit Russia at Any Time, Khrushchev Tells Newsman," *Boston Globe*,
June 3, 1955, 5.

"That is because": Ibid.

"Is he English?": Ibid.

"*Amerikanski*": Ibid.

"You can come": Ibid.

"You can come tomorrow": Ibid.

"You can all": "Yugoslavia: The Rover Boys in Belgrade," *Time*, June 13, 1955.

"Come on": Ibid.

"You can all come tomorrow!" Ibid.

"Can I come too?": Ibid.

"Oh sure": Ibid.

"We are not afraid": Ibid.

"Our agreement with Yugoslavia": Ibid.

"What did he say?": Ibid.

"He said peace": Ibid.

"'Yes, yes": Ibid.

"Come on, Khrushchev": Ibid.

"peace, peace": Ibid.

"There is a visitor": Edgar E. Clark Collection, Box 4, Folder 1, "Associations with Milovan Djilas,"
December 1976, Georgetown University Library, Booth Family Center for Special Collections.

"My wife and I decided": Ibid.

FIVE

"I am going to work": Ibid.

SIX

"gloomy and somber": Djilas, *Conversations with Stalin*, 22.

"In his stance": Ibid, 60–1.

"Small stature": Ibid, 61.

"Mixture": Ibid.

"Was not quiet": Ibid.

"Couldn't we somehow trick": Ibid., 62.

"No, that is impossible": Ibid.

"He in": Ibid., 66.

"I realized": Ibid., 57.

"the greatest possible": Ibid.

"I felt": Ibid., 57–58.

"a world of": Ibid., 66.

"A tall": Ibid., 53.

"sketched a picture": Ibid., 54.

"refusing to": Ibid., 54.

"Such a": Ibid., 76.

"I might conclude": Ibid., 82.

"Even then": Ibid., 83.

"No": Ibid.

"The Comintern": Ibid.

"The problem": Ibid., 88.

"I protest": Ibid.

"the cause": Ibid., 89.

"You have, of course": Ibid., 110–11.

"in one": Ibid., 107.

"the more": Ibid., 124.

SEVEN

"Such haste": Ibid., 142.

"Members of the Central Committee": Ibid., 143.

"We have no special": Ibid.

"personally write": Ibid., 146.

"the Yugoslavs": Ibid., 147.

"this apportioning": Ibid., 151.

"Everyone paid": Ibid., 153.

"there was": Ibid., 161.

"above and": Ibid., 159.

"You didn't": Ibid., 175.

"once again a dream": Ibid, 186.

"I was": Edgar Clark, "Uneasy Session with Stalin Recounted by Author Djilas," *Washington Post*, April 7, 1962, in Edgar E. Clark Collection, Box 4, Folder 1, "Associations with Milovan Djilas," December 1976, Georgetown University Library, Booth Family Center for Special Collections.

"When Djilas": "The Man in the Dock," *Time*, January 25, 1954, 27.

"Most sensational": Ibid.

"When a revolution": qtd. in Ibid.

"Djilas' attack": Ibid.

"I arrived": Djilas, *Rise and Fall*, 359.

"Though I": Ibid., 359–60.

"a piece ": Ibid, 360.

"ideas": Ibid.

"The longer": Ibid.

"He should not": Ibid., 363.

"to remain": Ibid., 369.

"But, Milovan": Edgar E. Clark Collection, Box 4, Folder 1, "Associations with Milovan Djilas,"
   December 1976, Georgetown University Library, Booth Family Center for Special
   Collections.

"Well, I guess": Ibid.

"to Milovan Djilas": Ibid.

"Well if you don't": Ibid.

EIGHT

"Dear Mr. Dodd" : Edgar E. Clark Collection, Box 1, Folder 1, "Letter from Katharine Clark to Allen
   Dodd April 7, 1956," December 1976, Georgetown University Library, Booth Family Center for
   Special Collections.

"A woman" : Edgar E. Clark Collection, Box 2, Folder 11, "Original of Katharine's report to INS on
   UDBA attempt to frame Steffie," December 1976, Georgetown University Library, Booth Family
   Center for Special Collections.

" My wife" : Ibid.

"part of a campaign": Sydney Gruson, "Ex-Aide to Tito Sees New Smear: Djilas' Wife in Court in Row
   with Professed Mistress of Former Vice President," New York Times, April 21, 1956, 5.

"gave Mr. Djilas" : Edgar E. Clark Collection, Box 2, Folder 11, "Original of Katharine's report to INS on
   UDBA attempt to frame Steffie," December 1976, Georgetown University Library, Booth Family
   Center for Special Collections.

"frameup": Edgar E. Clark Collection, Box 4, Folder 1, "Associations with Milovan Djilas," December
   1976, Georgetown University Library, Booth Family Center for Special Collections.

"part of a" : Sydney Gruson, "Ex-Aide to Tito Sees New Smear: Djilas' Wife in Court in Row with
   Professed Mistress of Former Vice President," New York Times, April 21, 1956, 5.

"Dear Katharine" : Edgar E. Clark Collection, Box 1, Folder 1, "Letter from Joseph Kingsbury Smith to
   Katharine Clark, April 24, 1956," December 1976, Georgetown University Library, Booth Family
   Center for Special Collections.

"Dear Sirs" : "Ousted Official Says Tito Regime Prevents Publication of His Book: Djilas Declares Curb

   Blocks the Only Means He Has of Earning a Living," *New York Times*, May 31, 1956, 2.

"May 15th": Ibid.

" I stress": Ibid.

"This prevention": Ibid.

NINE

"pleasant shock": Katharine Clark, "Sofia Proves Happy Shock to Visiting US Tourist," INS, *Kingsport

   Times* (Kingsport, TN), June 21, 1956, 14.

"A thaw is taking place": Katharine Clark, "Inside Bulgaria No. 1," INS, *The Daily Times* (New

   Philadelphia, OH), July 2, 1956, 14.

"difference between communist plans": Katharine Clark, "Communist Plan and Reality Prove Different

   for Peasant," INS, *The Lima News* (Lima, OH), July 2, 1956, 32.

"compelled to join": Ibid.

"held out against": Ibid.

"the amount of produce": Ibid.

"what we really get": Ibid.

"a step toward the industrialization": Katharine Clark, "Inside Bulgaria No 3", INS, *The Daily Times*

   (New Philadelphia, OH), July 5, 1956, 17.

"standing on a derrick": Ibid.

"articles splendid" : Edgar E. Clark Collection, Box 1, Folder 1, "Cable from Joseph Kingsbury Smith

   to Katharine Clark, June 1956," December 1976, Georgetown University Library, Booth Family

   Center for Special Collections.

"A Top Communist Exposes": Milovan Djilas, "A Top Communist Exposes Kremlin Danger," INS, *San

   Francisco Examiner*, June 10, 1956, 1.

"I think respect": Edgar E. Clark Collection, Box 1, Folder 1, "Letter from Joseph Kingsbury-Smith to

   Katharine Clark, June 13, 1956," December 1976, Georgetown University Library, Booth Family

   Center for Special Collections.

"The Unyielding Man": "The Unyielding Man," *Time*, June 4, 1956, 37.

"came to power," "were held down," "now that Stalin": Milovan Djilas, "A Top Communist Exposes
  Kremlin Danger," INS, *San Francisco Examiner*, June 10, 1956, 1.

"time life": Edgar E. Clark Collection, Box 1, Folder 1, "Telex," December 1976, Georgetown University
  Library, Booth Family Center for Special Collections.

"same theme": Ibid.

"a campaign organized": Ibid.

"jim am worried": Ibid.

"everything fine": Ibid.

TEN

"Before the war": Katharine Clark, "Poland Heartbreaking to American Visitor; War has Left Deep
  Scar," INS, *Courier Post* (Camden, NJ), July 11, 1956, 2.

"This correspondent estimates": Katharine Clark, "Reporter at Poznan Rioting Says at Least 400 Killed:
  Even Reds Talk of Underground," INS, *The Nashville Tennessean*, July 1, 1956, 6A.

"Oh, you": Katharine Clark, "Poland Heartbreaking to American Visitor; War has Left Deep Scar," INS,
  Courier Post (Camden, NJ), July 11, 1956, 2.

"My son was killed": Katharine Clark, "Graves Contradict Polish Denial of Child Slaying," INS, Poznan,
  Albuquerque Journal, July 8, 1956, 28.

"How old is a child": Ibid.

ELEVEN

"The average Pole": Katharine Clark, "Sky High Inflation Seen Cause of Polish Food Riots," INS, *The
  Times Record* (Troy, NY), August 16, 1956, 4.

"Frequently one sees": Ibid.

"We don't think": Katharine Clark, "Silesian Miners Among Favored Ground in Poland," INS, *The
  Corsicana* (Corsicana, TX), July 20, 1956, 14.

"We do a lot of work": Ibid.

"as it did": Katharine Clark, "Destruction of War Can Be Seen Now in Wrocław," *Anderson Herald*
(Anderson, IN), August 5, 1956, 37.

"for ten years" : Ibid.

"No one builds": Ibid.

"at the bottom": Ibid.

TWELVE

"I don't find these": Edgar E. Clark Collection, Box 1, Folder 1, "Letter from Katharine Clark to Joseph
Kingsbury-Smith, August 15, 1956," December 1976, Georgetown University Library, Booth
Family Center for Special Collections.

"to be careful": Ibid.

"the first time": Ibid.

"that all such money": Edgar E. Clark Collection, Box 1, Folder 1, "Letter from Milovan Djilas to
Katharine Clark, June 17, 1956," December 1976, Georgetown University Library, Booth Family
Center for Special Collections.

"I'm sorry": Edgar E. Clark Collection, Box 1, Folder 1, "Letter from Katharine Clark to Joseph
Kingsbury Smith, June 20, 1956," December 1976, Georgetown University Library, Booth Family
Center for Special Collections.

"I will try": Edgar E. Clark Collection, Box 1, Folder 1, "Letter from Joseph Kingsbury-Smith to
Katharine Clark, June 28, 1956," December 1976, Georgetown University Library, Booth Family
Center for Special Collections.

"your friend": Edgar E. Clark Collection, Box 1, Folder 1, "Letter from Katharine Clark to Allen Dodd,
April 7, 1956," December 1976, Georgetown University Library, Booth Family Center for Special
Collections.

"You can imagine": Edgar E. Clark Collection, Box 1, Folder 1, "Letter from Steffie and Milovan Djilas
to Katharine Clark, September 26, 1956," December 1976, Georgetown University Library, Booth
Family Center for Special Collections.

"There is no answer": Edgar E. Clark Collection, Box 1, Folder 1, "Letter from Katharine Clark to Joseph

Kingsbury Smith, September 8, 1956," December 1976, Georgetown University Library, Booth Family Center for Special Collections.

"At Poznan": "Justice at Poznan," *The Manchester Guardian*, October 9, 1956, 6.

"Communism today has lost": Milovan Djilas, "Russian Communism Bites Its Nails as Outside World Prospers," *Lansing State Journal* (Lansing, MI), October 2, 1956, 5.

Edgar E. Clark Collection, Box 1, Folder 1, "Letter from Katharine Clark to Felix Morrow, October 23, 1956," December 1976, Georgetown University Library, Booth Family Center for Special Collections.

THIRTEEN

"ten abreast": Katharine Clark, "Hungary Revolt Set Off by Smoldering Freedom Spirit," INS, *Indianapolis News*, December 3, 1956, 25.

"By the God": qtd. in "Reawakening of Hungary," *Des Moines Tribune*, November 1, 1956, 22.

"Russians go": Katharine Clark, "Hungary Revolt Set Off by Smoldering Freedom Spirit," INS, *Indianapolis News*, December 3, 1956, 25.

"We are Communists": Katharine Clark, "Writers Paved Way for Uprising in Hungary with Early Criticism," INS, *Kingsport Times* (Kingsport TN), October 26, 1956, 2.

"Our poets": Ibid.

"The anti-Communist": Katharine Clark, "Report High Casualties in Budapest: Jet Planes are Reported Strafing Mountain Revolters" INS, *Corsicana Daily Sun* (Corsicana, TX), October 24, 1956, 1.

"A Swiss businessman": Katharine Clark, "Nagy Pledges Withdrawal of Red Units: Stalinist Gero Replaced in Move to Curb Disorder," INS, *Corsicana Daily Sun* (Corsicana, TX), October 25, 1956, 1.

"Oh excuse me": Katharine Clark, "Stray Bullets Worried INS Reporter in Budapest," INS, *The Nashville Tennessean* (Nashville, TN), December 17, 1956, 2.

"The trick": Katharine Clark, "Stubborn Resistance Led to Victory for Budapest Youths," INS, *The Courier* (Waterloo, IA), December 5, 1956, 11.

"after as little": Ibid.

"I have been sick": Katharine Clark, "Cardinal Mindszenty Makes Triumphal Return to Budapest," INS, *St. Louis Dispatch*, October 31, 1956, 12D.

"mopping up": Katharine Clark, "Stubborn Resistance Led to Victory for Budapest Youths," INS, *The Courier* (Waterloo, IA), December 5, 1956, 11.

"rebel bands": Ibid.

"Each Hungarian": Katharine Clark, "People of Budapest Find Freedom Good," INS, *Clarion-Ledger* (Jackson, MS), November 2, 1956, 25.

"We are only temporary": Ibid.

"What do you": Ibid.

"Excuse me, Madam": Ibid.

"Madame, please": Ibid.

"The thing": Katharine Clark, "Mindszenty Calls on American People to Help His Country," INS, *The Times* (Munster, IN), November 2, 1956, 25.

"promised" : "27 Yanks, Held by Russ, Reach Safety," UP, *San Bernadino Daily Sun* (San Bernadino, CA), November 6, 1956, 36.

"made fine progress": Ibid.

"Go back": Katharine Clark, "American Families Captives of Russian for 31 Hours in Hungarian Border Town," *Cincinnati Enquirer*, November 6, 1956, 3.

"nyet" : Edgar E. Clark Collection, Box 4, Folder 1, "Associations with Milovan Djilas," December 1976, Georgetown University Library, Booth Family Center for Special Collections.

"I am a minor": https://sprague.com/scopia.

"all would": Katharine Clark, "American Families Captives of Russian for 31 Hours in Hungarian Border Town," INS, *Cincinnati Enquirer*, November 6, 1956, 3.

"If you want fresh air": Katharine Clark, "INS Girl Reporter Tells of Hours Spent As Captives of Russians As Convoy Tries to Get out of Hungary," INS, *Corsicana Daily Sun* (Corsicana, TX), November 6, 1956, 3.

"[W]e all": Ibid.

"[G]et upstairs": Ibid.

"Won't you help": Ibid.

"[I]n the name": Ibid.

FOURTEEN

"the atmosphere": Katharine Clark, "New Cominform Along Stalin Line Forecast," INS, *The Minneapolis*

Star, November 19, 1956, 16.

"Khrushchev's line": Ibid.

"purely normal": Katharine Clark, "Action Is in Wake of Kremlin Blast," INS, *The Miami News (Miami,*

FL), November 19, 1956, 1A.

"a fatal" :Ibid.

"the revolution": "Yugoslav Rebel," *New York Times*, November 20, 1956, 20.

"come to" : Edgar E. Clark Collection, Box 4, Folder 1, "Associations with Milovan Djilas," December

1976, Georgetown University Library, Booth Family Center for Special Collections.

"police had searched": Djilas, *Rise and Fall*, 387.

"purposely left" Ibid.

"They didn't get this": Edgar E. Clark Collection, Box 4, Folder 1, "Associations with Milovan Djilas,"

December 1976, Georgetown University Library, Booth Family Center for Special Collections.

FIFTEEN

"This is to": Edgar E. Clark Collection, Box 1, Folder 1, "Letter from Frederick A. Praeger to Katharine

Clark, December 4, 1956," Georgetown University Library, Booth Family Center for Special

Collections.

"was not a book": Edgar E. Clark Collection, Box 1, Folder 1, "Letter from Felix Morrow to Katharine

Clark, October 31, 1956," Georgetown University Library, Booth Family Center for Special

Collections.

"very much interested": Ibid.

"gone": Ibid.

"in view of ": Ibid.

"one of this country's": Edgar E. Clark Collection, Box 1, Folder 1, "Letter Sol Stein to Katharine Clark, December 10, 1956," Georgetown University Library, Booth Family Center for Special Collections.

"of Montenegrin origin": Ibid.

"Harcourt, Brace": Ibid.

"A Swiss newspaper": Edgar E. Clark Collection, Box 1, Folder 1, "Letter Katharine Clark to Joseph Kingsbury Smith, December 11, 1956," Georgetown University Library, Booth Family Center for Special Collections.

"In other": C. L. Sulzberger, "The Moment of Truth for Milovan Djilas?," *New York Times*, November 24, 1956, 18.

"Is this": Ibid.

"the moment": Ibid.

"There was the everlasting": Katharine Clark, "Getting News Out Proved Problem to Correspondents in Budapest," INS, *The Tribune* (Scranton, PA), December 17, 1956, 1.

"You never knew": Ibid.

"For the": Ibid.

"a little like": Ibid, 2.

"coaxing": Ibid, 1.

"so heavily": Ibid.

"I got very tired": Ibid, 2.

"always, always": Ibid.

"pushing a": Katharine Clark, "Budapest Short on Glass, Long on Russian Troops," INS, *Democrat and Chronicle* (Rochester, NY), December 2, 1956, 16A.

"the right": Katharine Clark, "Getting News Out Proved Problem to Correspondents in Budapest," INS, *The Tribune* (Scranton, PA), December 17, 1956, 1.

"Dear Mr. Morrow" : Edgar E. Clark Collection, Box 1, Folder 1, "Letter Katharine Clark to Felix Morrow, December 26, 1956," Georgetown University Library, Booth Family Center for Special Collections.

"Dear Mrs. Clark" : Edgar E. Clark Collection, Box 1, Folder 1, "Letter Frederick A. Praeger to Katharine

Clark, December 31, 1956," Georgetown University Library, Booth Family Center for Special Collections.

SIXTEEN

"a grave violation": "Senators Join Plea for Djilas' Freedom," *New York Times*, January 13, 1957, 22.

"crossed her": Djilas, *Rise and Fall*, 388.

"This is for": Ibid., 388.

"This is to authorize": Edgar E. Clark Collection, Box 1, Folder 2, "Letter Steffie Djilas to Katharine Clark, February 25, 1957," Georgetown University Library, Booth Family Center for Special Collections.

"This is to give": Edgar E. Clark Collection, Box 1, Folder 2, "Letter Steffie Djilas to Katharine Clark, February 25, 1957," Georgetown University Library, Booth Family Center for Special Collections.

SEVENTEEN

"Dear Mrs. Clark" : Edgar E. Clark Collection, Box 1, Folder 3, "Letter from Jean Wilcox to Katharine Clark, April 8, 1957," December 1976, Georgetown University Library, Booth Family Center for Special Collections.

"The Communist revolution": Djilas, *The New Class: An Analysis of the Communist System*, 36.

"the fact": Ibid., 62.

"persecution": Ibid., 144–5.

"history": Ibid., 146.

"in any case": Ibid., 214.

"again and again": Edgar E. Clark Collection, Box 1, Folder 3, "Telex Katharine Clark to Ed Clark, May 24, 1957," December 1976, Georgetown University Library, Booth Family Center for Special Collections.

"The social, economic": Katharine Clark, "Prostitution Flourishes in Misery Behind Iron Curtain, Irks Kremlin," INS, *Corsican Daily Sun* (Corsican, TX), May 17, 1957, 14.

"a health resort": Ibid.

"In an atmosphere": Ibid.

Edgar E. Clark Collection, Box 1, Folder 3, "Letter Felix A. Morrow to Katharine Clark, May 25, 1957,"
December 1976, Georgetown University Library, Booth Family Center for Special Collections.

Edgar E. Clark Collection, Box 1, Folder 3, "Letter Jean Wilcox to Katharine Clark, May 28, 1957,"
December 1976, Georgetown University Library, Booth Family Center for Special Collections.

Edgar E. Clark Collection, Box 1, Folder 3, "Letter Katharine Clark to Jean Wilcox, June 5, 1957,"
December 1976, Georgetown University Library, Booth Family Center for Special Collections.

"Nor is it possible": Katharine Clark, "Former Top Yugoslav Communist Indicts Communism as Brutal,
Inhuman," INS, *The Daily Reporter* (Greenfield, IN), July 26, 1957, 5.

"Wouldn't it be paradise": Katharine Clark, "Reporter Compares Housing in Poland with US Home
Shown at International Trade Fair," INS, *The Palladium Item* (Richmond, IN), June 27, 1957, 5.

"Yes": Ibid.

"filled": Ibid.

"It is still": Edgar E. Clark Collection, Box 1, Folder 3, "Letter Frederick A. Praeger to Katharine Clark,
June 7, 1957," December 1976, Georgetown University Library, Booth Family Center for Special
Collections.

"It has happened": Ibid.

Edgar E. Clark Collection, Box 1, Folder 3, "Letter Frederick A. Praeger to Katharine Clark, June
16, 1957," December 1976, Georgetown University Library, Booth Family Center for Special
Collections.

Edgar E. Clark Collection, Box 1, Folder 3, "Letter Frederick A. Praeger to Katharine Clark, July 15, 1957,"
December 1976, Georgetown University Library, Booth Family Center for Special Collections.

Edgar E. Clark Collection, Box 1, Folder 3, "Letter Katharine Clark to Felix A. Morrow, July 15, 1957,"
December 1976, Georgetown University Library, Booth Family Center for Special Collections.

Edgar E. Clark Collection, Box 1, Folder 3, "Letter Katharine Clark to Joseph Kingsbury-Smith July
15, 1957," December 1976, Georgetown University Library, Booth Family Center for Special
Collections.

"was to be": Edward Crankshaw, "A Communist Strikes at Heart of Communism: Smuggled Book by

Milovan Djilas, a Tito Prisoner, Shows That Marxist System Not Only Has Evil Results But Is Evil by Nature," *Life*, July 29, 1957, 43.

"The New Class": Ibid.

"one of the most tragic": Ibid., 45.

"A Smuggled Book": cover of *Life*, July 29, 1957.

"The first half": Edward Crankshaw, "A Communist Strikes at Heart of Communism: Smuggled Book by Milovan Djilas, a Tito Prisoner, Shows That Marxist System Not Only Has Evil Results But Is Evil By Nature," *Life*, July 29, 1957, 45.

"absolutely jubilant": Edgar E. Clark Collection, Box 1, Folder 3, "Letter Katharine Clark to Felix A. Morrow, August 15, 1957," December 1976, Georgetown University Library, Booth Family Center for Special Collections.

"it is not much": Ibid.

"At present": Edgar E. Clark Collection, Box 1, Folder 3, "Letter Katharine Clark to Felix A. Morrow, July 31, 1957," December 1976, Georgetown University Library, Booth Family Center for Special Collections.

"devastating criticism": Harry Schwartz, "Red Rule Scored in Book by Djilas: Yugoslav Once Close to Tito and Now Jailed Assails 'Despotic System'", *The New York Times*, July 26, 1957, 1.

"This is one": *The New Class* book jacket, First Harvest/HBJ edition.

"This is a book": *Ibid*.

"Every once": *Ibid*.

"the book is a fundamental": M. S. Handler, "Words of Djilas Beamed to Reds: Specialists Say Yugoslav's Criticism May Have Devastating Effect," *New York Times*, August 1, 1957, 5.

Edgar E. Clark Collection, Box 1, Folder 3, "Letter Frederick Praeger to Katharine Clark, August 29, 1957," December 1976, Georgetown University Library, Booth Family Center for Special Collections.

EIGHTEEN

"incorrect attitude": Elie Abel, "A Defiant Djilas Is Tried in Secret," *New York Times*, October 4, 1957, 15.

"What seemed": Ibid.

"If there is a secret": Ibid.

"I should like to state": Ibid.

"the peoples": Ibid.

"I protest": "Slav Author Given 7 More Years for Rapping Regime," AP, *Baltimore Sun*, October 6, 1957, 2.

"all foreign": "New book by Djilas Banned by Belgrade," *New York Times*, September 6, 1957, 5.

"We see": "Djilas Release Urged," AP, *New York Times*, October 7, 1957, 8.

"I should like": Edgar E. Clark Collection, Box 1, Folder 3, "Letter Felix Morrow to Katharine Clark, October 7, 1957," December 1976, Georgetown University Library, Booth Family Center for Special Collections.

"Although": Ibid.

"Dear Mr. Morrow" : Edgar E. Clark Collection, Box 1, Folder 3, "Letter Katharine Clark to Felix Morrow, November 19, 1957," December 1976, Georgetown University Library, Booth Family Center for Special Collections.

"the authorization": Edgar E. Clark Collection, Box 1, Folder 3, "Letter Felix Morrow to Katharine Clark, November 25, 1957," December 1976, Georgetown University Library, Booth Family Center for Special Collections.

NINETEEN

"INS turned" : Edgar E. Clark Collection, Box 1, Folder 4, "Letter Felix Morrow to Katharine Clark, January 6, 1958," December 1976, Georgetown University Library, Booth Family Center for Special Collections.

"I am certain": Edgar E. Clark Collection, Box 1, Folder 3, "Letter Katharine Clark to Joseph Kingsbury-Smith, August 6, 1956," December 1976, Georgetown University Library, Booth Family Center for Special Collections.

"As I understand": Ibid.

"you will": Ibid.

"writes of seemingly": Stoyan Christowe, "From Craggy Soil Sprang a Rebel," *New York Times*, April 27

    1958, BR 1.

"says, 'bravery'": Ibid.

"Dear Mrs. Clark" : Edgar E. Clark Collection, Box 1, Folder 4, "Letter Frederick A. Praeger to Katharine

    Clark, April 24, 1958," December 1976, Georgetown University Library, Booth Family Center for

    Special Collections.

"What particularly" : Edgar E. Clark Collection, Box 1, Folder 4, "Letter Frederick Morrow to Katharine,

    Clark June 30, 1958," December 1976, Georgetown University Library, Booth Family Center for

    Special Collections.

"At this moment": Edgar E. Clark Collection, Box 1, Folder 4, "Letter Frederick Morrow to Katharine

    Clark, July 10, 1958," December 1976, Georgetown University Library, Booth Family Center for

    Special Collections.

"Perhaps I exaggerate": Ibid.

TWENTY

"insoluble dispute": Edgar E. Clark Collection, Box 4, Folder 1, "Associations with Milovan Djilas,"

    December 1976, Georgetown University Library, Booth Family Center for Special Collections.

"overpaid driver": Ibid.

"notoriously cheap": Ibid.

"cardinal sin": Ibid.

"By telephone": Ibid.

"I should be glad": Edgar E. Clark Collection, Box 1, Folder 5, "Bill Jovanovich letter to Katharine Clark,"

    June 4, 1962, December 1976, Georgetown University Library, Booth Family Center for Special

    Collections.

"I have in my possession": Ibid.

"gone too far": Paul Underwood, "Tito Backs Curbs on Liberal Ideas," *New York Times*, July 24, 1962, 1.

"We shrugged": Ibid.

"We certainly do not want": Ibid.

"Dear Mr. Jovanovich" : Edgar E. Clark Collection, Box 1, Folder 5, "Katharine Clark letter to Bill
Jovanovich, August 15, 1962," December 1976, Georgetown University Library, Booth Family
Center for Special Collections.

"the general": Edgar E. Clark Collection, Box 1, Folder 5, "Bill Jovanovich letter to Katharine Clark,
August 24, 1962," December 1976, Georgetown University Library, Booth Family Center for
Special Collections.

"spirited": Ibid.

"she hoped": Edgar E. Clark Collection, Box 4, Folder 1, "Associations with Milovan Djilas," December
1976, Georgetown University Library, Booth Family Center for Special Collections.

"seriously": Edgar E. Clark Collection, Box 1, Folder 8, "Katharine Clark letter to Bill Jovanovich, May
16, 1964," December 1976, Georgetown University Library, Booth Family Center for Special
Collections.

"not so bad": Ibid.

"too good": Ibid.

"very important": Ibid.

"If you" : Ibid.

"would like": Ibid.

"Donovan is acting": Edgar E. Clark Collection, Box 1, Folder 7, "Bill Jovanovich letter to Katharine
Clark, May 27, 1964," December 1976, Georgetown University Library, Booth Family Center for
Special Collections.

"I've tried": Ibid.

"until Donovan returns": Ibid.

"a visit": "Donovan Hinds Success in Europe on Prisoners," New York Times, June 3, 1964, 4.

"some days": Edgar E. Clark Collection, Box 1, Folder 8, "Katharine Clark letter to Stella Alexander,
June 21, 1965," December 1976, Georgetown University Library, Booth Family Center for Special
Collections.

"not to worry": Ibid.

"I think": Edgar E. Clark Collection, Box 1, Folder 8, "Stella Alexander letter to Katharine Clark, June 23, 1965," December 1976, Georgetown University Library, Booth Family Center for Special Collections.

"was more": Edgar E. Clark Collection, Box 1, Folder 8, "Stella Alexander to Katharine Clark letter, July 20, 1965," December 1976, Georgetown University Library, Booth Family Center for Special Collections.

"Perhaps": Edgar E. Clark Collection, Box 1, Folder 8, " Katharine Clark letter to Bill Jovanovich, August 31, 1965," December 1976, Georgetown University Library, Booth Family Center for Special Collections.

"helpful": Edgar E. Clark Collection, Box 4, Folder 1, "Associations with Milovan Djilas," December 1976, Georgetown University Library, Booth Family Center for Special Collections.

"forget that": Ibid.

"I don't think": Edgar E. Clark Collection, Box 1, Folder 8, " Katharine Clark letter to Bill Jovanovich, August 31, 1965," December 1976, Georgetown University Library, Booth Family Center for Special Collections.

"the help": Ibid.

"Ed and Katharine": Ibid.

"were outside": Ibid.

"Stravo": Edgar E. Clark Collection, Box 4, Folder 1, "Associations with Milovan Djilas," December 1976, Georgetown University Library, Booth Family Center for Special Collections.

"keep up": Ibid.

"I learned": Ibid.

"Eureka": Ibid.

"watershed": Ibid.

"Come at once" : Ibid.

"for home" : Ibid.

EPILOGUE

"Dear Katharine" : Edgar E. Clark Collection, Box 1, Folder 11, "Milovan and Steffie Djilas letter to
    Katharine Clark, February 25, 1967," December 1976, Georgetown University Library, Booth
    Family Center for Special Collections.

"the highest": Ibid.

"I don't": Ibid.

"The 1951": Edgar E. Clark Collection, Box 1, Folder 12, "Editors Draft of Reader's Digest article,"
    December 1976, Georgetown University Library, Booth Family Center for Special Collections.

"Today": Ibid.

"somber warning": qtd. in Milovan Djilas *Reader's Digest* article: Dr. George A. Benson, "Looking
    Ahead," *Martinsville Daily Reporter* (Martinsville, IN), January 25, 1969, 3.

"the fact": Ibid.

"naked": Ibid.

"the margin": Ibid.

"command": Edgar E. Clark Collection, Box 4, Folder 1, "Associations with Milovan Djilas,"
    December1976, Georgetown University Library, Booth Family Center for Special Collections.

"dedicated": "Djilas Gets Freedom Award," AP, *The Morning Record* (Meriden, CT), December 10, 1968,
    13.

"recognition": Ibid.

"to seek": Ibid.

"All of ": Ibid.

"heroic": Ibid.

Djilas, *Land Without Justice*, 188.

"I honor,": John Chamberlain, "Tito's Enemy Honored," *The Monroe News-Star* (Monroe, LA), December
    16, 1968, 4.

"Katharine": "Katharine Clark, Prize-Winning Journalist, Dies," *Washington Post*, February 3, 1986, D4.

SELECTED BIBLIOGRAPHY

BOOKS

Djilas, Milovan. *Rise and Fall*. Orlando, FL: Harcourt, Brace Jovanovich, 1983.

—. *Conversations with Stalin*. New York: Harcourt, Brace & World, 1962.

—. *The New Class*. New York: Frederick A. Praeger, 1957.

—. *Memoir of a Revolutionary*. New York: Harcourt, Brace Jovanovich, 1973.

—. *Land Without Justice*. New York: Harcourt, Brace Jovanovich, 1958.

SPECIAL COLLECTIONS

The Office of President William Allan Neilson files, Smith College Archives, CA-MS-00013, Smith College Special Collections, Northampton, Massachusetts.

Edgar E. Clark Collection, Georgetown University Library Booth Family Center for Special Collections.

GOVERNMENT DOCUMENTS

Yugoslavia Country Reader, Association for Diplomatic Studies & Training, https://www.adst.org/Readers/Yugoslavia.pdf.

INTERVIEWS

Aleksa Djilas

David Jablonsky

Lea Uhre

NEWSPAPER ARTICLES

AP

INS

Life

The New York Times

The Morning Herald (Hagerstown, MD)

The New Criterion

Time

UPI

ONLINE

https://www.broadcastpioneers.com/wcauhistory.html

www.newspapers.com

The New York Times

Time

INDEX

ABOUT THE AUTHOR

Katharine Gregorio was inspired to write *The Double Life of Katharine Clark* when she uncovered a family secret about her great-aunt who worked as a foreign correspondent in Europe during the height of the Cold War. Years in the making, Katharine leveraged her degrees in history from Dartmouth College and international relations from The London School of Economics & Political Science in her quest to unravel the story. She also holds a master's in business administration from The University of Chicago Booth School of Business. Katharine resides with her family in San Francisco.